Tourism Ethics

TOURISM ETHICS

Vivek Verma

CENTRUM PRESS
NEW DELHI-110002 (INDIA)

CENTRUM PRESS

H.O.: 4360/4, Ansari Road, Daryaganj,
New Delhi-110002 (India)
Tel: 23278000, 23261597, 23255577, 23286875

B.O.: No. 1015, Ist Main Road, BSK IIIrd Stage,
IIIrd Phase, IIIrd Block, Bengaluru-560085 (INDIA)
Tel: 080-41723429

Email: centrumpress@gmail.com
Visit us at: www.centrumpress.com

Tourism Ethics

First Edition, 2012

ISBN 978-93-81293-86-7

PRINTED IN INDIA

Printed at Tarun Offset, Delhi

Contents

Preface

Tourism Ethics discusses the tendency of tourism researchers to examine impacts as the traditional root of ethical issues in tourism. It is also analyzes alternative tourism and sustainable tourism paradigms as the field's most frequently used means by which to alleviate the negative impacts of the industry. Tourism Ethics provides a generalized snapshot of the range of studies undertaken to date in addressing ethical issues in tourism.

The objective of the book is to bring together a balanced selection of core concepts as well as new perspectives that collectively articulate a knowledge-based view of tourism. This book's aim at enriching knowledge about the key issues related to sustainable development of our tourism systems. Our goal is to provide a realistic view point touching deeply the core issues and suggest solutions in different perspectives. This book would certainly help create knowledge and inculcate wisdom at all levels of society. We hope that the discussion made in this book will help the readers to understand and learnt about the different aspects of "Tourism Ethics" in a most comprehensive way.

Author

1

Introduction

AN OVERVIEW

BACKGROUND TO RESEARCH

Tourism is the world's largest industry and predicted to double in size in the next 20 years. It has the potential to bring major benefits to destinations, but can also be damaging to the people living there and to their environment. Other industries have already understood this ambivalent nature of trade and have adopted the triple bottom line of social, environmental and economic responsibility. It is now time for the tourism industry to rise to this challenge–the challenge of ethical tourism.

The big question, though, is how to put these ethics into practice. As a development charity, Tearfund is concerned to increase the positive impact of tourism to developing countries, particularly on the lives of the poor, and to mitigate any negative effects. In January 2000, Tearfund carried out some market research, which showed that the majority of tourists want a more ethical tourism industry, and would be willing to pay more for it. This current report, one year on, asks how the industry is responding.

It looks at 65 UK-based tour operators, highlights examples of their good practice in ethical tourism and suggests ways in which this can be replicated and built upon. Ethical tourism is in the best interests of all involved. It offers tour operators a competitive advantage and safeguards the future of the industry by ensuring the long-term sustainability of a destination. It offers the tourists a richer experience, as holidays will draw on the distinctive features of a destination. It is also in the interests of those living there and those working for development, as it can help to combat poverty and contribute to sustainable development.

TRENDS IN THE TOURISM INDUSTRY

The tourism industry is highly competitive and tour operators are under increasing pressure to differentiate their products. Research suggests that once the main criteria for a holiday are satisfied (location/facilities, cost and availability), clients will make choices based on ethical considerations such as working conditions, the environment and charitable giving. Clients are also looking for increased quality and experience in their holiday. In this climate, companies would do well to differentiate their products according to consumer demand ie based on ethical criteria.

The industry is already responding. Some operators are moving from a cut-price to an experience-focused approach, and there is a rise in small-scale and specialist operators. Since the Earth Summit in 1992, many operators have started to address their environmental responsibility. AITO (Association of Independent Tour Operators) have been working over the past year to produce a responsible tourism code for their members.

In November 2000 ABTA (Association of British Travel Agents) published their own detailed research into clients' ethical preferences. Any tour operator who fails to respond risks being left behind. They also fail to fulfil their role as a responsible company in the 21st century. Furthermore, they risk damaging the very resources upon which the industry depends–people and their environment. This report offers some ways forward for those who wish to rise to this challenge.

BRINGING BENEFITS TO THE LOCAL COMMUNITY

This stage highlights the benefits tour operators bring to local communities, the factors that enable this to happen and some of the barriers that operators face. It considers whether these benefits can be replicated elsewhere, and places these findings in the context of increased consolidation in the industry and consumer pressure for change. It then suggests some initial steps that companies can take to increase benefits they bring.

FINDINGS

Do you have any Examples of where your Company has had a Positive Impact on Local Communities

Many companies had positive stories to tell about supporting the local economy. This focused on using locally-run hotels and service providers, sourcing goods locally, and training and employing local people. It enabled the money from tourism to go directly to people in the destination and support their development. For some operators it included a year-round commitment to the destination, which helped to provide secure employment and ensure that tourism was a viable way of earning a living. In rural communities, tourism helped reverse the flow to the cities to look for work and enabled people to remain in their families and communities. There were also examples where the income from tourist visits had directly contributed to better standards of health and education. Some of the larger operators provided a significant proportion of employment in some destinations.

What Factors are Necessary for Local People to Benefit

When asked what key factors are necessary in order for people in the destination to benefit from tourism, there were some very clear views expressed across the industry.

Support for the Local Economy

This was considered most important. The emphasis was on using locally-owned and locally-run accommodation and transport, employing and training local people, and giving tourists the confidence and information to use local restaurants and buy local crafts. It confirms 'conventional' wisdom that strengthening local linkages will have the greatest positive impact in the tourism industry.

Good Relationships and Long-term Investment

This included the benefits of a long-term partnership, working with hotels or ground handlers over many years, and the need to build trust between tour operator and supplier. It also focused on the desire for good and regular communication.

Quality and Commercial Viability

This was central as operators stressed the necessity of an attractive product which will sell. There is no use having a product that could potentially bring enormous benefit to the local area, if no-one is interested in going and no-one uses it! Many also stressed the need for an interesting product, different from what others may be offering. This difference and added quality is based on a good knowledge of the area and time spent doing the necessary research. Smaller operators felt that the time invested up-front paid off later on in terms of clients' enjoyment and repeat visits.

Positive Attitudes of Clients

This was included by over half the respondents, emphasising the need for clients to be educated about the destination, the culture and the people, and to know how to behave in a way that respects the environment.

Other Areas

These included tour operators understanding and responding to local need, and the government providing support to local businesses.

Would it be Possible to do Something Similar Elsewhere

When asked if their good examples could be repeated in other settings, the overwhelming response was yes, given the right conditions. Out of the 54 companies with good examples, nearly 90% (47) said that this could be done in other places, showing a strong optimism that change is possible and that as suggested, be able to see many more of these good examples in the future.

What are the Barriers to Bringing Benefits

However, despite all of these potential benefits that tourism can bring, many of the tour operators expressed frustration at the difficulties in implementation.

Profit-driven

This is clearly important as tour operators need to make money to stay in business. Many of those interviewed simply said, 'We are a commercial company, we need to make money and therefore cannot do as much as we would like to.' Often the biggest operators are working on such small margins (typically around 2%) that they use economies of scale to reduce costs wherever they can.

This means that smaller, local service providers in the destinations miss out. Also, the larger operators often do not allow the time to do the research to find viable alternative service providers. Resort reps may have a few days to find all of the necessary information in a destination and therefore go to the places that others are already using.

Client Expectations

The high demands by clients for Western standards was cited by nearly half of the operators as a barrier to bringing greater benefits to the destination, as was the fact that few clients are talking directly to the companies themselves to demand holidays that bring more benefits to the local economy. A significant minority of operators mentioned the tourists' lack of awareness of the economic reality in a destination ie tourists may spend two weeks in a hotel in the Caribbean without realising the extent of the poverty a few hundred metres away. Some also mentioned that tourists may fear the poverty that exists because it is new to them and they are unsure how to cope with it. Significantly, ten operators spoke of a lack of respect by tourists for local people, and relationships having broken down as a result.

Provision on the Ground

The supply side was cited by the majority of operators

with a third of operators complaining that they could not find good quality ground agents, and almost the same number saying that the local government could be doing more to encourage local business through training and affordable loans. Others spoke of the poor communications to remote towns and villages, the lack of marketing of local features, and the lack of understanding of client expectations.

Bureaucracy

The fact that under the EU Package Travel Directive a tour operator may be liable for anything that happens to their clients when they are on holiday, has made many operators much more cautious about what they do, and the local services they recommend to clients. Many of the bigger operators who arrange package tours said they were keen to promote local restaurants and services, but were afraid that if something went wrong, they would be sued when the client came back to the UK. The high standards of health and safety required by the legislation means that Western-owned hotels are often favoured as they are already known to meet these standards. 20% of operators mentioned difficulties working with local or national governments, particularly when offering to clean up a particular beach or river, or helping with the rebuilding of a local site of interest.

How much Money Remains in the Local Economy

When asked what percentage of the holiday, excluding the flight, remains in the local economy, most operators found this difficult to answer. Many of the answers were very rough estimates. None of the bigger, mass tourism operators were able to give us an estimate of what remains locally. This was partly due to the many different holidays they offer, and partly due to the fact that hotels and local services are often owned by people who live outside the local area. Medium-sized companies (taking more than 5,000 people per year, but fewer than 100,000) gave an average estimate of 35% of the cost of their trips remaining locally. The smaller, more specialist operators gave an average estimate of around 70%.

COMMENTARY

Industry Trends

The tourism industry is undergoing an unprecedented period of consolidation. This can work against quality, as costs are cut through economies of scale and standardisation. Only the biggest operators will be able to win in terms of price, and others will need alternative strategies in order to ensure their future survival and success. Recent research into the industry has shown that clients choose their holidays on the basis of destination, price and availability.

Tearfund research in January 2000 found that clients choose their holidays in terms of cost, weather and facilities/ location. Although slightly different, both of these pieces of research showed that once the main criteria are satisfied, clients start to base their choices on other more ethical issues. For many larger companies, cost does not vary much, and many will offer similar holidays in similar destinations so clients' main criteria can be satisfied reasonably easily.

How they choose their holidays will then come down to issues such as how the company treats the environment, the working conditions and wages of the staff, local cultural experiences or the information and advice made available. Although clients may not be choosing their holidays at the moment on these criteria, this is probably because such holidays are not available or, if they are, they are not well advertised.

However, if the recent market research has accurately predicted future trends, companies who take the lead on ethical issues are likely to be rewarded with increased sales. The research findings show that most tour operators have some good examples of where their operations are making a positive difference to the lives of local people. They believe that this can be replicated in other places, and that this is best achieved by supporting the local economy wherever possible, educating tourists and long-term investment in the destination.

The mention of a long-term commitment to a destination is encouraging, because this is vital to enable tour operators to bring more investment, help local businesses to develop and meet clients' needs, and will ensure that tourism is viewed favourably by local people. However, this professed long-term commitment is in stark contrast to the current activities of some operators, who may move on very quickly to new destinations.

Problems encountered include time and financial pressure on the industry, the quality of local services, the increased liability due to the EU Package Travel Directive and tourist attitudes (whether ignorance or very high expectations). The frequency with which operators mentioned the lack of good-quality services is surprising, given that few operators are doing much to help with training and building the capacity of local service providers.

In terms of customer expectations and understanding, companies need to respond to two main challenges. In a market that is demanding a high-quality experience, companies that make stronger connections with local people and their culture will become increasingly appealing, as they will draw on the distinctive features of a destination, and offer a richer holiday experience. Tour operators are also in a unique situation to provide information and advice to ensure that tourists travel in an informed way, and operators have a responsibility to ensure that this happens.

Finally, many operators complained that they could not afford to change, as it cost too much money and took too much time. However, as the industry moves in this direction and clients increase their pressure for change, the question is increasingly likely to be 'can we afford not to change?' Ethical issues may not be mainstream at the moment, but the move is certainly in that direction. Companies that fail to respond to this change are likely to be left behind in five or ten years' time.

RECOMMENDATIONS

Action

Companies cannot do everything at once. Change comes gradually and sustainable change needs to be integrated into normal business practice.

Possible initial action includes:

- *Share best practice*: Tour operators can start by writing down more examples of where their operations have had a noticeable and positive impact on the local community. This will help to see which factors are important to bring benefits, and what can be done elsewhere.
- *Speak to local groups*: For new destinations especially, companies can make an effort not just to speak to the big hotel owners, but to speak to local community representatives, tourism associations and environmental groups as well as the hotels. They can find out about some of the local issues, details of local businesses and possible ways that they can be more integrated into the tourism industry. Development and environment charities in the UK working in these destinations may be able to help with contact details. This process is likely to add an extra day or two onto a trip, but the initial extra cost will be more than recouped later. Companies will be able to provide better-quality holidays, which draw on more of the local character, and ensure that local people benefit from tourism.
- *Consider how to overcome barriers*: Rather than accepting barriers to bringing greater benefits, tour operators can seek to overcome them eg by supporting local training initiatives, providing more detailed information for clients, and taking a longer-term approach to a destination.
- *Experiment with a few examples*: Companies can start in one or two destinations to experiment with using smaller operators and providing a more unique service that reflects the character of the destination. They can then get feedback to check whether this is the kind of holiday that is appealing to their clients.
- *Integrate into normal business processes*: No movement towards more responsible tourism will be sustainable unless change becomes integrated into normal

business processes. Companies therefore need to take a long-term view of their future, and of how they will operate in a changing industry.

CHARITY BEGINS OVERSEAS

This stage looks at which companies give money to charity, how much they give and whether they favour charities based overseas or in the UK. It shows how tourism companies encourage tourists to give to charities, and what sort of advice they offer to them. It places this charitable giving in the context of trends across many industries (not just tourism) and draws out some recommendations on how to give effectively, and advice to give to tourists

FINDINGS

Does your Company Donate Money to Charity

Information on charitable giving was relatively hard to come by. Few companies could provide the exact details for the previous year. Some were involved in charitable activities in the host destinations but had no records of this in the head office. Other companies gave donations in kind but did not seem to know if a record was kept or, if one was kept, where this might be. However, out of the 61 companies whom we interviewed (excluding the four who are actually charities), over three quarters (46) said they donated money to charity.

In what ways does your Company Give to Charity

There were almost as many ways of distributing charitable money as there were companies engaged in the activities. There were also strong ideas about what was good to do and what was not, with some of these ideas in direct contradiction to each other. Examples were: setting up a charitable trust which the tour operator administered eg MasterSun, Specialist Trekking Co-operative; giving to global environmental or development charities based in the UK but working overseas such as Friends of Conservation, WWF-UK and Survival International; giving £1 or £2 from every booking to a specified charity; giving to a well-known UK charity working in the UK;

using money to buy things that are needed by projects that the tour operator visits; matching 'pound for pound' the donations that tourists give; and donations in kind in the form of training or advice.

To which Type of Charities did you Donate Money

Out of the 46 companies who gave money, the majority (33) gave directly to projects in the destinations in which they were working, often projects that they visited or used or had a long-term relationship with. Half gave money to UK-based charities working overseas, either in development work in the destination or with a global environmental remit. Six operators (mainly the larger ones) gave to charities working in the UK.

How much Money did you Donate During the Previous Financial Year

A total of £700,000 was given to charity in 1999/2000 (by the 46 companies who could provide information). The bigger the company, the more money they gave away. Big companies gave on average £43,000 in the financial year, whereas medium companies gave £13,000 each and the smaller ones each gave £5,300 away.

However, when this was considered in relation to profit, the smaller and medium-sized companies paid a higher proportion of profits to charity. Some of the larger companies gave as little as £1 for every £1,000 pre-tax profit, which is about 0.1%. The medium-sized operators who did give to charity gave an average of 1% pre-tax profit. The smaller operators gave varying amounts. From the data we were able to use, these companies gave the equivalent of around 5% pre-tax profits away to charity.

Several of the smaller companies did not give to charity as they placed an emphasis on paying fair prices throughout the whole operation and viewed this as a more sustainable and long-lasting contribution of the company to development in the destination. For example, Tribes Travel, who advertise themselves as the UK's only fair-trade tour operator, integrate their ethical principles throughout their operations by favouring locally-owned and locally-run businesses and community initiatives, and paying a fair wage for the expertise and services they use.

Do you Encourage your Clients to Give to Charity

Of the 46 companies who give money (and two that do not), two thirds offer some sort of advice or encouragement to tourists about how to engage in charitable giving.

- *Giving direct to projects*: Some operators encouraged tourists to give money when they visited projects, or to bring out goods that they could give to the people they visited.
- *Giving money away in the street*: Some operators gave advice to tourists not to give money out in the street, especially to children. Some then added that it is better to bring pens to give away while some said that tourists should speak to the rep or to their tour leader about possible local projects to support.
- *Optional donations*: A few operators added an optional extra charge on the invoice, and specified which charity it would go to.
- *Contact with tourists when they returned*: Many of the smaller companies, particularly those who are keen to encourage repeat visits, will send out a newsletter or new brochure to all clients when they are back in the UK. This often has details of projects to support.

COMMENTARY

Industry Trends

The nature of charitable giving has changed significantly in the past few years.

The main changes are:

- *Strategic approach*: Companies have aligned their giving with long-term business objectives by funding projects that directly impact key stakeholders eg suppliers, customers, employees. This allows more focused giving, which is integrated into business processes and therefore more likely to last, even when margins are tight.

- *In-kind contributions*: In addition to giving money away, companies are giving time, expertise and equipment which is often more focused on specific business needs and therefore more valuable in bringing about long-term change and building partnerships.
- *Evaluation*: Various tools have been developed to measure the impact of giving, and therefore to be able to continuously increase the impact, and determine the most strategic and relevant inputs.
- *Participation*: More and more companies are including different stakeholders (eg non-governmental organisations, employees, local communities) in designing and implementing their giving activities, so that they are more effective in meeting real needs, more integrated into community activities and therefore more sustainable.
- *Terminations*: It is encouraging that so many companies are giving money to charity. It is also encouraging that over half of those giving money are targeting charities in destinations in which they are operating. This means that the tour operators are contributing in a positive way to those whose lives may be adversely affected by any tourism development in their area, or who may be missing out on direct economic benefits. They are also helping to reverse some of the decline of the natural environment. However, the larger companies are more likely to give to charities operating in the UK. While these charities may be doing good work, the tourism industry surely has a responsibility to support people overseas whose lives they are affecting by their presence in their communities? With increasing pressure for profits, charitable giving that is more targeted and aligned with business interests is likely to be more sustainable, both for the

industry and for the charities themselves. There is a wide variety of ways of engaging in charitable giving, and a range of advice given to tourists. Advice from one company may contradict advice from another, which shows the potential usefulness of some basic guidelines. These would give operators confidence in their charitable activities, and encourage consistency and adherence to good practice across the industry. However, charity is no substitute for ethical practice. So, while charitable giving is to be encouraged, it can only ever be seen as one part of a company's responsible behaviour.

RECOMMENDATIONS

Actions to Ensure More Effective Charitable Giving by Tour Operators

Below are ten suggested steps that companies could take to ensure that their charitable giving is integrated, effective and sustainable. They draw on the Business for Social Responsibility website and The Cause Related Marketing Guidelines.

- Integrate charitable giving into the overall company mission and objectives. Develop a clear understanding and articulation of how it fits into normal business operations, and ensure support at the highest level. This will help establish a clear set of values by which to decide where and how to give.
- Appoint a staff member who will have specific responsibility to oversee and develop charitable giving activities.
- Initiate effective research into the possibilities of funding, particularly in the destinations in which you work. Take some time to speak to staff and to the development and environment charities there. Find out their views on the real problems and ways they think you can best help. It is better to give less money in the first year and to spend time doing the initial

research well, in order to ensure that future money is spent well. Consider working with a local organisation that can help you with the research and distribution of funds. UKbased development and environment groups may be able to help you find suitable partners.

- Commit to a funding level and stick to it. This will enable you and the charities to plan better. Possible methods to decide a suitable level include: fix a set level of pre-tax profits either using a sliding percentage based on profitability, or a fixed percentage; set an amount for each year, regardless of profit; or give a per capita rate for each employee or visitor.
- Combine charitable giving activities with other company activities such as provision of training, in-kind donations, shadowing and placements. Consider how you can help to build the capacity of local entrepreneurs who could be integrated into the tourism industry in the destination. Fund projects that directly impact key stakeholders eg suppliers, customers, employees. This will strengthen your supply chain and help bring sustainable change.
- Develop long-term partnerships with the charities you are working with. This will ensure that the giving brings lasting change. Develop a formal agreement so that both sides know what to expect from the relationship. Ensure that regular communication happens.
- Focus on the poor as they will often be left out of any tourism activities, and may bear the brunt of any negative effects. Try to support some charities that are working with the poorest people in the destinations.
- Focus on the destination and try to give to charities that are either UK-based and working in the destination, or are based in the destinations themselves.

- Evaluate your activities regularly to ensure that you are doing the most with your money, and to make changes if necessary. Consider bringing in an independent assessor.
- Brief your staff in the destinations and in the UK about your charitable giving policies and the information you offer to clients.

Actions to Ensure more Effective Charitable giving by Clients

Below are some ways to encourage clients to give to charity, and to help them respond compassionately when they encounter poverty in the destinations.

- *Before they go*: Publicise the charities you support in your brochure and include fuller information in your pre-departure pack. Consider collecting charitable donations before the tourists travel, possibly through a voluntary supplement to the invoice.
- *Bringing goods to give away*: If you think that tourists may bring goods for local people, find out beforehand what is most suitable to bring and let them know. Arrange for any goods that they have brought to be collected by the rep or tour guide and distributed through a local agency once the tourists have gone.
- *Understanding and responding in the destination*: Use the welcome meeting to help tourists understand the extent of poverty or other problems in the destination eg environmental destruction. Explain the causes of the problems and what they are likely to encounter eg begging, children asking for money. Inform tourists about possible responses they can make, including giving to local charities when they are there, giving when they get back home and giving away goods.
- *Responses to begging*: Begging is often the greatest concern for tourists. Encourage people to seek local advice on how to respond and place begging within

its local cultural context. Some may choose to give to local charities, others may choose to buy food, or give money. Whatever they choose to do, encourage a compassionate and respectful attitude. Help them to be sensitive about how giving away money or sweets to children may affect their attitudes towards school ie they could see begging as more rewarding than gaining an education.

- *Visiting local projects*: Offer the opportunity for tourists to go to visit any projects you support. However, actively discourage ostentatious shows of charity when they are there, as this can reduce the dignity of the beneficiaries. Collect a fee from each tourist beforehand, which will go directly to the development work in the project.
- *Collecting and distributing money*: Encourage the local rep to collect any money in the destination and to distribute it discreetly through a local agent once the tourists have gone.
- *Back in the UK*: Provide information and advice for tourists for when they return home so they can continue to support the charities that are connected with your business.

DEVELOPING LOCAL PARTNERSHIPS

This stage looks at whether tour operators consider themselves to be in partnership with businesses in the destinations, and what they mean by the word 'partnership.' It also considers what type of training and advice they offer. It puts this in the context of increased community involvement across all industries, and suggests some principles that should underpin this, and some possible actions to take now.

FINDINGS

Would you use the Word 'Partnership' to Describe the Relationship with your Suppliers

When asked whether tour operators would consider their

relationships with their suppliers as a partnership, the overwhelming majority (80%) said yes.

What do you Mean by Partnership

When asked to define what this meant for them, a variety of different answers were given, but many strong common themes appeared.

Relationships at the Centre

Over 70% of those questioned who considered themselves to be in a partnership with their ground operators, spoke of this in terms of long-term commitment. The other areas of a good relationship were spending time together, trust, listening and good communication. This emphasises the importance of good relationships in tour operating, an industry still characterised as exploitative of its purchasing power. Breaking this down according to company size, roughly half of all of the small and medium-sized operators placed a significant emphasis on the centrality of good relationships, whereas the larger operators barely mentioned it.

Joint Business Approach

It is common that tour operators will work closely with ground operators or service providers to develop the necessary services in the destination. Many of the smaller specialist operators plan their trips together with those in the communities they visit. This ensures that the communities are happy with the way tourism develops, and can cope with the number of tourists coming. For the larger groups, partnership often focused on sharing the same view of customer service and being able to provide the necessary standard of service, but little more than that. A few of the smaller UK operators also mentioned financial openness, but this was a low priority.

Local Community Involvement

One third of those who answered emphasised the need to properly recognise skills and experience and to pay a fair wage for them. This focuses on paying for quality as opposed to paying the lowest price possible. Other operators, mainly those set up with strong development aims in mind, thought it was vital that a partnership would meet local needs, particularly those of the poor. Finally, a significant minority emphasised the need for local communities to be able to determine the direction of their tourism development. The emphasis on local community involvement came almost exclusively from the smaller operators, with one mention from a medium-sized operator and no mention from any of the larger operators.

What Type of Training do you Provide

Many of those who spoke of being involved in partnerships were involved in some form of training. However, for most it was a relatively small part of their operations, and it was not seen as a high priority. Some of those who did not provide training said that the relationship with their ground handlers overseas was so close that they discussed everything and worked together in all aspects of the business. Others operators did not provide any training as they tried to find service providers who could already provide the services they wanted.

Skills Development

This ranges from working with guides to improve their skills (including bringing some to the UK, or paying for others to shadow those who were already trained), paying for reps to have language training, and working with people in villages to help them prepare food in a way that clients will like.

Understanding Consumers and Customer Service

This involves training staff, particularly those in hotels, to treat tourists in a way that they expect. It enables both tour operator and local business to be confident that their services meet the clients' expectations. Some companies also give more general advice to smaller, community tourism initiatives to help them pitch their product at different operators in the European and North American travel market. (Companies also offer advice to tourists on how to treat those in the destination, but this is covered in the next stage on responsible tourism.)

Health and Safety

Many operators provide advice and training to hotels so that they can meet the health and safety requirements of the EU Package Holiday Directive. This may involve written guidelines or sending experts to those hotels to run training workshops eg on food preparation.

Product Development

Operators who are in long-term relationship with groups or service providers may help them to develop their product to increase the quality of experience for the client. In many cases this involves helping communities develop a series of activities, which can be done in a single day or in two days. This enables a visit to rural village or community tourism initiative to become viable as part of a standard package tour, and is not just limited to those wanting to have a completely alternative holiday.

Bureaucracy

This involves helping suppliers to undertake the necessary paperwork in registering themselves and in meeting the legal requirements of being a business.

Environment

This is mainly working with rural groups to support them in maintaining their wilderness and local environment to ensure that tourism does not do any damage.

COMMENTARY

Industry Trends

The role of the company in modern society is changing. It used to be acceptable to see a company's role as providing jobs and making a profit for its shareholders. However, the economic bottom line (profit) has given way to the triple bottom line (economic, social and environmental) and a company's responsibilities are now to its stakeholders, not only its shareholders. There is a growing body of research to suggest that responsible organisations are already more commercially successful. Part of this overall trend is increased involvement with the local community.

This spans a wide range of activities and includes developing local infrastructure, enhancing jobs skills of local residents, introducing technology, sharing business practice and supporting local business development. If done well and in partnership with the local community, it has the potential to bring many benefits. However, if done badly, it can further marginalise local groups. Increased involvement with the local community also brings benefits to the companies involved.

It provides a trained local labour pool that will be able to meet the company's needs, and increases understanding of local cultures and norms, so that local operations are smoother and more integrated. It also improves relationships with the community, supports the local infrastructure to improve logistics and service provision and increases employee skills and training. Finally, it enhances brand image which will, in turn, increase competitive advantage as clients include ethical principles in their purchasing decisions. Community involvement is a forward-looking activity for companies that want to be successful in ten or 20 years' time. It is a process of long-term investment, which will enhance the quality of the product and the competitiveness of the company.

Terminations

It is encouraging that so many tour operators spoke in terms of partnership with local communities or local service providers. Many of the smaller specialist operators saw this partnership in terms of a long-term commitment to a destination and the people there, with a strong emphasis on the centrality of good relationships at the heart of tourism, and a fairer distribution of any benefits. Medium-sized operators did also consider long-term relationships to be important. However, many of the more mainstream operators saw 'partnership' only in terms of providing a good-quality service that met the standards of the UK market, and made no mention of community involvement or developing good relationships. This seems to be little more than a new word for 'sub-contracting'. These bigger operators said that they would need so many local partners that they simply opt for the large, usually Western-owned hotels, which they know will already be able to meet their demands for quantity and quality.

Training features on many tour operators' agendas and includes skills development, customer service, product development, understanding the UK market and health, safety and environmental training. However, this was one of the most disappointing results of the questionnaire. One of the main barriers to improving local benefits was identified as lack of capacity or quality of local suppliers and ground agents, and yet the training that operators were offering in this area was limited.

On the whole, where training was offered, it was mainly done by the smaller, specialist operators who were committed to a particular group of people for many years. However, many of these smaller operators said that they were simply too small and could have only limited impact in a destination that they could not afford to provide any training. One even suggested that all operators be encouraged to contribute to a fund in the destination that could help to provide the necessary business training. Finally, developing local partnerships and providing training is often much better than charitable giving in terms of sustainable development. Partnerships and training, by their very nature, are integrated into business activities and their success can be easily be shown to contribute to the overall success of a tour operator in terms of its image, profitability and quality of a product. This is one of the most important areas in which operators could invest more time and effort to make a positive difference.

RECOMMENDATIONS

Principles

These key principles behind developing partnerships and increasing community involvement draw heavily on

Tearfund's Operating Principles for community development.

- *Long-term commitment*: A partnership takes time, to develop, and both sides need to know that the other is committed to the relationship.
- *Mutual respect*: Although the relationship is likely to have a power imbalance because the UK tour operator will have most of the money, mutual respect is vital if the partnership is to be successful. It acknowledges that both sides have something to bring, and both sides are likely to benefit and be changed in the process. It also includes respecting cultural differences and trying to come to a compromise, as opposed to imposing a Western approach. It may involve making initial contact through someone who is trusted by both sides of the potential partnership.
- *Accountability and transparency*: There needs to be a clear agreement about what any partnership involves, where different responsibilities lie and how the partnership will operate. There should also be clear understanding of what happens when things do not go exactly to plan, with the commitment to rectify any mistakes if possible, as opposed to abandoning a partnership at any sign of trouble. Where possible, decision-making should be a joint process.
- *Integrated into the whole community*: It is important that benefits are widely distributed so that any partnership can be seen to enhance community development and not just the livelihoods of a few people within a community.
- *Training and development*: Any partnership will need to include an element of training and development. This will be based on needs that have been identified together by both sides of the partnership. It will enable the ground agent, service provider or local community to provide a better service for tourists, and will help them maintain control of their lives as tourism develops.

- *Fair price and adherence to labour standards*: As a minimum, any tour operators should pay a good wage for a full-time job and a fair price for any services provided. This could mean paying above the local rate. It will also mean a bare minimum of adherence to international labour standards, but a responsible company should be seeking to implement the highest possible standards in labour, as it does in health and hygiene. They should seek to adhere to the same standards overseas as they do in the UK.

Action

Developing good-quality, long-term partnerships can be time time-consuming if done in a way that respects the other party. However, the initial investment of time will bring dividends in the future in terms of the increased quality of the product, experience for the tourists and benefits to the local community.

Possible activities for tour operators to undertake towards effective partnership with the community are:

- Integrate community involvement goals into the overall company mission and objectives. Develop a clear understanding and articulation of how this fits into the company strategy for providing good-quality holidays. Ensure that there is support at the highest level.
- Appoint a staff member for each destination area who will have responsibility for developing better local partnerships.
- Take a long-term view and consider using some of the money you would have given to charity to invest in training and business development for local communities in the destination. Develop a five or ten-year plan outlining what you hope to achieve.
- Seek local advice on the best way to develop partnerships. Consider working with a local organisation to make the necessary contacts, or with a UK-based group with the necessary expertise and

contacts. Develop a clear set of ground rules for the partnership.

- Focus the training input by working with local businesses to identify the barriers they face and the best ways to overcome them. Speak to the local tourism association and consider how you could work together. Support any local training institutions there may be which focus on business development or the hospitality industry. Speak to local government about the issues you face as an operator in using local services and supporting local development. Seek to work with them to support local businesses.
- Take a supply chain perspective and seek opportunities within the supply chain to make a difference and increase the quality of the tourism services you offer.
- Try a pilot project in one or two of the destinations in which you operate and seek your clients' opinions on the service provided and the experience they enjoyed.
- Focus on the poor and investigate how community involvement can integrate them into the tourism industry or provide them with some benefits from it.
- Evaluate your activities regularly to ensure that you are doing the most with your money, and to act to bring improvements if possible. Consider bringing in an independent assessor from time to time.
- Brief the staff in the destinations and in the UK about your community involvement and ensure that they have adequate information with which to brief clients.

RESPONSIBLE TOURISM POLICIES

This stage looks at whether companies have a written responsible tourism policy, the reasons for producing the policy and whether it focuses on the operations of the company, the supply chain or on tourists themselves. This policy may include reference to components mentioned in the previous three parts of the report, namely supporting the local economy, developing partnerships and charitable giving, but is not restricted to these areas of activity. Understanding that responsible tourism involves both companies and tourists, this part concludes with the possible components for a responsible tourism policy for the industry and a code for tourists.

FINDINGS

Do you have a Responsible Tourism Policy

Nearly 50% (32) of those asked claimed to have some form of responsible tourism policy.

What Form does this Policy Take

The responsible tourism policy took a variety of different forms.

Set of Principles within the Company

The most popular type of policy companies had was a set of written principles that underpinned their operations. Some published this in their brochure, others just kept it as an internal document.

Series of Activities

Other operators laid out a list of actions that they would do, and what they would not do.

Aspirations

A few companies had a written set of aspirations ie principles that they were aiming for, and what these might look like in practice. One operator even mentioned in their brochure that 'we don't pretend to be getting everything right' but that they are committed to doing as much as they can.

Code for Tourist Behaviour

Many companies said that their responsible tourism policy was a sheet of suggestions for how tourists should behave.

Responsibility was therefore shifted away from the operations of the company, on to the behaviour of tourists.

Do you Plan to Produce a Policy in the Future

Of the 33 who did not have a policy, over half of them (17) said they were planning to produce some form of policy in the future.

Why did you Produce your Policy

Companies had produced policies for all sorts of reasons:

- *Integral to the principles of the company*: When this was the case, it was common that tour operators had developed the set of principles right from the start. This was usually the case for smaller specialist operators, who had been established with the aim of promoting development in a region, or whose growth depended on a deep knowledge of a few areas eg Tribes Travel, Rainbow Tours.
- *To educate tourists*: The focus of policies on educating tourists is not surprising, considering the earlier results that mentioned unprepared tourists as being a key barrier to bringing more benefits to local people.
- *Way of differentiating themselves*: Some of the smaller operators had produced a policy either to react against mainstream tourism, or as a way of celebrating what they were doing and differentiating themselves. Dragoman wanted a policy as a reaction against the accusations that overland operators cause the most destruction. Discovery Initiatives set up and developed a policy as a reaction against the destruction to the environment of mainstream tourism and many socalled 'ecotourism' initiatives.
- *To integrate the ethos into business*: Some of the tour companies wanted all suppliers and staff to know their policy so that they could ensure that it was implemented right down to ground level. These companies had produced policies in a way that was

easy for suppliers and staff to understand and therefore implement.

- *External pressure*: Only three operators mentioned external pressure, from NGOs or from tourists, as a motivating factor for producing a policy. However, when asked if companies were thinking of producing a policy in the future, over half who did not have a policy already, said that they were. Pressure from NGOs or an awareness that clients' expectations were changing were frequently cited as reasons for doing this, even if the clients had not directly approached the companies themselves.

Why have you not Produced a Policy

Integrated into Business

Many of the specialist companies said that their policies were integrated into their operations, that they had only a few staff and that these staff were so involved in the company that they had no need for a written policy. One company previously had a responsible tourism code, but no longer used it.

Time to Explain to Ourists

Again, many of the specialist companies said that a verbal briefing to clients about the issues is better than a written one eg Sunvil Africa will spend an average of 2-3 hours overall on the phone to each client, answering their questions, and educating them about the place they are going to.

Lack of Priority

Some companies simply said that it was not a priority, that their clients were not interested and that they were simply in the business to make money.

Appears throughout the Brochure

Finally, a few companies who did not have an explicit policy, mentioned that their values and principles appeared scattered throughout the brochure, and integrated into what they had written.

Are more Clients asking about Responsible Tourism

Despite a recognition by many companies that there is increased interest (especially in the media) in holidays that are more ethical, few companies reported that their clients were asking more about it. Only about 30% (19 out of 61) said that clients were asking more about some of the social, environmental and economic issues in tourism.

However, a significant number of the specialist operators said that clients were certainly more interested in the issues when they came back from a holiday and had seen the situations for themselves, and seen the benefits that tourism can bring, and the potential negative effects.

COMMENTARY

Industry Trends

It is increasingly common across all industries for companies to have responsible business policies. Examples include environmental policies of various oil companies, labour standards and ethical sourcing policies of UK supermarkets, a commitment to avoid the use of child labour by textile companies and statements against the use of animal testing by cosmetic companies.

Some companies have their practices independently verified and are awarded a mark eg the fairtrade mark. Others simply produce a policy for public relations purposes and do little to ensure that it is implemented. In the tourism industry there are numerous schemes and awards, recognising various different aspects of responsible business practice.

British Airways Tourism for Tomorrow Awards have annual awards in six categories including accommodation, tourism organisation and mass tourism. Green Globe certifies for their view of sustainable tourism and allows operators to use one logo if they join the programme and another one if they reach the required standard.

AITO have developed a responsible tourism policy and plan that it will become a condition of membership in the future. Even if some of these schemes could still go further in embracing all aspects of responsible tourism practice, they serve to highlight good practice that is happening at the moment and are encouraging more operators to develop their responsible tourism policies and practices.

Terminations

Many tour operators claim to have some form of responsible tourism policy, although these appear in widely different forms and are aimed at different people. Some are aimed at staff, others at suppliers and others at tourists themselves. Reasons for producing these were to educate tourists, suppliers and staff, as a reaction against the mainstream industry, and because the principles are integral to the operation of the company. Only a few tour operators are up-front about their policies or make them explicit and easy for clients to access. Although the policies may appear in their brochures, many are scattered throughout the brochure so they are difficult to understand fully, and some are so brief as to be virtually meaningless. Some very good and detailed policies do exist, and the best ones include a broad set of principles with details about how these will be implemented in practice right throughout the supply chain eg The Imaginative Traveller.

However, over half of the operators asked still have no policies (although half of these said they planned to develop one in the future). It is likely that more and more tourists will be asking for the responsible tourism policies of companies, so there will be a mounting pressure to produce them. However, tourists are increasingly discerning, and will need to see evidence that the policy is not just for show, but is actually implemented on the ground. Companies will need to show evidence of good practice examples where they are behaving responsibly and making a real difference to the lives of people on the ground.

Many tour operators also see themselves as having a strong educational role in helping tourists to understand the people and culture in the destination they will be travelling to. A number of well-developed policies exist in this area, based on work over many years. Sending out a basic code to tourists to encourage them to think about their behaviour is such a well-established practice in some parts of the industry, and it is a relatively straightforward thing to do, that it is surprising that so few operators do it.

RECOMMENDATIONS

Possible Components of a Responsible Tourism Policy for Industry Operations

Many of the principles behind a responsible tourism policy will be similar to the principles involved in setting up partnerships. They have also been covered extensively elsewhere, so as suggested, not attempt to replicate previous work. What makes a policy meaningful is the details of how it will be put into practice, and below we have offered some suggestions.

- *Support local links*: Use locally-owned accommodation and service providers wherever possible, and support local artisans and craft producers. Favour ground operators who use local transport providers, source food locally and source guides locally. Work with already established local businesses, service providers, co-operatives or associations who favour employment of local people, pay adequate wages, and have good working conditions and employee relations.
- *Clear contract*: Negotiate clear terms and conditions of operation with service providers, recognising the power imbalance that exists and allowing for this while undertaking negotiations.
- *Social and environmental audits*: Extend health and safety audits of hotels to include environmental and social issues, and recommend changes based on your findings.
- *Culture*: Respect the local traditions and culture in the places where you operate, and allow workers and staff to observe their religious and cultural practices.

- *Community partnerships*: Identify community initiatives with which you can form a partnership, and establish what training they will need
- *Charitable giving*: Develop a clear policy on charitable giving and integrate this with your normal business activities and training of local suppliers and service providers.
- *Monitoring*: Monitor your activities regularly to assess their impact and see if there are any areas for improvement.
- *Code for tourists*: Produce a code for tourists in order to encourage responsible behaviour from all those who travel with you. This code may vary between destinations.
- *Training staff*: Train your staff in how to implement the responsible tourism policy.
- *Implement policy through the supply chain*: Make your responsible tourism policy clear and available to service providers with whom you are working, and provide the necessary support and training for them to implement any changes.

2

Ethics in Tourism

INTRODUCTION

The tourism industry is one of the largest industries in the world, and despite recent events that have made its operating environment more complex, the industry continues to grow. It has the potential to bring major benefits to destinations, but can also be damaging to the people living there and to their environment. Other industries have already understood this ambivalent nature of trade and have adopted the triple bottom line of social, environmental and economic responsibility.

It is now time for the tourism industry to rise to this challenge–the challenge of ethical tourism. Ethical tourism is in the best interests of all involved. It offers tour operators a competitive advantage and safeguards the future of the industry by ensuring the long-term sustainability of a destination. It offers the tourists a richer experience, as holidays will draw on the distinctive features of a destination.

It is also in the interests of those living there and those working for development, as it can help to combat poverty and contribute to sustainable development. The tourism industry is highly competitive and tour operators are under increasing pressure to differentiate their products. Research suggests that once the main criteria for a holiday are satisfied, clients will make choices based on ethical considerations such as working conditions, the environment and charitable giving. Clients are also looking for increased quality and experience in their holiday.

In this climate, companies would do well to differentiate their products according to consumer demand *i.e.* based on ethical criteria. In this respect, especially in recent years a new issue is under discussion called "ethics in tourism" and it calls all the people involved in tourism industry to follow its codes and help the sustainable development of this industry. This research is concerned with the issue of the ethics in tourism industry and it focuses on the Global Code of Ethics for tourism set by the Worlds Tourism Organization.

SUSTAINABLE TOURISM

Taking into account the swift and continued growth, both past and foreseeable, of the tourism activity, whether for leisure, business, culture, religious or health purposes, and its powerful effects, both positive and negative, on the environment, the economy and the society of both generating and receiving countries, on local communities and indigenous peoples, as well as on international relations and trade, Aiming to promote responsible, sustainable and universally accessible tourism in the framework of right of all persons to use their free time for leisure pursuits or travel with respect for the choices of society of all peoples, But convinced that the world tourism industry as a whole has much to gain by operating in an environment that favours the market economy, private enterprise and free trade and that serves to optimize its beneficial effects on the creation of wealth and employment.

Also firmly convinced that, provided a number of principles and a certain number of rules are observed, responsible and sustainable tourism is by no means incompatible with the growing liberalization of the conditions governing trade in services and under whose aegis the enterprises of this sector operate and that it is possible to reconcile in this sector economy and ecology, environment and development, openness to international trade and protection of social and cultural identities.

Considering that, with such an approach, all the stakeholders in tourism development–national, regional and local administrations, enterprises, business associations, workers in the sector, non-governmental organizations and bodies of all kinds belonging to the tourism industry, as well as host communities, the media and the tourists themselves, have different albeit interdependent responsibilities in the individual and societal development of tourism and that the formulation of their individual rights and duties will contribute to meeting this aim.

Today, some new concepts as "sustainable tourism", "tourism morality", "ethics in tourism", "visiting nature", "green tourism", "responsible tourism", "people-oriented tourism" and "parallel tourism have emerged in tourism industry. Emergence and development of the tourism thought which could adapt itself in terms of social affairs with all ecological features of the touristic regions is the outcome of such discussions. Figure shows the most important traits of touristic products known as the "Magic Pentagon of the tourism development".

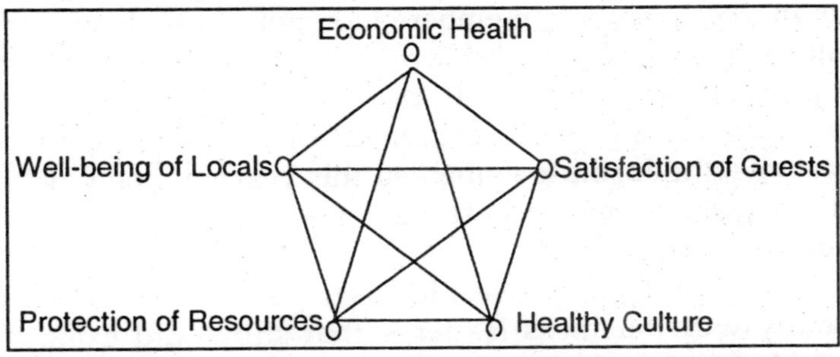

Based on recent strategies implemented, the desired development is the one that all its affecting and affected factors develop in the same level *i.e.* this magic pentagon seeks to establish the highest balance between tourism and social-ecological features of the touristic regions.

GLOBAL ETHICS

The international community regularly calls for global action to provide more decent lives for more of earth's inhabitants, while securing the future for everyone. Those common calls to action invoke a set of global moral practices–practices like economic development, public health, human rights regulation, and environmental protection. Most countries rely on their local legal and ethical systems to try to solve global problems.

In order to achieve the leadership which is needed, we need to cooperate globally. This cooperation, using respectful dialogue to search for common spirituality, will enable us to go beyond national leadership and achieve global ethics for business. Organizations whether they want to or not provide a cultural setting within which their individual members work. This setting may or may not be conducive to ethical decision making and ethical actions. In some organizations, people are clearly important and valued; while at the others they seem less valued.

The environmental impact of one company's work processes is addressed with attention and a sense of responsibility, while other companies invest in obfuscation and evasion. What are the requisites for an ethical culture? How can an organization's members incorporate the language of ethics into their day-to-day work? What conversations must be encouraged and what processes utilized to build community within the organization? To address these questions, the Institute embarked this year on a new field of exploration, which we are currently calling Cultures of Integrity.

The steps taken this year led us to a series of interviews—initially with business leaders—that show and exemplify current practices that encourage and promote sound ethical judgment. Some of these organizations have firmly established their culture and reputation over decades; others are more cutting-edge entrepreneurs. As we deepen our understanding around how cultures of integrity are established, grow, and thrive, a bank of new knowledge will accrue to the Institute.

Books, conferences, and other marketable products will follow with broad application in both of our key sectors—business and education. "We live in a time when the products of our private and governmental organizations have become so technologically powerful that they can have almost instantaneous national or global effects. The size of these organizations and the reach of these technologies mean that ethical failures can have worldwide consequences. That's why an understanding of organizational ethics and culture is so crucial now."

ETHICS AND TOURISM

The substantial growth of tourism activity clearly marks tourism as one of the most remarkable economic and social phenomena of the past century. The number of international arrivals shows an evolution from a mere 25 million international arrivals in 1950 to over 700 million in 2002, corresponding to an average annual growth rate of 6.6%. In addition to the numerical growth of tourism, there has been an increasing geographic spread of tourism to encompass almost all the reaches of the globe.

Simultaneously, there has been a diversification of the tourism product from the traditional sun, sea and sand offering to a product that can be potentially more intrusive or more beneficial for those living in the tourism destination. Tourism's expansion has meant the industry now represents the leading source of foreign exchange in at least 38% of countries, and ranks in the top five industries for exports in 83% of countries.

However, in addition to the cited economic indicators displaying the dominance of the tourism industry, there has been a commensurate and almost equally well-publicized rise and recognition of the potentially negative impacts of the burgeoning tourism industry. Researchers have been critical of the pernicious social and environmental impacts the industry can have from reinforcing western domination over developing countries through the 'host/guest' relationship to the visual scars on the landscape caused by ski resorts or golf courses.

This has led to calls for the industry to exercise greater responsibility and "professionalism' in order to protect the "golden goose" and mirrors the arguments for greater corporate and social responsibility in other industries. Corporate Social Responsibility is a specific application of the notion of environmental and social auditing to business practice. The technique is strongly promoted by Fair Trade in Tourism which suggests that the technique of CSR emerged in the late 1990s out of NGO efforts to create a more equitable international trade system. According to Mowforth and Munt the tourism industry is well behind other industries in terms of CSR, and the absence of ethical leadership in the tourism industry has been 'astounding'.

However, in the last few decades, responsible tourism has emerged as a significant trend in the western world, as wider consumer market trends towards lifestyle marketing and ethical consumption have spread to tourism. Tourism organizations are beginning to realise that promoting their ethical stance can be good business as it potentially enhances a company's profits, management effectiveness, public image and employee relations.

Yet, although more attention is now being paid to ethics in tourism there is a very weak foundation of research into tourism ethics studies to date. The consequence is that the arguments presented for and against CSR in tourism are often simplistic and largely without any practical evidence.

PRINCIPLES OF THE GLOBAL CODE OF ETHICS FOR TOURISM

- The understanding and promotion of the ethical values common to humanity, with an attitude of tolerance and respect for the diversity of religious, philosophical and moral beliefs, are both the foundation and the consequence of responsible tourism; stakeholders in tourism development and tourists themselves should observe the social and cultural traditions and practices of all peoples, including those of minorities and indigenous peoples and to recognize their worth;
- Tourism activities should be conducted in harmony with the attributes and traditions of the host regions and countries and in respect for their laws, practices and customs;
- The host communities, on the one hand, and local

professionals, on the other, should acquaint themselves with and respect the tourists who visit them and find out about their lifestyles, tastes and expectations; the education and training imparted to professionals contribute to a hospitable welcome;

- It is the task of the public authorities to provide protection for tourists and visitors and their belongings; they must pay particular attention to the safety of foreign tourists owing to the particular vulnerability they may have; they should facilitate the introduction of specific means of information, prevention, security, insurance and assistance consistent with their needs; any attacks, assaults, kidnappings or threats against tourists or workers in the tourism industry, as well as the willful destruction of tourism facilities or of elements of cultural or natural heritage should be severely condemned and punished in accordance with their respective national laws;
- When travelling, tourists and visitors should not commit any criminal act or any act considered criminal by the laws of the country visited and abstain from any conduct felt to be offensive or injurious by the local populations, or likely to damage the local environment; they should refrain from all trafficking in illicit drugs, arms, antiques, protected species and products and substances that are dangerous or prohibited by national regulations;
- Tourists and visitors have the responsibility to acquaint themselves, even before their departure, with the characteristics of the countries they are preparing to visit; they must be aware of the health and security risks inherent in any travel outside their usual environment and behave in such a way as to minimize those risks;
- All the stakeholders in tourism development should safeguard the natural environment with a view to achieving sound, continuous and sustainable

economic growth geared to satisfying equitably the needs and aspirations of present and future generations;

- All forms of tourism development that are conducive to saving rare and precious resources, in particular water and energy, as well as avoiding so far as possible waste production, should be given priority and encouraged by national, regional and local public authorities;
- The staggering in time and space of tourist and visitor flows, particularly those resulting from paid leave and school holidays, and a more even distribution of holidays should be sought so as to reduce the pressure of tourism activity on the environment and enhance its beneficial impact on the tourism industry and the local economy;
- Tourism infrastructure should be designed and tourism activities programmed in such a way as to protect the natural heritage composed of ecosystems and biodiversity and to preserve endangered species of wildlife; the stakeholders in tourism development, and especially professionals, should agree to the imposition of limitations or constraints on their activities when these are exercised in particularly sensitive areas: desert, polar or high mountain regions, coastal areas, tropical forests or wetlands, propitious to the creation of nature reserves or protected areas;
- Nature tourism and ecotourism are recognized as being particularly conducive to enriching and enhancing the standing of tourism, provided they respect the natural heritage and local populations and are in keeping with the carrying capacity of the sites;
- Tourism professionals have an obligation to provide tourists with objective and honest information on their places of destination and on the conditions of travel, hospitality and stays; they should ensure that the contractual clauses proposed to their customers

are readily understandable as to the nature, price and quality of the services they commit themselves to providing and the financial compensation payable by them in the event of a unilateral breach of contract on their part;

- Tourism professionals, insofar as it depends on them, should show concern, in cooperation with the public authorities, for the security and safety, accident prevention, health protection and food safety of those who seek their services; likewise, they should ensure the existence of suitable systems of insurance and assistance; they should accept the reporting obligations prescribed by national regulations and pay fair compensation in the event of failure to observe their contractual obligations;
- Tourism professionals, so far as this depends on them, should contribute to the cultural and spiritual fulfillment of tourists and allow them, during their travels, to practice their religions;
- The public authorities of the generating States and the host countries, in cooperation with the professionals concerned and their associations, should ensure that the necessary mechanisms are in place for the repatriation of tourists in the event of the bankruptcy of the enterprise that organized their travel;
- Governments have the right–and the duty-especially in a crisis, to inform their nationals of the difficult circumstances, or even the dangers they may encounter during their travels abroad; it is their responsibility however to issue such information without prejudicing in an unjustified or exaggerated manner the tourism industry of the host countries and the interests of their own operators; the contents of travel advisories should therefore be discussed beforehand with the authorities of the host countries and the professionals concerned; recommendations formulated should be strictly proportionate to the

gravity of the situations encountered and confined to the geographical areas where the insecurity has arisen; such advisories should be qualified or cancelled as soon as a return to normality permits;

- The press, and particularly the specialized travel press and the other media, including modern means of electronic communication, should issue honest and balanced information on events and situations that could influence the flow of tourists; they should also provide accurate and reliable information to the consumers of tourism services; the new communication and electronic commerce technologies should also be developed and used for this purpose; as is the case for the media, they should not in any way promote sex tourism;

CONSUMERS OF TOURISM PRODUCTS

Research on marketing of tourism products in the recent years has showed that consumers of such products tend to pay much more for products in which ethical values are considered. Based on numerous researches in this field, commitment of tourist agencies to ethical principles has had a significant and positive effect on the marketing of their products.

HOLDERS OF TOURS

Attention of holders of ensemble tours to ethical issues would definitely affect the increase in the quality and added value of tourism products. Agents of such institutes, especially in marketing field, even for achieving their commercial goals and competing with other institutes can rely on this approach, as the behavioural manner of the responsible agents of such institutes often based on the "work ethics" can lead to higher benefits in their business.

PROVIDING THE NATIVES WITH NECESSARY INFORMATION

Of the important affecting factors in the success of tourism in a region is to try to encourage the natives of the region to contribute in tourism activities and this will lead in sustainable development of tourism industry. It is thus strongly recommended to employ natives of a developing touristic region in the agencies rather than non-natives and inform them with the tourism advantages and potentials and train them to cooperate in such activities.

STAFF OF THE TOURISM AGENCIES

Tourism is one of the biggest industries in the world which offers the biggest number of employed people in the world. More than just an industry, tourism is a cultural activity able to change the world in which we live in. It's exactly this cultural dynamic which makes tourism interesting and even more important. Tourism agencies serve as a connecting bridge between tourism and products of travel which are offered. To have an economy with high standards, the development of tourism must be planned, controlled and "sold" to tourists in the best way possible.

Tourism agency is the business which sells travel packages to destinations around the world which are connected to the products and services, especially the airline, hotel, travel company etc. A lot of travel agents have a special department which deals with reservations; meanwhile tourism agencies are specialized for business trips. Productivity and output of tourism agencies has a close relationship with the work quality of the individual workers in tourism industry. Involving non-experienced human resource in these agencies will be a negative factor impeding the development of this industry.

CONCLUSION

Considering the growth and development of tourism industry in recent years and its positive consequences in developing countries in terms of the increase in currency resource, diminution of unemployment rate, increase in foreign investment and public welfare and income of the residents and finally in terms of the sustainable development of this industry, following the ethical terms made by the WTO seems necessary.

These ethical terms are summarized as follows according to principles of the Global Code of Ethics for Tourism:

- The public and private stakeholders in tourism development should cooperate in the implementation of these principles and monitor their effective application;
- The stakeholders in tourism development should recognize the role of international institutions, among which the World Tourism Organization ranks first, and nongovernmental organizations with competence in the field of tourism promotion and development, the protection of human rights, the environment or health, with due respect for the general principles of international law;
- The same stakeholders should demonstrate their intention to refer any disputes concerning the application or interpretation of the Global Code of Ethics for Tourism for conciliation to an impartial third body known as the World Committee on Tourism Ethics.
- States Members or non-members of WTO, without being obliged to do so, should accept expressly the principles embodied in the Global Code of Ethics for Tourism and to use them as a basis when establishing their national laws and regulations and to inform accordingly the World Committee on Tourism Ethics.
- Tourism enterprises and bodies, whether WTO Affiliate Members or not, and their associations should include the relevant provisions of the Code in their contractual instruments or to make specific reference to them in their own codes of conduct or professional rules and to report on them to the World Committee on Tourism Ethics.

3

The Ethics of Poverty Tourism

INTRODUCTION

Reality tourism in impoverished areas goes by several names; critics call it "poorism;" a more neutral term is "poverty tourism." Articles in The New York Times, Smithsonian Magazine, Newsweek, The Wall Street Journal, The Huffington Post, and other popular media characterize these as trips as morally controversial. Critics attack not just actual visits, but also virtual poverty tourism through film.

In the film Slumdog Millionaire, the protagonist is an orphan from Mumbai's Dharavi slum. Shyamal Sengupta, a film professor at the Whistling Woods International Institute in Mumbai, condemns the film for being a poverty tour. In the month before it won the Oscar for Best Picture, Slumdog Millionaire was derided as "poverty porn" in the pages of the London Times. National Public Radio even ran a lively episode of "Talk of the Nation" devoted to the topic called "'Poverty Porn': Education or Exploitation?".

Are poverty tours really the moral equivalent of pedophiliac tourism in Southeast Asia? Far from being a trendy and short-lived topic of conversation, the debate over poverty tourism reaches back at least to Victorian London, where "slumming" was both vilified and celebrated, fueling both prostitution and significant social welfare institutions. In all likelihood, poverty tourism is much older than critics acknowledge. Since most of the criticisms of poverty tourism occur in journalistic contexts, the leading arguments espouse personal convictions that fall short of the criteria that typifies scholarly debate. Indeed, most of the contributors to poverty tourism discourse do not reconstruct opposing views charitably. Perpetuating one-sided polemics, they fail to satisfy the demands of communal justification. Furthermore, most contributors to poverty tourism discourse do not comment on whether other people already have advanced similar, if not identical, views. Given these problems of subjectivism and redundancy, the poverty tourism debate requires reorientation if it is to become a topic of mature deliberation.

With the hope of moving beyond the impediments just outlined, the purpose of this thesis is to reconstruct and assess core moral issues surrounding poverty tourism, giving special emphasis to the most frequently cited problem, voyeurism. Not only should this reconstruction and assessment benefit the general public, but it should be of special interest to readers of Environmental Philosophy. The debates about poverty tourism concern judgments about conduct that takes place in a distinctive environment. Were that environment to lose its defining characteristics, the conduct would cease.

This collaboratively written thesis draws from different academic backgrounds and personal experiences. One author, Boston University law professor Kevin Outterson, has taken graduate students to Brazilian favelas. He has also taken religiously sponsored trips to colonias and garbage dumps in Mexico, and impoverished religious minority communities in Egypt. While journalistic coverage reduces Outterson's views to titillating talking points, people who read articles that quote him are given less restrictive opportunities to judge his conduct and values.

For example, The NY Times provided an online discussion board for readers respond to "Slum Visits: Tourism or Voyeurism," an article that quoted Outterson. By addressing some of the central points that were posted there, we are introducing overdue parity. The other author, Evan Selinger, is a philosopher. His training in phenomenology—the branch of philosophy that analyses embodied first-person experience—enables him to discern ambiguity and nuance in ethical dilemmas that mainstream discussions fail to detect.

While Selinger has not gone on a poverty tour, his expertise in phenomenology can:

- Enhance our understanding of experiences that Outterson and others share,
- Clarify how the poverty tourism debates revolve around phenomenological concepts that have been subject to more sophisticated analysis in academic literatures than public editorials.

First, we describe Outterson's experience of preparing law students to visit favelas, and account for the significant interactions that transpired while there. Second, we address the charge the debate about poverty tourism is a journalistic red herring that distracts the public's attention from more pressing issues. Third, we reconstruct and assess the leading moral criticisms of poverty tourists that centre on the allegation of voyeurism.

As a caveat, we should note that while as suggested, be pursuing a deflationary agenda, what follows does not amount of a moral defence of most poverty tours that currently are being conducted. To the contrary, we acknowledge that many of the current tours are, in fact, morally questionable. When we defend poverty tourism, we do so with an eye towards a minority of actual of actual practices that are structured around fairly robust educational ideals and reflexive moral considerations.

WHAT HAPPENS DURING A FAVELA TOUR? PROFESSOR OUTTERSON'S EXPERIENCE

The students were nervous about the favela. Most came from middle class backgrounds from one of the poorest states in the United States. We were in Brazil for a three-week foreign study trip sponsored by the West Virginia University College of Law. The programme was codirected with a colleague, Professor andre cummings. For some of these students, this was their first trip outside the U.S. Our pedagogical goal for the foreign study programme was to expose the students to Brazilian legal culture, forcing them to think more deeply about the relationship between law and society.

Before we left, we spent two semesters exploring Brazilian history and culture, using both critical and conventional materials, assisted by Brazilian graduate students at WVU. While in Brazil, we attended classes with students at two Brazilian law schools (in Rio de Janeiro and in Vitória, Espírito Santo). Most of the classes were comparative in focus and we enjoyed extensive discussions with our colleagues. A favela tour was not part of the original syllabus. But a unique teaching moment emerged.

We were staying in Ipanema, an energetic beachfront neighbourhood in Rio. Ipanema is an expensive place to live, more residential and less touristy than nearby Copacabana. One key to Ipanema is the access to cheap labour from nearby Rocinha, a large hillside favela in Rio. It is an incomplete picture of Brazil to enjoy Ipanema's beautiful beaches, hotels and restaurants without seeing the poor people who make it all possible: the people who swept the streets at dawn, who cooked the food, cleaned the rooms, and sold things on the beach.

The danger of voyeurism and reinforcing stereotypes concerned me, but our students were well prepared for this experience, and we would have ample academic time to process the experience critically and personally. We asked for a few student volunteers to come into the Rocinha favela with a local operator of a poverty tour. We chose this tour because he did not offer a "safari" experience from a tour bus, but led small groups, on foot, with some connection to the community.

We began with a van ride from Ipanema to Rocinha, a short 15-minute ride across a gaping social gulf. Rocinha is a hillside favela, home to perhaps 200,000 people. We ascended to the top of Rocinha using "motoboys"–small motorcycle taxis driven by young men. From the top, we walked down very small pedestrian streets for the next three hours, with the guide explaining his view on how the favela worked. We saw small shops, ate sonhas from a bakery, walked past tidy homes, bars, and impromptu laundries.

The longest stops were at an artists' studio and a community centre that some donors have supported. We have returned several times over the years, and have seen the growth of the community centre and its programmes. The guide has built some financial relationships with the people along the route. All undoubtedly enjoy the tourist money, but we also experienced something more personal. The guide paused several times to explain how Rocinha operates with very little government assistance.

Basic public health facilities are modest; sewage runs in open gutters; water is piped in plastic pipes above ground; he reports that even the postal service stops at the road and residents have to pay extra for delivery to their homes. For law students, many interesting questions follow–Do the residents own their homes? (Yes, in a practical sense.) Do they have legal title? (Not really, but the local community association functions as a semi-formal real property registry.) Is there much robbery or rape? (Not really, the drug gangs keep the peace unless a rival gang or the police enter the favela.)

After three hours, we emerged at the bottom and caught vans back to Ipanema. For many students, it was the highlight of their time in Brazil. We debriefed the students afterwards, to help process the experience. Students consistently noted that their expectations were challenged. They were nervous about poverty, crime, and despair and expected to encounter things they had seen on film. What they saw instead was community, homes, and dignity in the midst of poverty.

They interacted with real people, instead of images in a movie like City of God. They also improved their understanding of the connection between rich and poor communities, both as a local process and in the context of globalization. The long-term effect on the students is still unknown, but the post-tour seminars we held with our students were some of the best discussions we had in law school. Many students appear to be deeply affected by the experience and report the experience as valuable.

The West Virginia programme is primarily educational, and therefore may not be representative of poverty tourism in general. The programme certainly can be improved. Others in Rocinha criticize the tour we took, and we have modest abilities to confirm many of the statements offered as "facts" along the tour without deeper ties to residents of Rocinha. It is possible to imagine ways to improve this experience for all concerned, especially for the residents of Rocinha.

One can also find other forms of poverty tourism that would be easier to attack, such as "Ugly American" tours on a safari bus. We deliberately avoided those models. A second, briefer example is in Mazatlan, Mexico, another tourist destination. The poor of Mazatlan live in colonias. We have visited nearly a dozen different colonias, which range from working poor to extremely poor. The poorest colonia was at the base of the city's garbage dump, until the local government evicted them in 2008. These visits were not academic, but were sponsored by the La Viña church, a Protestant church with ties to many U.S. and Canadian churches. Church-sponsored mission trips are a huge undertaking in the U.S. Tens of thousands of churches send small teams out each year, generally to less affluent communities for a week or two. Some destinations are foreign such as Mazatlan; others are domestic, like rebuilding projects in New Orleans.

Some focus on evangelism; others on service projects. At La Viña, service and evangelism are seen as two sides of the same coin: serve and love, following the example of Jesus. In Mazatlan, some teams focus on primary care medical clinics; others work with children and adults; Bible studies and prayer ministry occurs in an open shed while other volunteers prepare meals for colonia feeding centres established by the church. Everything is done in the name of Jesus.

The Mazatlan church itself is an interesting partnership, with two congregations meeting in the same building. The English-speaking members are generally snowbirds, retired Canadians and U.S. citizens with some money who spend the winter in Mazatlan. They hail from many church backgrounds or no particular church, but winter at La Viña.

The Mexican-speaking congregation is made up of local people, generally with less wealth. These two groups partner together in the outreach efforts to the colonias, supported by the mission trip teams from the U.S. and Canada. Certainly these trips are also open to critique. Christianity Today, a leading evangelical magazine, asks whether some mission trips are "religious tourism." In our context, perhaps we should evaluate them as a subset of poverty tourism.

IS THE DEBATE ABOUT POVERTY TOURISM UNSEEMLY

Some see the debate about poverty tourism as unseemly. These critics allege that the debate diverts attention away from more significant moral and political issues, and even encourages the people who think about it to turn a blind eye to the injustices that affluent Western countries have committed against developing countries in the past, and continue to commit in the present. One of the readers who posted a response to "Slum Visits: Tourism or Voyeurism" makes this case in especially stark terms.

The reader alleges that because debates about poverty tourism focus exclusively on the current behaviour of a few individuals who are engaged in unusual activity, they:

- Obscure the relevant large-scale issues concerning how European and the United States policies have been and continue to be responsible for creating global inequality,
- Obscure the rationalizations that Europeans and Americans come up to justify why they are not willing to further global justice by accepting a lower standard of living.

We acknowledge the importance of questions concerning what obligations are entailed by "backwards" (*e.g.*, potentially rectification) and "forwards" (*e.g.*, potentially compensation) looking dimensions of justice at the large-scale. Nevertheless, we suggest that debates about poverty tourism actually enrich discussions about global ethics. Globalization reduces the difficulty and cost for tourists to travel the world—in both virtual (*e.g.*, via Internet and film) and more robustly corporeal (*e.g.*, via air and ground transportation) ways.

If we take global tourism as a given, then it becomes increasingly important to determine which values and ideals should guide a traveller's conduct. The importance of providing careful ethical reflection on tourist conduct is heightened by the fact that the present is marked by the growth of "tourism reflexivity," a concept that sociologist John Urry defines as "the set of disciplines, procedures, and criteria that enable each...place to monitor, evaluate, and develop its 'tourism potential' within the emerging patterns of global tourism."

The combination of ease of travel, enhanced tourism reflexivity, persistence of differences in cultural practices, and changes in material culture make it likely that the foreseeable future will be plagued by normative concerns related to tourism, especially as it relates to matters of poverty, indigenous rights, natural resource use, and biodiversity. Comprehensive analysis of global justice requires analyzing poverty tourism.

In anticipation of possible objections, let us note that we would be willing to withdraw our claim about the merits of poverty tourism discourse if someone were to establish that:

- The public is capable of cognitively processing only a single debate about global justice at a time,
- Debating poverty tourism diminishes how the public addresses pressing matters of global justice. With respect to (1), no empirical evidence exists that validates the patronizing charge that discussions of poverty tourism detrimentally monopolize public attention.

To be sure, good reasons exist for being skeptical about how informed the general populace is on a number of issues that are central to social welfare. Nevertheless, such skepticism only validates the argument being made by sociologist Harry Collins who insists that better tools need to be developed for analyzing the role that technical expertise should play in policy formation.

That is, while the public can entertain multiple policy issues, the level of technical detail surrounding any one of them may be beyond the scope of what the average person can grasp. Likewise, no compelling logical, conceptual, or causal relation has been established that validates (2). Now, a bias may very well exist that inclines the general public to view responsibility primarily as a matter of assessing individual conduct, and not judging institutional structures and collective behaviour.

Anthropologist Allan Hanson makes a compelling case that this bias exists because assumptions related to "methodological individualism" have informed historical conceptions of responsibility. But even if such bias is pervasive, partisans can enhance discussions of responsibility by framing the debate over poverty tourism as an issue that remains contentious largely because large-scale issues of global justice have not been satisfactorily addressed.

THE CHARGE OF VOYEURISM

Poverty tourists regularly are denounced as immoral voyeurs, and the charge of voyeurism has fueled the recent debate over audience response to Slumdog Millionaire. As mentioned in the Introduction, critics like Shyamal Sengupta condemn the film for being a poverty tour; Alice Miles labeled it "poverty porn." Are state universities and church groups engaged in the global pornography business? Since critics presuppose different meanings when they use the term "voyeur," it can be difficult to assess which of their appraisals, if any, are valid. Moreover, inadequately formulated theses tend to accompany the prevalent linguistic impression.

To overcome these impediments, we proceed by:

- Providing a taxonomy of the circumstances in which observing others has been construed as an immoral use of the gaze;
- Appealing to this taxonomy to clarify which observational circumstances should be deemed relevant to the poverty tourism debate.

Taxonomy of Voyeurism

No one argues that it is inherently demeaning to look at others. That view would be so extreme as to be the expression of deep pathology. However, some contexts of observation are seen as morally troubling.

Claims about immoral behaviour have been leveled at the following scenarios:

- Immoral voyeurism occurs when undetected glances invade other people's privacy and take advantage of their vulnerability.
- Immoral voyeurism occurs in some instances where people perceive that they are being observed for demeaning purposes.
- Immoral voyeurism occurs when observers are motivated to look at others to further demeaning ends.
- Immoral voyeurism occurs in some instance where observers are dishonest about their reasons for observing others.
- Immoral voyeurism occurs in some instances where the mere presence of a distinctive group of observers makes people who are observed and not members of that group feel demeaned.
- Immoral voyeurism occurs in some instances where members of a privileged group misrepresent the values and beliefs of an underprivileged group on the basis of selective observations of their lives.
- Immoral voyeurism occurs when people view inappropriate events and images.

In the next three parts we clarify what each of these contexts entails and discuss whether they apply to the poverty tourism debates.

Voyeurism and the Undetected Glance

Let us start by examining the first charge that immoral voyeurism occurs when undetected glances invade other people's privacy and take advantage of their vulnerability. The tradition of existential phenomenology provides us with some insight into this issue, especially a frequently cited passage of Being and Nothingness (1943) in which Jean-Paul Sartre describes his experience of being startled by a walker's approaching footsteps as he covertly peeps at someone through a keyhole in a door.

Sartre emphasizes feeling shame, and suggests that the emotion is triggered by recognition that his gaze took advantage of another's vulnerability: "It is shame which reveals to me the Other's look and myself at the end of that look. It is shame...which makes me live, not know the situation of being looked at". In characterizing the situation of shame as one that is "lived" and not "known," Sartre makes the anti-intellectualist point that his recognition of harm does not occur via an inner monologue that is expressed in propositional form.

Rather, the recognition occurs in the visceral experience of a stinging emotional state. In identifying emotional experience with moral awareness, Sartre appears to be suggesting that non-pathological people inevitably will feel deserved shame if they find themselves caught (or on the verge of being caught) being "Peeping Toms." However, at the time that Being and Nothingness was written, Sartre had not yet fully clarified the moral dimensions of existentialism.

One way to attribute a moral interpretation to Sartre's description of voyeurism is to follow a line of thinking that Leon Kass, a contemporary bioethicist, advances. In Life, Liberty, and the Defence of Dignity (2002) Kass refers to emotional expressions of a distinct class of moral judgments as the "wisdom of repugnance." As Kass sees it, certain negative emotional responses offer evidence that an action or characteristic is intrinsically bad.

In differentiating the evidentiary statuses of reasoned and emotional responses to moral harm in "crucial cases," he goes so far as to privilege emotional attunement: "In crucial cases...repugnance is the emotional expression of deep wisdom, beyond reason's power fully to articulate it". Deep debate exists as to whether intuitive moral judgments of the sort designated by Kass are objective, or whether they merely reflect the contingent values that subjects internalize through cultural discipline.

As suggested, return to this issue in the next part. For now it suffices to note that the context under review does not apply to the poverty tourism debates. If poverty tourists are guilty of any moral infractions, these infractions occur in contexts where poor people realise that they are being observed. No one is accusing poverty tourists of engaging in surreptitious peeping.

Voyeurism and Demeaning Ends

We turn now to second and third contexts in which voyeurism has been seen as immoral: instances where people perceive that they are being observed for demeaning purposes, and instances where observers are motivated to look at others to further demeaning ends.

The following reader comments on "Slum Visits: Tourism or Voyeurism" are illustrative examples of how critics see both of these contexts as applicable to the poverty tourism debates:

- "Poverty tourism is simply the racist Othering of post-colonial societies by a metropolitan elite. It treats individuals as objects in a zoo, not as empowered agents."
- "I lived in Mumbai in 2003, close to the world trade centre in a large and beautiful residential tower. It was only a couple of streets away from the nearest slum and the people that lived there were essentially the 'support staff' of the wealthy who lived in the towers. They were cleaners, cooks, garbage collectors, elevator operators and street sweepers, keeping the district and its wealthy residents in tip top shape. I was always fascinated with the slums of Mumbai and would walk my shirts down to the local ironing men, on the edge of the slum to have them pressed. One day, my curiosity got the better of me and instead of handing over the clothes and turning back, I headed in, winding my way through the tiny lanes. I hadn't been walking for two minutes when a young man stopped me—and in halting English asked me what I was doing there. I said I was just walking and looking. He looked at me, then at the ground and replied, madam, you not see this. In an instant I was looking at the ground. I apologized, turned on my heel and left. My curiosity got the better of me, I

wanted to see inside those homes, look through the doorways, see what 'they' did in there. I didn't think about their dignity, that these shacks were someone's home. I would never walk through a neighbourhood in the US to see how the people lived, to look through their doors, to see what 'they' did in there. That young man taught me something about myself that day, I thank him for it, and I will never forget him."

In "Shocked by Slumdog's Poverty Porn," Times Online columnist Alice Miles clarifies how the third context extends beyond the initial poverty tourism debates to other contexts of where poverty is observed. Many people suggest that poverty tourists treat poor people as "as objects in a zoo, not as empowered agents." Unfortunately, most of these denunciations fail to clarify whether they are stating that poverty tourists intend to demean poor people, or whether poor people feel demeaned when observed by tourists. There is an important difference between the two scenarios.

In the first scenario, the problem lies with the tourists' intentions, and we note our agreement with those who believe it is immoral for tourists to go on poverty tours in order to demean the poor. An elaborate justification of this condemnation is not necessary, given how easily different moral theories justify condemning the intention to demean marginalized people.

However, we would add that no evidence exists that all poverty tourists or even a high percentage of poverty tourists have such despicable motivations. Crucially, it is an open empirical question as to how frequently such ill intentions exist. Critics thus are not justified in equating the practice of poverty tourism with immoral intention.

A problem similar to the confusion of likely with inevitable intentions plagues Miles's denunciation of Slumdog Millionaire and A Thousand Splendid Suns. Miles presumes that since these artworks graphically depict violence against poor people, well-off audiences will be inclined to experience them with a sense of Schadenfreude. Now, Miles correctly recognizes that information often is structured in a non-neutral manner that "invites" viewers to respond in patterned ways. Recently, this thesis about constrained intentionality has extended beyond philosophical circles—where debates occur about Don Ihde's phenomenological conception of "technological mediation"—to mainstream understanding through the widespread reception of Cass Sunstein and Richard Thaler's jointly authored book Nudge: Improving Decisions About Health, Wealth, and Happiness (2008).

In this text, the legal scholar and behavioural economist appeal to such concepts as "choice architecture" and "default settings" to challenge readers to think about how design configurations interact with our perceptual and cognitive systems so as to "nudge" us in biased directions. They make their point by discussing a range of provocative examples, including ranging from fly-etched urinals in the men's restrooms at Schiphol Airport (that minimize spillage) to strategically arranged cafeteria displays (that incline kids to select healthy food).

They also feature insightful studies about how the format in which information is presented influences people's decisions, including which mortgages and medical insurances they select, how much money they save, and which investments they target. The problem, here, is that Miles' cinematic and literary examples bear little resemblance to the instances of informational "nudging" that Sunstein and Thaler emphasize.

By characterizing Slumdog Millionaire and A Thousand Splendid Suns as "poverty porn," Miles implies that the depictions of violence against poor people there are so sensationalized as to likely arouse the vile viewer/reader response of enjoying the depicted miseries. Contrary to this view, we contend that neither logical nor empirical necessity supports such a cynical link between the content of violent media (of this kind) and the perceptions of those who view violent media (of this kind).

The only response that can be reasonably inferred to follow from exposure to such emotionally powerful content is an emotionally powerful response. Of course, it could be argued that in a culture typified by widespread sadism, those emotions readily are readily expressed as pleasure in the other people's pain. But while some cultural critics identify U.S. culture with a sadist sensibility, we find that that such a sweeping generalization is too reductive to be informative.

It is more useful to posit that while some people will, in fact, feel better about their privileged lives as a result of being exposed to these stories, others will feel sympathy for the victims that these stories portray. Knowing that sympathetic viewers of these media do exist, the well-respected non-profit organization Save the Children is using Slumdog Millionaire as an educational tool to raise awareness of global poverty. In short, then, Miles does not provide good reasons for assuming the perverse response.

The second scenario concerning how poor people respond to being observed suffers from the same problem as the first. It also conflates possible with actual intentions by presuming that poor people necessarily must feel demeaned when observed by tourists. As the reader's comment about visiting Mumbai in 2003 establishes, some poor people do feel that being observed demeans their existence. Nevertheless, it is presumptuous to assume that all poor people necessarily must feel demeaned when observed by or interacting with tourists. Such presumptuousness is ironic because it actually deprives poor people of the very "agency" that it intends to safeguard. To this end, one of the readers of "Slum Visits: Tourism or Voyeurism" leveled moral accusations at the author, journalist Eric Weiner, and commentators who condemned poverty tourists as immoral voyeurs without actually consulting with the poor people who were observed and supposedly harmed.

The following response is illustrative:

- "Here's a really novel idea. To New York Times reporters like Eric Weiner, the tourists, tour organizers and all you fine folks who are commenting. Why not ask the residents themselves? This object appeared not to interview a single resident to ask their opinion on tourism vs. voyeurism. Nor has anyone in the commentary

> suggested that the object should have done so. Even those who are arguing for residents' dignity. Failing to grant residents' the agency of making that choice is the greatest transgression. Shame on all of you."

Having agreed that it is immoral for people to go on poverty tours with the intent of demeaning others, having rejected the thesis that one can make valid a priori assumptions about the intentions of poverty tourists and readers of poverty media, and having rejected the thesis that one can make valid a priori assumptions about how poor people feel about being observed, we now have to address the matter of what judgments are appropriate to the cases where poor people do feel demeaned by being observed.

Should tourists in this circumstance feel the shameful "wisdom of repugnance" akin to the experience had by person who looked at the ground in shame after realizing that a poor person felt it was inappropriate of him/her to be in slums of Mumbai? Does it matter, morally speaking, that he/she did not intend to be demeaning? Both effect and intention should matter, in different ways. Some people will feel demeaned by some poverty tourists, while others will not. This is an empirical question, but to the extent people do not actually feel demeaned, the objection fails. For those who do feel demeaned, we might ask whether all poverty tourists would elicit the same response to the same degree. Perhaps the objection is not to poverty tours as such, but only badly executed poverty tours, just as some tourism has a much larger carbon footprint than others.

This is a helpful exercise, as it makes us ask what aspects of poverty tourism elicit the strongest negative reactions from the residents, or does the greatest harm to everyone involved. The next question then becomes how the tours could be modified to reduce or eliminate the harm. As for intention, few would defend a tourist who was intentionally demeaning another person.

As suggested, assume that the remainder either have good intentions (the road-paving kind) or perhaps are clueless. Either way, when confronted with the unintended demeaning effect of their actions, these tourists and tour operators will have an opportunity. They can continue to act in the face of what is now a known harm (and become an intentionally demeaning tourist) or they can modify their behaviour with the intention to reduce the harm. Whether they are successful in the latter is again an empirical question, which might trigger an iterative action/reaction process.

This process is a path to ethical improvement in tourism practices, if well executed. One troubling assumption in this discussion is that the communities are homogeneous in their reaction to poverty tourism. Perhaps most residents of Rocinha are indifferent about the tourists; some are obviously pleased to see them. But what if one person is terribly upset by it? Is that enough to veto the visit? What if just one person is mildly annoyed by the tour? At this point, we look for individual answers in contract, and community answers in democratic consent. Certainly, if the residents have made a bargain (a sale, as in the artists' studio in Rocinha), some of the objections fall away. No one forced them to sell goods or services to the tourists, but having done so, they are not well positioned to complain that they feel demeaned by the transaction. Some might say that the concept of consent is invalid in the context of gross inequality, that residents who sell to tourists are coerced by the extreme wealth gap into a transaction that demeans them.

Such arguments are leveled at consensual sex workers, and capitalism in many contexts. We acknowledge this argument, but will not address it here, as it applies in many contexts well beyond poverty tourism. In any event, the vast majority of Rocinha residents do not consent by contract to poverty tourism, nor do they benefit directly. Perhaps consent (or the absence of dissent) derived from the community through customary or democratic processes can bridge the gap.

If a tour has permission from the community's legitimate leaders, or is otherwise permitted under local law and custom, then we might overlook the mild annoyance of the solitary objector. That person's difficulties have been weighed in the balance and found wanting; not by an external value system or neocolonial power, but by the legitimate and internal governance system in the community itself. And if that is true for the mildly annoyed, it is also true of the deeply disturbed minority, so long as the legitimacy of the leadership structure can bear the weight of the aggrieved minority.

In short, the consent of the community matters greatly, and complaints and suggestions from residents and their leaders should shape poverty tour practices. The absence of formal consent should not hinder tourism, so long as the community is not objecting. A legitimate community decision to ban tourists should be respected, and a visit in violation of that ban would be unethical. Identifying a "legitimate" decision is more difficult. Democratic structures have the capacity to evaluate the relative merits of restrictions on travel and tourism. In the United States, those opposed to freedom of travel bear a heavy burden to justify restricting such a fundamental right, which encourages us to operate with the presumption that consent is not needed until objections are voiced. As Gregory Hartch stated, "the right to travel has been recognized by American courts for more than 150 years." It was the first fundamental right recognized under the Fourteenth Amendment.

The right to travel is fundamental to our national conception of freedom: "The rule of open travel on the roads was viewed as superior to freedom of speech, freedom of religion, and freedom of press throughout the late 1800s." "[T]he constitutional right to travel from one State to another... occupies a position fundamental to the concept of our Federal Union.... A right so elementary was conceived from the beginning to be a necessary concomitant of the stronger Union the Constitution created." The right to travel is an important component of personal autonomy. While the consent and participation of the community are ethically valuable, the mere absence of formal consent should not block the right to travel until legitimate objections are raised.

In the context of Rocinha, we have serious concerns about community consent, given the quasi-governmental role played by the drug traffic gangs, together with their erstwhile allies, the residents' associations. These institutions suffer significant democracy deficits, and yet one would be hard pressed to point to alternative institutions in a better position to govern Rocinha. In any event, the tours occur only because the gangs and the residents' associations tacitly allow them to continue.

Voyeurism

There is not much to say about the fourth context in which immoral voyeurism is said to occur. If poverty tourists are dishonest about their intentions, they deserve moral rebuke. For example, we should consider a tourist to be morally reprehensible if they proclaim motivation to learn more about poverty, but in fact their guiding intention is to acquire life experience that will make for interesting party stories, or to make a profit (using the funds only for personal benefit) by selling pictures of suffering people once home. Because this judgment can be justified by a variety of moral outlooks, it does not require elaborate justification.

The next context, however, calls for more nuanced considerations. It is quite possible that the mere presence of tourists will make poor people feel demeaned, even if the tourists have good intentions. This issue might tilt the balance towards virtual poverty tourism, especially through film, if the primary harm is the demeaning presence. In Rocinha, several tour operators lead small tour groups every day. With a documentary film, the intrusion would occur just once.

Of course, documentary films are exactly what send some tourists to the favela, sometimes with false impressions. Likewise, the New York Times article will undoubtedly spur some interest in these tours; some will go with inaccurate expectations. Leaving the question of virtual versus physical tourism unresolved for the moment, let us consider the underlying claim about demeaning presence. The following responses to "Slum Visits: Tourism or Voyeurism" defend the thesis that tourist's gaze demeans the dignity of the poor people who are observed because poor people are a marginalized group. The guiding idea in these responses is that poverty tourism is an unacceptable form of voyeurism because it displays an asymmetric presence that reinforces social stratification. The following sociological features are relevant to this issue: poor people cannot take a comparable tour of a rich neighbourhood; poor people who work in resorts are instructed not to make eye contact with rich guests; despite the legality of free-association, poor people have been rounded up by the police for being in neighbourhoods they do not "belong" in; and the conspicuous consumption of rich tourists can serve as a painful reminder of how much better off others are. No one is justified in assuming, a priori, that the presence of tourists must induce the harm and resentment that these quotes detail.

However, it is empirically possible that poor people will feel this way about being observed, regardless of the tourist's intentions. In the context of Rocinha, some of these concerns may not be well grounded. The theory of asymmetric presence as a damaging force loses power if you spend a few days watching television in Rocinha. Brazilian television is ubiquitous in favelas, and wealth is prominently on display.

If it is harmful for Rocinha residents to be confronted with wealth and inequality, poverty tours are not the primary cause. Likewise, the assumption that Rocinha residents cannot take a comparable tour of wealthy areas does not fit well with the Brazilian context. Many of the residents of Rocinha work in the homes and businesses of Ipanema.

They travel by public transit every day to the homes and workplaces of very wealthy people. We are not defending the income inequality in Brazil, but merely stating the obvious: income inequality is not news to Brazilian favela residents. Nor would a Hollywood-style tour of the homes of the rich and famous do much to restore the moral balance. Perhaps the argument is that Rocinha is a refuge for the poor, and should be protected as a safe haven from social difference.

This is a plausible argument. In other contexts, such as Native Americans, certain areas are preserved for the tribal members from external intrusions. If Rocinha's community leadership took such a position, then it would be entitled to respect. But the mere presence of inequality (absent other compelling circumstances) should not create a zone of non-autonomy around the poor and their communities, preventing other people from exercising their autonomy, including the right to travel.

The sixth context in which immoral voyeurism is said to occur are instances where members of a privileged group misrepresent the values and beliefs of an underprivileged group on the basis of selective observations of their lives. The phenomenological tradition presents rich insights into this issue, and we can gain clear sense of its basic parameters by reflecting on a summary presentation of the concepts of the "male gaze" and the "racial gaze".

In her feminist classic The Second Sex (1949), Simone de Beauvoir—Sartre's longstanding partner and collaborator—argues that women are defined as inferior "others" in male dominated cultures and socially disciplined to accept their second-class status as a natural state of affairs. By extending de Beauvoir's insights into the social construction of gendered identity, feminist scholars learned how to analyse a range of representations—including photography, cinema, painting, and even the history of philosophy itself—as manifestations of a "male gaze".

This reductivist gaze is defined by its tendency to view women not as subjects, but eroticized and fetishized objects; it is identified a leading cause underlying degrading depictions of women's lives, beliefs, and values—depictions that unduly demean political, moral, aesthetic, and worth, and which disregard the adverse psychological and social consequences that result from such abjection.

By the 1980s, Laura Mulvey's conception of "Woman as Image, Man as Bearer of the Look"—a part title found in her frequently cited thesis "Visual Pleasure and Narrative Cinema" (1975)—became an organizing principle of much feminist and cultural studies scholarship. In his seminal Black Skin and White Masks (1952), Franz Fanon offers a forceful articulation of the idea of a "racial gaze". This idea is so powerful that in the Preface Sartre himself writes: "The Third World finds itself and speaks to itself through his voice." Fanon explored the concept of the "racial gaze" by examining how "the black person is not only burdened by geography, history, and place" but also "most particularly saddled with the heavy weight of difference, difference exacted by the idea of race."

Fanon contends that white people routinely look at black people with a gaze that emerges from a dangerous "double consciousness". According to Fanon, the white racist who condemns black skin and African cultures simultaneously "secretly desires their black bodies and ways of doing things." Fanon insists that when black people begin to understand this paradox of desire and repulsion, they take a crucial step in developing an emancipatory psychology rooted in black pride.

This is a potentially damaging critique of poverty tourism, especially if the visits are superficial and poorly rooted in context–the "safari bus" rides again, now saddled with the "bourgeois gaze." Agencies serving the homeless in the U.S. are frequently inundated with requests for groups to provide dinner on Thanksgiving Day, but a dearth of volunteers in other months. Many challenge these holiday efforts as shallow and transient. Poverty tours are certainly exposed to the real possibility of superficiality and reinforcing of stereotypes. But all superficial experiences are not equally problematic. In the United States, many Native American tribes host gambling casinos, legally permitted because the tribes have some autonomous legal authority.

At some of these casinos, one will occasionally find a performance, replete with Native dancing and dress. In Boston, one can view an exhibition of Irish step dancing; in Houston, a rodeo; colonial re-enactments in Williamsburg; in Harlem, jazz and blues on Saturday night and Black gospel choirs on Sunday morning. Perhaps some of these are performances and not authentic cultural expressions. But if they are just images designed for consumption, that does not make them unethical.

They are what they are: entertainment for the tourist and perhaps a small dose of culture or education. This point emphasizes the value of linking quality teaching (*e.g.*, reflexive inquiry into the conditions under which identities and stereotypes are constructed) and tourism, rather than abandoning either teaching or tourism altogether. Also important are the consent of the observed.

Finally, the last context listed in our taxonomy of voyeurism is instances in which people conceive of certain events or images as inherently objectionable to observe. Outside of the tourism context, many examples meet this criterion. For example, some people consider pornography to be inherently immoral, other people consider public executions to be inherently immoral, and, as the recent controversy over the Danish political cartoon of the prophet Muhammad demonstrated, some cultures consider depictions of certain religious imagery to be profane.

In the tourism context, several examples are germane. To pick but a single salient one, we can note that according to a BBC News article, some Jewish settlers have offered special "terror tours" of the West Bank and Gaza where tourists receive training in hand-to-hand combat and weapon use, view Palestinian "terror enclaves" from a helicopter and suicide bomber belts that the Israeli army seized, and, finally, engage in a paintball fight in a simulated Arab village containing simulated Arab terrorists.

Not only does this practice raise questions about how tourism can exacerbate prejudices, but it also prompts us to consider whether it is inherently objectionable for people who are not journalists or soldiers to take a "tourist" attitude towards warfare. But why are actual preparations for real events acceptable, but mock preparations for the same events are condemned? People with money and time can put themselves through training camps as if they were minor league baseball players, racecar drivers, jungle mercenaries, or astronauts.

Why not Jewish West Bank settlers? Beyond this extreme example, many Israeli kibbutzes offer short term visits as a way to experience "real kibbutz life." Undoubtedly, some of that experience includes anti-terrorism training, formal or informal. If the underlying practice is defended solely on a ground of strict necessity, then the tourist may be acting unethically absent such necessity. But in most cases, necessity is not the explicit or implicit justification, and the ethical distinction between tourist and participant fades.

CONCLUSION

We do not defend all or even most poverty tourism practices. As noted in the Introduction, empirical work may find that most poverty tours are ethically objectionable as voyeuristic experiences. Our delimited task has been to bring some taxonomic order to the debate, and to resist categorical condemnation of poverty tours. Hopefully the structure and insights expressed in this collaborative paper will help the debates over tourism transition to a mature discourse.

Additionally, we hope that our thesis will advance inquiry into the following question—a question that is broader in scope than poverty tourism, but which has been central to the present discussion. In the context of domestic and global travel, who has the right to enter another community? Certainly a fire fighter or ambulance does when it responds to an emergency call.

Perhaps the President does when touring a disaster area; this visit can be a public act of solidarity, not tourism. But what of journalists, social workers, artists, documentarians, and students? If students are permitted, what possible difference could academic credit provide as an ethical justification? Indeed, it would seem that if the backpacker in Rio wants equal access to favela tours, he or she should not be afforded less liberty than U.S. law students.

Such interrogatives and observations ultimately prompt the following question: If ethical considerations are insufficient to warrant suspending the right to travel, do they amount to little more than reflexive reminders to maintain vigilant awareness of the complexity and ambiguity that attends to unequally structured social encounters?

4

Tourism Industry of Ethics and Tourism

ETHICS AND TOURISM

The substantial growth of tourism activity clearly marks tourism as one of the most remarkable economic and social phenomena of the past century. The number of international arrivals shows an evolution from a mere 25 million international arrivals in 1950 to over 700 million in 2002, corresponding to an average annual growth rate of 6.6%. In addition to the numerical growth of tourism, there has been an increasing geographic spread of tourism to encompass almost all the reaches of the globe.

Simultaneously, there has been a diversification of the tourism product from the traditional sun, sea ands and offering to a product that can be potentially more intrusive, or more beneficial for those living in the tourism destination. Tourism's expansion has meant the industry now represents the leading source of foreign exchange in at least 38% of countries, and ranks in the top five industries for exports in 83% of countries.

However, in addition to the of cited economic indicators displaying the dominance of the tourism industry, there has been a commensurate and almost equally well-publicized rise and recognition of the potentially negative impacts of the burgeoning tourism industry.

Researchers have been critical of the pernicious social and environmental impacts the industry can have from reinforcing western domination over developing countries through the 'host/guest' relationship to the visual scars on the landscape caused by ski resorts or golf courses. This has led to calls for the industry to exercise greater responsibility and "professionalism" in order to protect the "golden goose" and mirrors the arguments for greater corporate and social responsibility in other industries.

Corporate Social Responsibility is a specific application of the notion of environmental and social auditing to business practice. The technique is strongly promoted by Fair Trade in Tourism which suggests that the technique of CSR emerged in the late 1990s out of NGO efforts to create a more equitable international trade system. According to Mowforth and Munt the tourism industry is well behind other industries in terms of CSR, and the absence of ethical leadership in the tourism industry has been 'astounding'.

However, in the last few decades, responsible tourism has emerged as a significant trend in the western world, as wider consumer market trends towards lifestyle marketing and ethical consumption have spread to tourism. Tourism organizations are beginning to realise that promoting their ethical stance can be good business as it potentially enhances a company's profits, management effectiveness, public image and employee relations.

Yet, although more attention is now being paid to ethics in tourism there is a very weak foundation of research into tourism ethics studies to date. The consequence is that the arguments presented for and against CSR in tourism are often simplistic and largely without any practical evidence.

ETHICAL DECISION-MAKING

The two approaches to ethical decision-making which have received most attention in the literature are those reliant on the theories of deontology and teleology. A deontological approach enjoys a rich historical legacy, dating back to philosophers such as Socrates, 384 Simon Hudson and Graham Miller and more recently to the work of Kant.

Deontology is concerned with the idea of universal truths and principles, which should be adhered to regardless of the circumstances. Kant's categorical imperative states that a person faced with a problem should be able to respond consistently and in conformity with their moral principles and also feel comfortable with the decision being made in full view of others.

A teleological view can be understood as "consequentialism" following from the philosophical work of Jeremy Bentham and John Stuart Mill on utilitarianism. Thus, ethical decisions are made in view of expected outcomes, which eliminate the universality of decisions and subordinates principles to context. A common expression for the two approaches would be that deontology places the means as more important than the end, while for teleology it is the end that justifies the means.

Understanding these theories helps to successfully employ the various "tools" that exist to control the tourism industry, ranging from market-based instruments such as taxes through to more command and control instruments such as legislation. For a deontologist, breaking the law would contravene their view of ethics and so the legislation would be abided by almost regardless of the value of the legislation.

Yet, a teleologist would consider the consequences of not abiding by the law and would weigh this against the benefits of breaking the law. If tourism students seem to adopt a teleological approach to ethical dilemmas, then legislation can only expect to be effective if accompanied by stringent penalties that make the outlawed behaviour not worthwhile, and hence the need to understand how decisions are made.

Malloy and Fennell, Cleek and Leonard and Stevens all point to the increasing prevalence of codes of ethics employed by the tourism industry as a tool to provide guidance to employees when making decisions. An important contribution in this area has been made by the World Tourism Organization, who in 1999 approved the Global Code of Ethics for Tourism that consolidated and reinforced previous recommendations and declarations on sustainable tourism.

The Code aims to preserve the world's natural resources and cultural heritage from disruptive tourist activities and to ensure a fair and equitable sharing of benefits that arise out of tourism with the residents of tourism destinations. Yet the code is not supported by an understanding of how industry practitioners make their decisions. Indeed, the lack of awareness within the industry of the code would indicate the code is not a particularly effective tool.

INFLUENCES ON ETHICAL DECISION-MAKING

Previous theory suggests that there are a number of influences on ethical decision making of students, including nationality, the type of ethical dilemma, prior ethical education, and gender. Prior research in cross-cultural or cross-national ethical values of students has been quite contradictory. For example, Lysonski and Gaidis found that business students' ethical orientations were similar in the USA, Denmark and New Zealand.

However, Okleshen and Hoyt found that US students were less tolerant than New Zealand students of situations involving the ethical constructs of fraud, coercion and self-interest. Whipple and Swords suggest that the field of business ethics has not attracted the degree of academic interest in the UK as it has in the US, and that more business ethics courses are needed in Britain to counter the difference in ethical judgements found.

Ethical decision making is also likely to be influenced by the type of ethical dilemma faced. Jones showed ethical issues can be classified according to their intensity, with respondents more likely to respond according to ethical principles if the issue is deemed as important. Applied ethics has evolved for functions and aspects such as business ethics, marketing ethics, and accounting ethics, but discussion of sustainable tourism ethics and the moral appropriateness of sustainable tourism in various contexts is somewhat muted by comparison.

In western societies over the last few decades, an increased recognition that the world's resources are limited, has led to the strengthening of an environmental ethic, whereby the natural environment is recognized to have an intrinsic value which outweighs its value as a leisure asset. Yet, despite understanding the concept of the "triple bottom line", attention to the negative economic and socio-cultural impacts of tourism is less evident.

Indeed, a recent review of tourism journals shows a heavy bias in favour of Ethical Orientation and Awareness of Tourism Students 385 papers that focus on the environmental issues arising from the industry, reflecting the acknowledged predisposition NGOs have previously held towards the environment. Through exposure to these debates students are potentially more likely to be sensitive to environmental issues.

The level of ethical education is likely to have an influence on ethical decision making. The last decade has seen an increase in the demands for ethical training amongst tourism students. However, there is little evidence that tourism students are receiving ethical education, and no research has looked at the relationship between this training and ethical decision making. Singh's survey of Canadian management schools shows that nearly half of all those Universities surveyed did not offer a formal course in business ethics to their students.

Enghagen found a higher proportion of courses were offered in the US for hospitality education, although the majority of ethics courses offered were electives. Studies which have attempted to measure the impact of teaching ethics to students have shown improved, but short-lived improvements in the ethical values and reasoning skills of students. Harris found that business majors profess a teleogical approach, whereas non-business majors prefer a deontological approach.

Okleshen and Hoyt concluded from their study that educational experience in an ethics course produces homogeneity and is beneficial towards obtaining cross cultural understanding and congruence in ethical values. Finally, studies of ethics and gender have found females to be less tolerant than males of situations involving ethical dilemmas.

For example, Whipple and Wolf found that female students are more critical than their male classmates of questionable business practices. Others have found student females to have higher moral values than males. Galbraith and

Stephenson demonstrated that female business students prefer a utilitarian decision rule while male business students prefer an Egoist approach to evaluating ethical dilemmas.

As one of the world's truly global industries, working with a diversity of cultures, moral and ethical values, future business practitioners face the challenge of global ethics. In order to contribute to the development of understanding of global ethics, this study is responding to calls for the need to document existing ethical perspectives of individuals from around the world and to identify the determinants of ethical orientations.

CONCLUSION

The tourism literature makes a continual call for more decisions to be made that acknowledge the full impacts of the industry and yet little research has been conducted that attempts to establish the ethical framework the managers of the future will employ to approach these decisions. This research has drawn on the work of other subject disciplines and applied an established research methodology to tourism students in three different countries.

Such research has enabled more informed discussions about what is required from ethical instruction in the future. It should be noted that the intention of this research was not to determine what is ethical or unethical. Rather, it was to assess how the characteristics of issues influence ethical beliefs, how individuals think and devise what is ethical and unethical and how different variables influence ethical perceptions.

Once greater knowledge exists about how students and businesses are making decisions, then discussions of which tools are appropriate to enable or constrain those decisions become more apposite.

5

Ethical and Responsible Tourism

INTRODUCTION

There is increasing recognition of the significant shift away from the predominance of the traditional sun, sand and sea holiday towards more experiential vacations: holidaymakers are seeking holidays which provide them with more than two weeks on the beach and a tan. John King argued in this journal in March 2002 that 'successful destination marketers will need to engage the customer as never before, to be able to provide them with the type of information and experience they are increasingly able to demand'.

He went on to argue that travel is increasingly 'about experiences, fulfilment and rejuvenation' rather than about 'places and things'; and that the lifestyle market is of increasing importance. King argues that tourism and travel are more about lifestyle and personal enhancement than many other lifestyle products.

'Lifestyle marketing tends to focus on and confirm more of what the customer would like to see in and of themselves rather than on any physical properties of the product or service being promoted', King stated, concluding that this will require that destination marketing organisations (DMOs) reinvent themselves and the emphasis needs to shift towards 'creating holiday experiences and connecting them with the customer'.

This paper considers recent survey evidence of changes in consumer attitudes in the context of wider market trends towards more ethical consumption in the UK. Campaigns by Voluntary Service Overseas (VSO) and Tearfund contributed to the development of ethical and responsible tourism as a market segment—those campaigns are reported and the implications of these trends are considered. King is not alone in identifying these trends towards more experiential vacations.

Fifteen years ago Krippendorf placed his argument for responsible tourism in the context of Maslow's pyramid of needs, arguing that we would increasingly see 'emancipated tourists', and that once their needs for physical recreation (sleeping, eating and drinking) were satisfied tourists would seek 'emotional recreation', pursuing activities and experiences which were not available to them in everyday life. Tourists would increasingly seek 'the satisfaction of social needs: contact with other people and self-realization through creative activities, knowledge and exploration'.

He envisaged a movement towards a new holidaymaker, 'an independent and emancipated tourist, a critical consumer not only at home but also when travelling'.While in Krippendorf's terms passive and uncritical tourists still outnumber active and enlightened ones, there is mounting evidence of the pursuit of 'selfrealization and fulfilment in all spheres of life'. This market trend towards less passive holidaymaking and towards more active and experiential vacationing affects DMOs, tour operators and travel agents—all distribution agencies need to link the holiday experiences they sell to the aspirations and needs of customers.This trend is widely based. It is a specific example of the consumer trend towards the purchase of more ethically traded products and increasing pressure across most sectors for evidence of corporate social responsibility.

WIDER CONSUMER TRENDS

Work by the Co-operative Bank and the New Economics Foundation established the Ethical Purchasing Index, which is designed to measure the growth in the ethical marketplace. With a base of 100 in 1999, they calculated the index at 115 in 2000, suggesting an increase of 15 per cent in the ethical consumption market between 1999 and 2000.

In selected sectors: Those where there is an ethical alternative—ethical consumer purchases increased 18.2 per cent between 1999 and 2000 compared with a total market growth in the same sectors of only 2.8 per cent, suggesting that (in those sectors) ethical purchasing is growing six times faster than the overall market. But, the overall ethical market share in these selected sectors is only 1.6 per cent, up from 1.3 per cent in 1999.

Ethical investment and banking is also growing at a rate of 20 per cent per year. Doane concluded that health, environmentalism and concern for human rights are the main driving forces behind ethical consumerism and that globalisation and concerns about corporate power provide the backdrop. Traidcraft was founded in 1979 and has grown into the largest 'fair trade' company in the UK, joined by Oxfam and Cafe' Direct among others; the range of products now includes food, clothing, furniture, carpets and toys.

Datamonitor reported in October 2002 that the sector had grown 40 per cent in the previous 12 months and opined that 'paradoxically, the Fair Trade phenomenon surfs a wave of egocentrism. What has catapulted Fair Trade products into the mainstream are not the altruistic principles of those with whom the idea originated but the more widespread desire among consumers to make themselves feel good'.The aspiration to feel good is one of the main drivers of responsible tourism.

CAMPAIGNING FOR CHANGE

Krippendorf called for 'rebellious tourists and rebellious locals'.A number of UK NGOs have campaigned on the issue of tourism in the 1990s. Tourism Concern ran a long 'our holidays, their homes' campaign calling for just, participatory and sustainable tourism.

Action for Southern Africa (ACTSA) ran a campaign for 'people first' tourism which called upon British companies operating to South Africa to sign up to core labour standards, commitments to a living wage and racial and gender equity and sourcing goods locally wherever possible. In 1995, following a survey of its volunteers working in developing countries who were asked about the pressing problems confronting the communities with which it worked, VSO launched a campaign on ethical tourism.

- 'Many communities VSO works with have felt the sharp end of tourism and are desperate for change. Volunteers report that losing land, water and access to public places are common complaints, and tourism has very clearly been associated with serious social abuses such as child sex tourism and the eviction of people from their land.'

VSO's WorldWise campaign focused on the 'hidden extras' of holidays, echoing the concerns that holidaymakers have about the small print in the brochures. The campaign videos, postcards and leaflets raised the issues of cultural and environmental impacts dealing with photography, behaviour and dress codes, and encouraged visitors to spend time and money in the local community.

The WorldWise campaign encouraged holidaymakers to make an informed choice. The campaign pointed out that 'Every travel brochure says "meet our friendly local people, they are the warmth of our welcome". But will you actually meet any? Will you go beyond just ordering a meal or a drink?' The WorldWise campaign aimed to show tourists how they could get more out of their holiday.

Pointing out that 'many people travel to the most distant locations on earth and never eat, drink or shop outside the hotel', the campaign encouraged tourists to get more out of their holiday: 'there's probably a market just down the road—you can buy direct from the crafts people and see local traditions come alive. An experience for you. A livelihood for local people'. VSO pointed out to holidaymakers that their choice of holiday and the way they visit could make a difference. 'We found the real country beyond the beaten tourist track. You have to make some effort to get there and to make contact with local people. But the welcome we found and the kindness we were shown, I'll never forget.' Alex Knight, WorldWise tourist, Pakistan.VSO WorldWise advice to the tourism industry can be summarised as follows.

- *Travel agents*: Stock VSO's WorldWise leaflet, a print version of VSO's online Travel Advice Centre information, in the agency. Insert the leaflet into ticket wallets or flight confirmation envelopes for tourists travelling to the developing world.
- *Tour operators*: Give customers more information about the people and the places they will be visiting in brochures, including advice on how they can visit locally owned facilities and resorts. Develop a policy for the business on how the holidays it provides could be of more benefit to people living in the destinations it visits.
- *Hotels*: Start buying more goods and services locally and reducing imports. Start an environment management programme within the hotel.

VSO's WorldWise campaign encouraged consumers to demand holidays where more of the money tourists spend benefited local communities. VSO sought change from the industry. In order to engage more directly with individual tour operators, VSO conducted a survey of the travel advice provided by 50 operators which carried tourists to Kenya, Tanzania, the Gambia, India and Thailand, all developing countries in which VSO had volunteers.

Companies were then given a star rating for the quality of the advice on respecting local people, respecting local communities, interacting with the local economy and respecting the local environment—the themes of the WorldWise campaign. VSO adopted a consumer rights approach, arguing that holidaymakers are entitled to 'basic information about the country or people we are visiting'.

'We want to interact with local people and to enjoy a new environment when we visit a developing country, but all too often we don't have the guidance we need to get the most out of our holiday without undermining local customs and culture... Without the added confidence good information provides many holiday makers won't venture beyond the confines of the hotel, depriving local markets, restaurants and other businesses of essential income.'

VSO argued that for small steps there was potentially a big return: 'Tour operators have a lot to gain in terms of the good-will both of their customers and people who live and work in the resorts they use.' Richard Bowden Doyle, Managing Director of Thomson Holidays, endorsed this approach 'Our customers trust Thomson to provide them with enjoyable trouble-free holidays. We believe that providing good information and advice is essential to keeping that confidence.' VSO subsequently worked with the Association of Independent Tour Operators (AITO), which formed an ethical tourism committee to respond to the issues raised by the WorldWise campaign and the concerns of its own members about the impacts of tourism in destinations.

The AITO represents about 150 independently owned UK tour operators and it has formally adopted responsible tourism guidelines which are now part of its membership criteria backed by a rating system and an awards contest. In January 2003 it announced its first responsible tourism awards.

In 2000 Tearfund published 'Don't Forget Your Ethics', asserting that tourism is an ethical issue—that the way one travels to another country and comes into contact with people raises ethical issues about working conditions, employment and entrepreneurial opportunities; about who benefits; about the environmental consequences; and about whether or not travelling to a particular place supports democracy and human rights or undermines them.

Most radically, Tearfund posed the question 'Do local people want tourists visiting them?' Tearfund argued that holidays are a consumer item and that 'our choice of holiday, just like any other consumer choice, affects other people'. The principles of responsible consumption applied to tea and coffee can be applied to tourism. Tearfund pressed operators to move beyond the environmental agenda and to address the social and economic agenda.

They suggested that operators could ensure good working conditions, fair prices and that a greater share of tourism revenues go to local communities. Tourists, they argued, could use local services and stay in 'locally run guest houses, treating all those we meet with respect, learning about and honouring local customs and looking after the environment'. Tearfund published a ten-point list of things which tour operators could do to make a difference.

CONSUMER ATTITUDES TOWARDS RESPONSIBLE TOURISM IN THE UK

In November 1999 Tearfund commissioned a survey of consumer attitudes towards ethical issues in tourism amongst a nationally and regionally representative sample of adults (15+). Twenty-seven per cent of the respondents had never been on an overseas holiday; they were excluded from the data presented in the report. Twelve per cent reported that they regularly buy fairly traded goods or use an ethical bank or investment fund, and 8 per cent that they are members of an environmental, development or human rights group.

As might be expected cost, weather and the quality of facilities were judged by respondents to be of most importance when choosing a holiday but the quality of local social, economic and political information (42 per cent), opportunities to interact with local people (37 per cent) and environmental impact (32 per cent) were all judged more important than the ethical policy commitments of the company (27 per cent). But all of these concerns were regarded by this representative sample of travellers as more important than whether or not they had travelled with the company before (26 per cent).

This last point was not lost on many operators. Tearfund argued that 'Taken with the fact that there is little loyalty shown by tourists to tour operators, this shows that a company could gain a competitive advantage by adopting ethical policies.' Sixty-three per cent of respondents reported that they wanted information about at least one ethical issue, and nearly half wanted information about local customs and appropriate dress and behaviour for tourists.

Respondents were permitted to tick as many or as few items as they liked. Respondents identified 'tour operators including tour guides' (54 per cent) and travel agents (52 per cent) as primarily responsible for providing them with this information. Tearfund asked some specific questions about the willingness of travellers—package and independent travellers alike—to pay more money for holidays which had the ethical characteristics they aspired to.

Fiftynine per cent of respondents said that they would be willing to pay more for their holiday if money went to guarantee good wages and working conditions for workers in the destination, to preserve the environment and reverse some negative environmental effects or directly to a local charity. This means that 41 per cent would not be prepared to pay more for any of these reasons. Respondents could tick as many items as they wished. Only 45 per cent of respondents were prepared to admit that they were not willing to pay more for the guarantees in 43 per cent were prepared to pay at least 2 per cent more.

These figures are clearly aspirational—they record the views of respondents about how they would like to behave, and do not necessarily accurately forecast how consumers will actually behave when booking holidays. But, consumers provided with comparable holidays at similar prices where one operator meets the ethical agenda to some degree and the other does not can reasonably be expected to exercise their preference for a holiday that meets their ethical consumption aspirations. Tearfund asked the same question in 1999 and 2001, and over the two years the percentage aspiring to be willing to pay more for an ethical holiday increased by 7 per cent from 45 per cent to 52 per cent. By the end of 2001 52 per cent said that they would be more likely to book a holiday with a company with an ethical commitment. This aspiration is one that companies are increasingly responding to.

The Association of British Travel Agents (ABTA) has surveyed package holidaymakers consistently for many years, and in September 2000 and September 2002 it included some questions, which addressed the ethical and responsible agenda. As part of their regular annual survey ABTA asked a series of questions about tourism and the environment.

The results provide firm evidence that environmental issues are important to many package holidaymakers when they choose or recommend particular destinations. More than half the respondents said that the issue of food or water shortages for local residents mattered a great deal to them in choosing or recommending destinations, and there was an increase of 8 per cent in those saying that it mattered a great deal to them between 2000 and 2002.

The number saying that air pollution and the aesthetics of hotels mattered a great deal to them also increased by 5 per cent and 7 per cent respectively. Concern about crime also increased. ABTA also asked about the importance of a range of factors in determining the respondent's choice of holiday company. In September 2000, 78 per cent of package holiday respondents said that the provision of social and environmental information in tour operators' brochures is important; and 70 per cent said that the reputation of the holiday company on environmental issues is either very or fairly important in affecting their choice of holiday company.

In the repeat survey in 2002 both figures had fallen slightly by 3 and 5 per cent respectively. This may reflect either a slight reduction in the level of importance attached to the issues or recognition that the industry has made some progress in this area, or of course both. In 2000, 52 per cent of respondents said that they were interested in finding out more about local social and environmental issues in the resort before booking a holiday, in 2002 this had increased by 7 per cent to 59 per cent.

Asked in September 2000 the aspirational question 'How important is it to you that your holiday should...', 71 per cent of the sample said that it was either very important (27 per cent) or fairly important (44 per cent) to them that their holiday benefited the people of the destination they are travelling to through creating jobs and business opportunities; 85 per cent said that it was important to them that their holiday did not damage the environment; and 77 per cent said that they wanted their holiday to include visits to experience local culture and foods.

By September 2002 greater importance was being attached to all three aspirations, up by 5 per cent, 2 per cent and 4 per cent respectively. Through MORI, ABTA then asked in 2000 whether the respondents would be prepared to pay more money for various social and environmental elements to be guaranteed as part of the package holiday.

Fifty-three per cent said that they were prepared to pay more for their package holiday in order that workers in the destination could be guaranteed good wages and working conditions, and 45 per cent were prepared to pay more to assist in preserving the local environment and reversing some negative environmental effects of tourism.

In 2002 the same questions elicited more support and the aspiration to see local sourcing increased by 5 per cent; but the aspiration that workers in the destinations should be guaranteed good wages and working conditions declined by 4 points. ABTA then went on to ask how much extra package holiday travellers would be willing to pay for the guarantees each respondent had identified.

Accepting that these statements are aspirational and that there is a significant difference between what is said in response to a survey question and a decision to book a particular holiday at a particular price, there is a clear trend. While 94 per cent of respondents aspire to be willing to pay 1 per cent more in both 2000 and 2002, the proportion aspiring to pay 5 per cent more increased by 12 per cent and those willing to pay 10 per cent more by 6 per cent.

ATTITUDES TO RESPONSIBLE TOURISM AMONG UK TOUR OPERATORS

In 2001 Tearfund published 'Tourism Putting Ethics into Practice'. This report reviews practice in the UK industry and reports on benefits to local communities, charitable giving by companies in the destinations, the development of local partnerships and the responsible tourism policies of companies.

UK tour operators are beginning to respond to these campaigns and to changing consumer attitudes, although only about 30 per cent of Tearfund's good practice review respondents said that their clients were asking more about some of the social, environmental and economic issues in tourism. Tearfund conducted research into the responsible tourism policies of UK tour operators late in 2000. They surveyed 65 UK tour operators looking for examples of good practice, and their sample was skewed towards those companies thought most likely to be adopting responsible practices. In Tearfund's survey the medium-sized companies (carrying between 5,000 and 100,000 holidaymakers per year) estimated that about 35 per cent of the costs of their trips remained in the local economy (excluding the cost of the flight).

The smaller, more specialist operators estimated the equivalent figure at 70 per cent, while the larger mass operators were not able to estimate. Tearfund identified 46 tour-operating companies (71 per cent of its survey) which gave money to charities: 33 gave money directly to charities in the destination, half gave money to UK charities working overseas and six operators (mainly the larger ones) gave money to charities working in the UK. Thirty-two of the operators Tearfund surveyed looking for good practice said that they had a responsible tourism policy, and over half of the remainder were planning to develop a policy.

Those companies which had adopted responsible tourism policies said that they had adopted them because the principles were integral to the company (the majority of the companies with policies were independent and owner-managed) or to educate their travellers. Less than one-third of companies said that they produced a responsible tourism policy as part of the process of differentiating themselves from mainstream tourism, and none overtly said that it was for commercial advantage.

IMPLICATIONS

As Weeden has argued, ethical tourism 'can allow companies to compete on more than just price'. Krippendorf, too, argued that in a competitive market sales often dependent upon a unique selling proposition (USP), and a responsible tourism commitment is an 'added value' which may secure additional bookings. Where there is little to choose between competing holidays and trips, the responsible tourism aspects of a particular trip may provide competitive advantage. Research by Francis into attitudes towards responsible tourism among a range of large, medium and small operators concluded that while destination, price, services and departure date remain, in the view of tour operators, the tourist's key decisionmaking criteria, those operators practising responsible tourism stated that given broad parity on these criteria, their responsible tourism practices make the difference 'nearly every time'. All were endeavouring to create points of difference, USPs between their products and those of their competitors, and acknowledged that this was a key component in their product differentiation. Weeden argues that existing research in psychological studies highlights the problem of discrepancy between the conscience of the consumer and their actual purchasing behaviour. This is not unique to tourism. Consumers purchase holidays for a range of reasons and these coalesce at the moment of decision.

Consumer choice is constrained by price and availability, and the responsible elements of a tourism product are only a part of the motivation to purchase, but for an increasing number of operators a significant part. Rebellious consumers will expect the suppliers they purchase from to provide products, which are economically, socially and environmentally responsible. But they will not be prepared to pay any price for responsible ethically traded products.

They will pay a greater or lesser premium according to what they can afford and the priority which they accord to the ethical dimension for their purchasing as against more traditional criteria. The smaller the premium for a more responsible product, the more likely consumers are to purchase it. Noel Josephides, managing director of Sunvil Holidays, argued in the Travel Trade Gazette that British tourists have 'absolutely no interest in supporting a host country's economy, respecting local customs or acting responsibly while on holiday'. But, he reported in the same article that 8 per cent of Sunvil clients said that Sunvil's environmental initiative encouraged them to book with the company. In the highly competitive UK tourism market few operators can ignore the preferences and ethics of 8 per cent of their clients. It is also true that they cannot pay any price to satisfy their clients, as operators cannot be sustainable without making profits. There is a trade-off between economics and aspirations for operators as well as tourists. Where the responsible tourism elements make for a superior product it will attract consumers predisposed to purchase.

The responsible tourism product has one particular advantage over many other ethical products—the consumer will often experience the difference. A cup of fairly traded coffee or tea will not taste significantly different from other teas and coffees—it can taste as good but not better. Responsible tourism holidays which bring particularly high-quality engagement with local communities and their environments can provide a superior product, the life-enhancing experience which a growing sector of the market craves.

6

Conceptualizing Sustainable Tourism

INTRODUCTION

This paper will attempt to respond to an emerging area of growth within globalization debates which has as yet been subject to little academic attention–good ethical responses to the 'bads' of globalization. Globalization is a term used to refer to the way in which our lives increasingly rely on patterns of communication, interaction and exchange that transcend the times, spaces and places of local life from the home to the nation, incorporating technological, political, social, psychological, economic, ecological and cultural aspects of modern day life.

The nature, extent and benefits of globalization are still being fiercely contested in many academic fields and political movements. For example, it can be argued that what we now label as 'globalization' is in fact '...the continuation of base structures of capitalism or the power of nation-states'. However, on a global scale, it is argued that cheaper goods have led to improved standards of living for parts of the Global North population.

In addition, there is also an increased recognition that mass production and an international division of labour unfairly exploits some individuals and environments, particularly in 'Third World' countries. Such knowledge underpins movements with an explicitly ethical agenda, whether it be in terms of protecting the welfare of human beings (*e.g.* Fair Trade), or the welfare of the material environment (*e.g.* Greenpeace).

Ethical responses to the organisation of capital, even global capital, are nothing new. However, it could be argued that ethical responses to global capital loosely focused around consumption practices, despite having some precedence, are relatively novel. Work in disparate fields such as political geography and consumer studies have made some inroads in developing the study of ethical/political consumption.

Micheletti (2003) for example, considers such movements to be representative of collective individualization: a new way of doing politics individually which, at the same time utilises global networks. Cova (1997) emphasises the enshortening of supply chains to the point where producer and consumer may become mutually and transparently aware of each other while Wright (2004) argues more critically that the mediation of ethical consumption relies on a problematic refetishization of the commodities involved, reminiscent of colonial imagery.

Throughout this paper issues surrounding everyday ethics and consumption shall be explored. This paper will also approach tourism as a form of consumption: consuming places, spaces, environment and culture. This object will investigate if we can conceptualise sustainable tourism as an emerging form of ethical consumption in order to better understand it.

Sustainable tourism will be examined as a response to the growing cultural and environmental concerns expressed by the public regarding the impacts of mass consumption and mass tourism. Finally the paper shall offer a post-colonial critique of sustainable tourism in relation to two central concepts associated with the movement–ecological sustainability and human rights.

IS SUSTAINABLE TOURISM A FORM OF ETHICAL CONSUMPTION

In recent years, ethical consumption has been a growing phenomenon throughout the West and research into this trend has generated an increasing amount of attention over the past few decades. However, it is widely acknowledged that more extensive engagement with this trend is needed within the field. This object shall critically engage with sustainable tourism and discuss to what extent it might be understood as a form of ethical consumption. The following part shall offer an initial insight into the historical trajectories and key characteristics of both ethical consumption and sustainable tourism, highlighting possible commonalities and inconsistencies between ethical consumption and sustainable tourism.

A SHARED HISTORY

The historical origins of ethical consumption appear somewhat contested with various accounts presented from the activity of the Empire Marketing Board to the co-operative movement in the nineteenth century. Many argue that a key moment for ethical consumption was in 1942 in Britain when the Quakers founded Oxfam. Oxfam began purchasing goods such as handicrafts from the disadvantaged producers in the developing world at above-market prices. Purchasing products in such a way allowed for an increased income for the producers and the products were sold onto conscientious consumers in the UK wanting to reduce the impact of their consumption.

The concept was adopted across the Atlantic in 1946 in the USA with the retail outlet Ten Thousand Villages established and various faith groups and networks selling handicraft products with the ethos of a fair price for the producers. This growing concern for producers was coupled with an increasing awareness of environmental degradation from the 1960s onwards.

This attention to the environment was strongly influenced by Rachel Carson's book Silent Spring, and a growing concern about the detrimental effects of consumerism on the environment (with a particular focus on pesticides) developed across Europe and North America. It is argued that current levels of consumption in Western societies can be held partly responsible for inequality, environmental degradation, exploitation and socio-economic disparity. This represents a shift in ideology during the latter part of the twentieth century as it previously was production processes which were typically associated with environmental degradation, inequality and exploitation. It was only towards the end of the twentieth century that consumers and mass consumption (in the world's richest nations) began to be identified as major components of the problem.

In response to the growing concern towards the end of the twentieth century, ethical concerns about the exploitation of producers and the environment could now be registered through the purchase of ethical products. For example Cafédirect coffee was launched in 1992 and offered a fairer price (amongst other aspects) for small-scale coffee producers and was sensitive towards the environment in the production process.

Ethical consumption appears to have developed over the latter half of the last century through various movements both in Europe and North America. Further, it appears that ethical consumption has begun to appeal to a broader market with the introduction of fair trade goods in mainstream supermarkets, for example, Cafédirect. The next part shall briefly highlight a few key moments in the history of sustainable tourism and identify any possible similarities and differences with ethical consumption more generally.

Throughout the history of tourism there have been various shifts in tourism practices. From the Grand Tour of the 17th and 18th centuries to the emergence of the package holiday in the later part of the 20th century. More recently a new tourist practice has emerged offering a different outlook on the practices and responsibilities involved in tourism. Initially, tourism was viewed as a clean industry as it did not have such obvious effects on the environment compared to a factory or dock yard.

As Honey highlights '...mass tourism was originally embraced by many countries as a 'smokeless' (non-polluting) industry that could increase employment and gross national product'. However, it has now become apparent that tourism contributes to worldwide pollution, natural resources depletion, and the exploitation of host workers and local cultures. This shift in understanding of the effects of mass tourism appears to coincide with the broader environmentalist movement in the 1960s. As highlighted above, environmental concerns appeared to expand during the 1960s with consumption practices being examined in relation to the damage they cause to the environment. It would seem that these concerns expanded into the tourism industry and changed the historical perspective that tourism was a non-polluting industry.

In addition, the tourism industry was not only coming under pressure from the environmental movement but concerns were raised surrounding the cultural impact of travelling to foreign countries and the treatment of host country natives. Politically, concerns surrounding human rights and the environment were arguably brought to the forefront of global attention by the World Commission on the Environment and Development which is more commonly referred to as the Brundtland Report.

In this report the Commission argued that a developmental paradigm was needed in order to address issues of environmental degradation, preservation of human rights, address economic progress and alleviating poverty, which again reiterate the concerns of ethical consumption more generally. This paradigm is based around the notion of 'development that meets the needs of the present without compromising the ability of future generations to meet their own needs'. Following on from this the Agenda 21 strategy document was a result of the United Nations Conference on Environment and Development held in Rio de Janeiro in 1992. Agenda 21 was the first document to address issues surrounding tourism and sustainability, however within the report there were only a few incidental references to the social and environmental issues generated by international tourism.

Agenda 21 was received with severe criticism as it did not meet the aims of the conference mainly due to its non-binding treaties allowing most of the recommendations surrounding climate change and various other cultural issues to be ignored by the international community. Within academia, the Journal of Sustainable Tourism was first put to print in 1993 aiming 'to advance critical understanding of the relationships between tourism and sustainable development'.

During the same period the WTO pursued the issue of sustainable tourism and in partnership with the World Travel and Trade Council released Agenda 21 for the Travel and Tourism Industry in 1996 which influenced the UN Commission on Sustainable Development in 1999, focusing mainly on issues of sustainable tourism. Following the disappointing impact both Agenda 21 documents had on the implementation of international sustainable development a further UN World Summit on Sustainable Development took place in Johannesburg, South Africa, in 2002.

The discourse employed at the conference appears to highlight similar concerns to the previous summits with the conference concluding:

- 'From the African continent, the cradle of humankind, we solemnly pledge to the peoples of the world and the generations that will surely inherit this Earth that we are determined to ensure that our collective hope for sustainable development is realised

Concerns around implementing these visions have once again arisen surrounding the need for policies to force change on the international community rather than adopting an opt-in system. With this brief history in mind, it is suggested that there appears to be some commonalities between ethical consumption and sustainable tourism: increased awareness regarding the detrimental effects of consumerism on the environment has influenced the growth of ethical products such as Cafédirect coffee from the 1960s onwards.

These concerns are mirrored in relation to the growing acknowledgement of the environmental impact of the tourism industry generating political and academic attention towards the latter part of the twentieth century; in addition, cultural concerns in relation to mass consumerism are at the heart of the development of ethical products and this is also highlighted in the need for culturally sustainable forms of tourism which attempt to reduce the impact of tourism on host communities.

Although there appear to be clear commonalities between ethical consumption and sustainable tourism it is not suggested they are exactly the same as they both have their own distinct histories, motivations and practices. The following part shall develop this idea by examining what is meant by ethical consumption and investigate if sustainable tourism shares any of these characteristics.

A COMMON DEFINITION

Ethical consumption is a concept incorporating a number of aspects such as ethical product purchase, boycotts, investment in ethical funds and deposits in ethical banks. When we talk of these different aspects in terms of 'being ethical' a number of key features appear consistently throughout the corpus of definitions. For consumption practices to be defined as ethical they need to incorporate at least one of the key principles surrounding environmental, social concerns/human rights, animal welfare concerns and economic sustainability.

More broadly ethical consumption is defined as '...any practice of consumption in which explicitly registering commitment towards distant or absent others is an important dimension of the meaning of activity to the actors involved'. Cowe and Williams extend the definition of ethical to incorporate 'self-interested health concerns' and use the expansion of organic foods to highlight this as they are not only concerned with the environment through pesticides but also the detrimental effects these chemicals have on the individual's personal wellbeing.

Further, the ethical concept does not simply mark the production process or the values of the consumer, but is also subject to companies acting ethically across the board including their investment strategies. Following this broad definition of ethical consumption, it appears that it represents a complex set of practices addressing different concerns in a variety of different ways.

In relation to this definition, initial suggestions regarding the ethical trajectories of sustainable tourism shall be presented in order to examine the possibility of understanding sustainable tourism as an emerging form of ethical consumption. Sustainable tourism could be understood as an emerging form of ethical consumption as it adopts social, environmental and economic concerns which are also expressed through the form of consumption. Further, within the sustainable tourism domain we have identified four dominant forces as influencing sustainable tourism which may help to show the parallels between it and ethical consumption.

Whilst I also acknowledge there may be additional forces or motivations influencing sustainable tourism in comparison to ethical consumption it would appear that these four forces enable a better understanding of sustainable tourism:

- *Climate change*: Due to the rapid growth in international tourism transport concerns have been raised regarding the environmental impact of such travel. For example, according to the WTO in 1950 there were around 25 million international arrivals compared to 806 million international arrivals in 2005-representing an average annual growth rate of 8.6%. Further, it is now argued that the transport sector of the tourism industry is a major contributor to international greenhouse gas emissions.
- *Impact of mass tourism on landscapes*: Tourist destinations in countries such as Spain and Thailand provide excellent examples of how mass tourism can change the natural landscape, from high-rise hotels to mass backpacker hostels.
- *Growing interest in environmentalism*: Sustainable tourism appears to have grown alongside environmental and conservation concerns with an increasing emphasis on conservation work or environmental tours whilst on holiday.
- *Cultural and human rights*: Cultural sensitivity appears

at the forefront of a sustainable holiday. The protection and celebration of indigenous cultures and their traditions appears to have influenced the emergence of sustainable tourism. Further, through cultural projects tourists are able to provide the host communities with the advanced knowledge to develop and enter the post-modern world with the protection of human rights providing the foundations for such values.

Therefore, with a broad definition of ethical consumption presented, followed by forces which have influenced sustainable tourism, similarities between ethical consumption and sustainable tourism will now be discussed. Within the definition of ethical consumption it was noted that the environment or green concerns are a key factor in defining a form of ethical consumption.

From the forces influencing sustainable tourism the first three factors appear to fit within the environmental and green concern paradigm through carbon emission concerns, natural landscape concerns and the conservation of natural environments. The social/human rights concerns of ethical consumption in general appear to be expressed through the fourth force influencing sustainable tourism which addresses issues such as cultural sensitivity, cultural protection, development and the protection of human rights.

Therefore it would appear that the ethical consumption paradigm could provide a useful framework through which to develop a better understanding of sustainable tourism. However, referring back to the definition of ethical consumption offered by Barnett *et al*, it appears that other theories maybe needed to further develop this understanding as there appears to be inconsistencies with the fit.

For example, a key aspect of ethical consumption is the concern with distant or absent others, within the sustainable tourism paradigm it would appear that the others are not distant or absent, at least physically, as the tourists are actually visiting the other. Having established a deeper understanding of ethical consumption and offered suggestions as to how sustainable tourism could be conceptualised as an emerging form of ethical consumption, the paper will challenge and critique some of the fundamental assumptions of sustainable tourism by drawing on current post-colonial critiques.

The following part of this paper will critically engage with two central themes of sustainable tourism, ecological sustainability and human rights, and apply a post-colonial critique to these concepts.

SUSTAINABLE TOURISM: AN OXYMORON—A POST-COLONIAL CRITIQUE

One of the key aims of ethical consumption is to tackle the inequalities that the global capitalist free market is said to create. Within this paradigm there seems to be contradictory ideals. Firstly, it would appear we are turning to consumption in order to tackle the inherent problems with consumption, this can clearly be seen as a problematic approach.

In addition, it is argued that ethical consumption is a form of technological competition in the global market whereby producers must exploit technological advances in order to reduce their impact on the environment and reduce the waste commonly associated with production.

However, this generates its own inequalities as smaller producers are said to be unable to invest the necessary capital into new technologies and the larger companies are able to exploit the gap in the market, therefore the small producers that ethical consumption is said to be helping may in fact be the ones that suffer. These arguments could be applied to the technologies surrounding sustainable tourism, for example, eco lodges using solar panels etc.

More broadly, Goodman and Goodman argue that ethical consumption simply provides a "green gloss" to the inequalities of production in the current capitalist system. These assessments are by no means an exhaustive account of the critiques surrounding ethical consumption and sustainable tourism; debates surrounding the expense and time constraints of the labelling process are also dominant to mention but a few.

This part will add to these contemporary debates by putting forward a postcolonial critique of sustainable tourism. Critiques of third world tourism in general have tended to focus on tourism as signifying a new form of colonialisation: for example by demonstrating how 'third world' tourism infrastructures are often owned by developed countries and the suggestion that first world tourists consume 'third world' places, spaces and cultures.

This part shall develop the concept of re-colonialisation through the tourism industry in relation to sustainable tourism. This argument shall start by examining the problematic power dynamics in relation to the current conceptualisation and implementation of ecological sustainability.

Following this, the argument shall be extended to unpack the cultural or human rights basis that informs sustainable tourism and will look critically at human rights in relation to the fundamental assumptions the human rights paradigm is based on. From this investigation it is suggested that these central themes to sustainable tourism embody characteristics of colonialism.

ECOLOGICAL SUSTAINABILITY, PRESERVATION AND WESTERN IDEALS

Within the sustainable tourism definition it was proposed by the author that there are four key motivations or forces which have been central to the development and conceptualisation of sustainable tourism. Further, it was argued that the first three forces are directly concerned with the detrimental effects the tourism industry has on the natural environment; for example, the effects of tourist transport on climate change, the impact of mass tourism on landscapes and the growing interest in environmentalism from the 1960s onwards.

These concerns appear to be relatively neutral in their assumptions and focus solely on the preservation and conservation of the natural environment; however the relationship between humans and the environment within this context warrants further analysis. Within the sustainable tourism domain regarding the impact of tourism on the environment there are fundamental assumptions made by western societies as to what constitutes ecologica sustainability and how we are to further knowledge and thus move closer to achieving it.

In order to develop knowledge around ecological sustainability, the environment is analysed through western scientific methods which assume an objective, value-free view of the natural world. Within tourism it is now apparent that certain forms adopt this objective view on the environment and promote their products as 'sustainable' or 'eco'. It is within the labelling framework that the western nations can inflict their concepts of what nature should be onto the poorer countries and seemingly cover-up such implementation of power under the green, eco or ethical guise.

These unequal power relations can be seen as a new form of colonialism, or what Sachs refers to as eco-colonialism with the survival of the planet providing the perfect backdrop to implement these western values and motivating the world to conform. Consequently, it is through the ideals of ecological sustainability and sustainable tourism that western standards and ideals are imposed on developing nations with conscientious consumption choices enforcing these ideals.

Therefore, the objective view of nature and the environment adopted by sustainable tourism to achieve ecological sustainability through sensitivity to the effects of tourism is not objective and does not provide a real view of the natural world. The reliance upon science to provide an objective evaluation of the environment and allow for the preservation of natural areas can also be seen as the pursuit of technological control over the environment in which capital generated from the development of scientific methods and technology is the primary driving force and therefore constantly reinforcing the capitalist system whilst also imposing the ideals of capitalism on previously untouched cultures and environments. Further, ideals of what constitutes the natural environment and natural beauty are based on aesthetic assumptions which are arguably socially constructed, and therefore historically and culturally specific. In our drive to preserve the natural environment we are attempting to freeze or fix biodiversity to what science currently deems as 'natural'.

Moreover, although the motivations are different, it is not only the natural environment that we wish to freeze frame, but also the cultures living within the environments. For example, Kuhn argues that sustainable tourism attempts to preserve traditional cultures in a way that the western tourist deems as 'authentic'.

Using the example of an Aboriginal community, she suggests that when tourists are first to encounter a community they deem this as the communities' natural way of being and if that community is to change due to western influence then the community is no longer as natural or authentic; as Kuhn notes: 'We cannot expect indigenous peoples to remain forever frozen as that exotic other that we might wish them to be'.

This preservation of authenticity can be seen in terms of sustainable tourism applying pressure, and thus power, to keep cultures in a particular way and removing the choice and agency of that culture, which reiterates the unequal power relations reminiscent within the colonial period. This idea of visiting untouched or primitive cultures under the guise of culturally educational and sustainable holidays appears to reinforce unequal power relations whilst sampling cultural traditions and ceremonies.

For example, these ceremonies and dances are often packaged up, with the inclusion of some local food and transport to the area and sold to the tourists. In addition, the timings of traditional ceremonies are sometimes altered to fit within the tourists schedule and in some cases the traditions altered completely. As such, it is suggested that there is a need for a critical analysis of not only the practices involved in sustainable tourism but also a critical analysis of the promotional material surrounding sustainable tourism to establish if these power relations are represented, as has been attempted in relation to ethical consumption more generally.

For example, Wright argues that through attracting potential consumers, advertisements for ethical products draw on certain cultural representations which partially re-present colonial imagery, embedded within unequal power relations. Therefore, ethical labelling and advertising, be it under the guise of the environment or culture, can be seen as a force to reproduce the unequal power relations between the developed and developing world despite the assumption that it is said to be challenging these historical colonial relationships.

CULTURAL AND HUMAN RIGHTS AS AN ENFORCER OF UNEQUAL POWER RELATIONS

Another emerging criticism surrounding sustainable tourism in relation to colonialism boasts similar concerns to the implementation of western ideals on developing countries, but rather than the focus being on the environment and nature, or our desire to freeze frame cultures for our consumption this critique addresses the very essence of human rights promotion.

In the definition of ethical consumption listed earlier in this object, the forth force of motivational factor influencing sustainable tourism, human rights, was identified as a central concept to the ethical or sustainable arena. The following part will offer a critical approach to the universalistic assumptions of human rights. Human Rights in lay thinking appear to be universal values which form the essence of each and every human being.

Common understandings about what a 'human right' actually is appear to be founded on the lay assumption that '...human rights are based on human needs'. This assumption appears attractive to many when conceptualizing basic human rights as human needs can be scientifically determined, for example, you need food and water to live.

It is this conception of human rights, allowing an individual to the right to live, that forms the basis of the human rights concept. Moreover, the basic right to food and water is argued to be a belief or moral value that no human should deprive a fellow human from having. Therefore, the assumption is made, that it is within the human nature of all individuals to respect the right of others' basic need to survive, as Donnelly notes, '...socially shared moral conceptions of the nature of the human person and the conditions necessary for a life of dignity are the source of human rights'.

However, the Western origins of human rights is said to be problematic due to its claims of total universality. It has been argued that far from creating a sense of inclusive justice and equality for all human beings, it is human rights that reinforce the power relations that exist in the modern world.

In his paper Savages, Victims, and Saviors: The Metaphor of Human Rights, Mutua argues that human rights and human rights discourses are based around a three dimensional prism. It is this three dimensional prism that is the structure of human rights but also the reason why human rights are not truly universal and are cementing the social and political divisions between the west and the rest.

He argues that the first dimension of the prism positions the savage, exemplified by non-western states and developing cultures which within the sustainable tourism domain could be viewed broadly as the primitive host cultures with their outlandish traditions. The second dimension in the prism is the positioned victim that is submissive and their 'naturalist attributes have been negated by the primitive and offensive actions of the state or the culture foundation of the state'.

This second dimension not only presents the victim as somewhat helpless with no power, but also ostracises the primitive nation and their cultural foundations implying they are backward or inferior. Within the sustainable tourism domain this dimension could be viewed as individuals within the host cultures or on a more abstract level, the natural environment. Mutua then highlights the third dimension, that of the 'saviour or the redeemer, the good angel who protects, vindicates, civilizes, restrains, and safeguards'.

Of course, the dimension of the prism being referred to here is that of the ethical, moral, liberal, and enlightened western individuals/states that see themselves as the rescuers for these less-fortunate others living in a state of moral or intellectual darkness. This third dimension could easily be describing the western tourists who embark on a sustainable or ethical holiday to help or save the 'third world' victim.

This three dimensional prism of human rights gives an ethical or moral guise to a system which enforces unequal power relations between the west and the rest which were emblematical within colonisation. Encompassed in the aims and objectives of ethical consumption and sustainable tourism is the promotion of demographic participation.

However, Buchanan highlights that the right to democratic participation should not be viewed as a universal human right, but rather an ideal of western societies. Buchanan uses the example of Asian values and notes that 'The implication is that societies in which "Asian values" are predominant can achieve prosperity (that all their members can have the opportunity for a decent life) without democracy'.

In addition, Taylor claims that due to the western liberal basis for the current human rights concept, there is too much emphasis on individualistic values. The idea of individualism leads rights to be viewed as something individuals can claim from society. Taylor argues that this concept of claiming rights conflicts with the values of different cultures, such as, Islamic and African, where rights are perceived more as responsibilities and what the community owes to each other.

Therefore, if we are to adopt the promotion of human rights and demographic participation through the aims and objectives of our ethical products including sustainable tourism, we must also consider just whose rights are we protecting, whose values are we promoting, and are we really offering and equal/fair exchange in this process?

CONCLUSION

Throughout this object sustainable tourism has been conceptualised as a form of ethical consumption. Following a deeper exploration into the history, aims and objectives of ethical consumption and sustainable tourism it was argued that sustainable tourism shares a number of characteristics with ethical consumption. These similarities include some of the fundamental goals both are striving to achieve, which include a primary concern with regards to both environmental and cultural impacts of mass consumption. Although sustainable tourism has been conceptualised as a form of ethical consumption throughout this object, the author does not intend to claim that this is the only way of conceptualising sustainable tourism and acknowledges variances between the two, particularly in relation to concern for the distant other.

It is suggested here that further work into conceptualising sustainable tourism is essential if we are to fully understand and develop the notion. Following a conceptualisation of sustainable tourism, a post-colonial critique was applied to sustainable tourism in direct relation to ecological sustainability and human rights–both aspects central to sustainable tourism and ethical consumption more broadly. This critique allowed for the examination of power relations within the global society which can operate through seemingly ethical products and labels.

This paper does not intend to argue that sustainable tourism is in no way an improvement on previous production-consumption relationships. Rather the author wishes to suggest that a critical approach to sustainable tourism and ethical consumption in general is essential if we are to seriously challenge current global inequalities and fundamentally shift the production-consumption relationships typically associated with the capitalist free-market system. The question still remains regarding the philosophy that consumption itself can offer the solution to the inequalities created by consumption. Currently this area of research is generating increased interest and it is proposed by the author that further research is needed in order to engage with issues of ethics, sustainability, inequality and consumption within tourism.

7

Reducing Poverty through Tourism

INTRODUCTION

There is enormous scope for the tourism industry to contribute better to less poverty in the world. This booklet outlines ways to do this on a larger scale than at present. It looks at the issues surrounding the subject, refers to the most recent research and suggests how both the tourism industry and the poor can benefit from an integrated approach to growth and equity.

It is still not widely recognized that travel and tourism is one of the world's biggest industries that creates vast economic growth, especially for poor countries. The wider travel and tourism industry now accounts for more than 10 per cent of global gross domestic product (GDP) and creates more than 230 million jobs. For developing countries, tourism generated foreign earnings of more than US$260 billon in 2007, more than six times higher than in 1990.

Tourism is one of the major export sectors of poor countries and the leading source of foreign exchange in 46 of the 49 least developed countries (LDCs). Yet, to date the link between tourism and poverty reduction has lacked focus in the development plans of many poor countries. Many development plans accept that tourism contributes significantly to economic growth.

However, economic growth does not necessarily lead to less poverty. Equally, while many small-scale projects have been developed to link tourism with poverty reduction, large-scale poverty reduction from tourism depends upon clear strategies consulted, articulated and monitored through national poverty reduction strategy plans.

TARGETED INTERVENTIONS

Economic growth is an essential but not a sufficient condition for poverty reduction. Poverty reduction involves growth with a substantial reorientation in favour of the poor. It includes changes in institutions, laws, regulations and practices that help create and perpetuate poverty. It includes targeted interventions to enable poor people to better integrate into economic processes and take advantage of opportunities to improve their economic and social well-being. It means ending harassment of the poor, and eliminating restrictions on how they make their livelihoods. This especially applies to the tourism sector. Interventions must be made to help poor people become part of the processes that drive the industry.

THE ILO

The ILO has always worked to address poverty. The notion that "poverty anywhere is a threat to prosperity everywhere" is part of its Constitution. This booklet aims to show how the potential of the tourism industry to reduce poverty can be realised through decent work in mainstream tourism and related sectors. It also aims to help developing countries highlight the sector in their national poverty reduction strategy plans and encourages international financial institutions to recognize the impact of travel and tourism in their support strategies. For the ILO and its in-country constituents, this booklet outlines how decent work fits with the United Nations Millennium Development Goals (MDGs) in tourism-related poverty reduction strategies, and shows how pro-poor tourism (PPT) projects can be articulated and supported in the development process.

BACKGROUND

The term "pro-poor tourism" is recent. The United Kingdom's Department for International Development (DFID) coined the phrase in the 1990s and many United Nations agencies adopted it this century. This part deals with some of the structures and concepts that relate to its development.

POVERTY REDUCTION STRATEGY PAPERS

In 1999, the World Bank and the International Monetary Fund (IMF) agreed that nationally owned, participatory poverty reduction strategies should be the basis for all concessional lending and debt relief. This approach is reflected in the Poverty Reduction Strategy Papers (PRSPs), which describe a country's economic, social and political policies and programmes over a three-to-five year period.

PRSPs are comprehensive plans prepared by governments, with support from development partners, which identify who the poor are and develop strategies for overcoming poverty, including policy and expenditure targets. PRSPs are supposed to be locally generated, owned and developed through wide participatory dialogue. PRSPs encourage accountability of governments to their own people rather than to external funding agencies.

In this way, the poor can become active participants in development, not just passive recipients. To date, about 50 countries have full PRSPs in place and a number of others have similar national planning instruments. The key difference between PRSP processes and the Structural Adjustment Programmes (SAPs) that preceded them is this national ownership based on an inclusive participatory process.

MILLENNIUM DEVELOPMENT GOALS

Consistent with their poverty reduction focus, PRSPs are also an instrument for achieving the United Nations MDGs. The MDGs are eight universal goals with global, regional and national application. The 189 member States of the UN endorsed them at the UN Millennium Summit in September 2000. The MDGs apply to the period 2000–15.

The MDGs are becoming even more significant as the world approaches the 2015 deadline. Increasingly development plans and poverty reduction strategies refer to them and incorporate them in their framework of action. The

"One UN" reform initiative, whereby all UN agencies deliver as one in each country, has further increased their practical importance.

DECENT WORK

The ILO's concept of "decent work" cuts across the MDGs. Through decent work, the ILO can contribute significantly to MDG achievement, especially to the major goal of halving the incidence of poverty by 2015. The Decent Work Agenda can also have major effects on the other seven goals. Within the list of MDG targets and indicators, the ILO is specifically responsible for indicator 11, on the share of women in waged employment in the non-agricultural sector, as well as indicator 45 on unemployment of 15–24-year-olds.

Target 16, on youth employment is also directly relevant to ILO activities. Work is central to people's well-being. As well as providing income, work can make for social and economic advancement. Work can strengthen individuals, their families and communities.

This, however, hinges on work that is decent. The ILO defines "decent work" as "opportunities for women and men to obtain productive work in conditions of freedom, equity, security and human dignity".

Decent work involves opportunities for productive work that delivers a fair income; security in the workplace and social protection for workers and their families; better prospects for personal development and social integration; freedom for people to express their concerns, organize and participate in decisions that affect their lives; and equality of opportunity and treatment for all. The Decent Work Agenda is an integrated approach to the objectives of full and productive employment for all at global, regional, national, sectoral (industry) and local levels.

It rests on four pillars:

1. Standards and rights at work
2. Employment creation
3. Social protection
4. Tripartism and social dialogue

THE ILO'S MISSION

The ILO's mission is to promote decent work within the context of poverty reduction strategies. In the tourism industry, the strategically important question for the ILO is how to move these activities from niche to mainstream tourism for development. Part of this is ensuring that developing countries highlight the potential of the sector for employment and poverty reduction in their national PRSPs.

It is also important that the ILO helps international financial institutions recognize the impact of tourism in their support strategies.

While there are links between decent work and the MDGs, the ILO and its constituents need to ensure stronger connections between the two frameworks when developing project proposals and strategies–especially in relation to poverty reduction. In particular, this means that the MDG framework should be used wherever possible in outlining project aims and in measuring project impacts.

The ILO's comparative advantage in the design and implementation of PRSPs lies in the integrated approach of decent work, which embraces rights, employment, social protection and (tripartite) social dialogue. Although the well-being of people depends not only on income, it is obvious that income from work is the most important means of survival for poor people.

SURPRISING

It is therefore surprising how few PRSPs include an analysis of labour markets and employment issues. This may be due to a common view that equates employment with waged employment.

In most PRSP countries, less than 20 per cent of the labour force is in waged employment. It is also consistent with the widespread notion that labour markets are best left to the market. In some cases, this neglect of employment policy probably reflects the relative absence of labour ministries and the social partners from the consultation processes for many PRSPs.

TOURISM JOBS

Travel and tourism is itself human-resource intensive due to the service nature of the industry. Further, one job in the core tourism industry creates about one and a half additional (indirect) jobs in the tourism-related economy. The wider travel and tourism economy creates (both directly and indirectly) more than 230 million jobs, which represents about 8 per cent of the global workforce. Half the workers in the industry are aged 25 or younger. Women make up between 60 and 70 per cent of the labour force in the industry. This gender dimension can be especially important: according to the United Nations Development Programme (UNDP), empirical evidence suggests that developing countries with less gender inequality tend to have lower poverty rates. Paid work by women reduces overall poverty and inequality.

In fact, eliminating barriers to women's participation in paid work (as is typical of the tourism industry) has a much stronger effect on poverty and economic growth than ending wage discrimination. In the hotel segment of the industry, globally there is an average of one employee for each hotel room. Further, there are three workers indirectly dependent on each person working in hotels, such as travel agency staff, guides, taxi and bus drivers, food and beverage suppliers, laundry workers, textile workers, gardeners, shop staff for souvenirs and others, as well as airport employees.

TOURISM AND POOR COUNTRIES

The World Economic Forum (WEF) recently produced a competitiveness study on tourism and travel (T&T). According to the report, the tourism industry creates most new jobs in developing countries. Tourism is also the major services export for many developing countries and has much potential to provide competitive advantage for them.

Tourism in developing countries is also growing rapidly. Developing countries' foreign earnings from tourism leapt from less than US$50 billion in 1990 to more than US$260 billon in 2007. For one third of developing countries, tourism is already the main income source. Tourism is also the main source of foreign exchange in 46 of the 49 LDCs. Further, in more than 50 of the world's poorest countries tourism ranks either first, second or third largest of their economic sectors.

Tourism is the only service industry to show a positive balance of trade, with flows from first world countries to developing countries exceeding those in the opposite direction by US$6.6 billion in the year 2000. By way of contrast, tourism accounts for between 3 and 10 per cent of GDP in advanced economies, and up to 40 per cent in developing countries. Yet some aid donors, international funding agencies, segments of the industry and even national governments have only very recently recognized tourism as an appropriate instrument for poverty reduction.

RECENT DEVELOPMENTS

As at 2008, the ILO was taking part in a global discussion and activities about PPT. It is actively involved in rural community tourism projects in 14 countries in Latin America. It has held several global meetings on the tourism industry, has an established web site on tourism issues relating to work and social dialogue and is developing PPT studies and projects in Africa.

The ILO works with the United Nations World Tourism Organization (UNWTO) and the International Hotel and Restaurants Association (IH&RA), as well as with the global union federation, the International Union of Food, Agricultural, Hotel, Restaurant Catering, Tobacco and Allied Workers' Association (IUF). The UNWTO recently launched a programme called "Sustainable Tourism–Eliminating Poverty" (ST–EP). This initiative focuses on long-term measures to encourage sustainable tourism–social, economic and ecological–and which specifically alleviates poverty, bringing development and jobs to people living on less than a dollar a day. A broader development has been the increasing importance of emerging economies in tourism as both destinations and sources of tourists.

According to The Economist magazine, the rise of emerging economies is the third revolution in the travel industry over the past 50 years. The first was during the 1960s with cheap air travel and package tours. The second was the Internet, which meant that travellers could book flights, hotels, cars and tours without using a travel agent.

Now people from high-growth emerging economies such as Dubai, Brazil, Russian Federation, India, China, Republic of Korea and Viet Nam are changing tourism again: These economies are both destinations and sources of newly affluent travellers. Often they visit similar emerging countries, rather than first-world destinations.

According to the UNWTO, while continued growth from emerging tourism will suffer from the economic downturn, fuel price rises and 'mega crises', the numbers of potential travellers are so huge and the logic of targeting tourism for development so pervasive that long-term growth prospects will remain "substantial by any measure". The Organization stresses the need for public-private partnerships to ensure that emerging states access funds for tourism development.

HOTEL, CATERING AND TOURISM SECTOR

For the ILO, the hotel, restaurant and tourism (HCT) sector includes:

- Hotels, boarding houses, motels, tourist camps and holiday centres;
- Restaurants, bars, cafeterias, snack bars, pubs, night clubs and other similar establishments;
- Institutions that provide meals and refreshments within hospitals, factory and office canteens, schools, aircraft, and ships;
- Travel agencies, tourist guides and tourism information offices;
- Conference and exhibition centres.

Other organizations concerned with tourism, including governments, intergovernmental organizations and non-governmental organizations (NGOs) often use much broader definitions of tourism than that used by the ILO. They include all services and products consumed by tourists, including transport. In the ILO HCT sector, the part referring to tourism only covers travel agencies and tour operators. According to the UNWTO, tourism includes the activities of people (visitors) travelling to and staying in places outside their usual environment for less than a year for leisure, business and other purposes. Tourists are people whose main purpose of visit is not an activity paid from within the destination. Most organizations consider hotels and catering, including restaurants, to belong to the industries with characteristic of tourism, although in some countries only a small part of their services is for tourists. The fact that the ILO definition of the sector is different from that used by other organizations does not prevent it sharing most concerns about tourism development. One such concern is the sector's potential to provide employment. Nevertheless, the ILO's focus on labour issues is unique as it includes all working and employment conditions in the HCT sector.

VISION

The vision embraced by this booklet is for a tourism industry that is both competitive and much more strongly linked to the well-being of poor people who live at the destination. This is consistent with the World Travel and Tourism Council's (WTTC) 2003 policy statement: Blueprint for New Tourism. The blueprint is a strategic framework for a travel and tourism industry that works for all stakeholders. This new tourism looks beyond the short term and focuses on benefits for travellers, as well as for local communities and their natural, social, and cultural environments.

The blueprint has three key components:

1. Governments recognizing travel and tourism as a top priority;
2. Business balancing economics with people, culture, and environment; and
3. A shared pursuit of long-term growth and prosperity.

The vision encompassed by this booklet is, however, more detailed.

Its key elements Are:

- Upgrades local skills;

- Creates decent local jobs;
- Uses local construction;
- Embraces the local culture;
- Improves local infrastructure;
- Helps sustain the local environment;
- Sources locally as much as possible;
- Plans to be inclusive over the long term;
- Provides a unique experience for tourists;
- Promotes itself as a top economic priority;
- Creates partnerships to improve livelihoods.

While some regard corporate social responsibility as a public relations exercise or simply providing charity to poor people, a genuinely inclusive tourism industry promises much more. The difference between a tourism industry that relies on charity and one that embraces inclusion is the results: Only an inclusive industry can achieve greater benefits and at the same time add to human dignity. And it is human dignity that guarantees the motivation and the security to benefit all those who are included, not least benefits for the industry itself.

ISSUES

There are many issues associated with mainstreaming this complex industry to better benefit the poor. There are disagreements about how much tourism benefits local people. Some issues result from mindsets that are out of touch with current reality. Some concern access, information and analysis. Others are more straightforward, practical issues of recognition, planning and implementation.

DEFINITIONS

Apart from the differing definitions of the tourism industry used by different organizations mentioned in the background part above, even definitions of PPT and poverty itself can be issues.

Pro-poor Tourism

According to the Pro-Poor Tourism Partnership, PPT is "tourism that results in increased net benefits for poor people.

PPT is not a specific product or niche sector but an approach to tourism development and management. It enhances the linkages between tourism businesses and poor people so that tourism's contribution to poverty reduction is increased and poor people are able to participate more effectively in product development.

Links with many different types of "the poor" need to be considered: staff, neighbouring communities, land-holders, producers of food, fuel and other suppliers, operators of micro tourism businesses, craft-makers, other users of tourism infrastructure (roads) and resources (water), etc. There are many types of PPT strategies, ranging from increasing local employment to building mechanisms for consultation. Any type of company can be involved in PPT–a small lodge, an urban hotel, a tour operator, an infrastructure developer.

The critical factor is not the type of company or the type of tourism, but that an increase in the net benefits that go to poor people can be demonstrated". Even this detailed definition has its limitations, however. Its weakness is that it remains oriented to single operations, rather than to the wider industry. Because tourism is such a large and growing industry, and so important to poor nations, large-scale strategies should now be emphasized in order to make real inroads into poverty.

Poverty

Who are poor people? The United Nations defines extremely poor people as those who live on less than the equivalent of one US dollar per day. This is measured in purchasing power parity (PPP), which is based on the cost of a similar basket of goods in different countries, expressed in United States dollars. Merely poor people are those who live on less than US$2 per day PPP. There are about 1.3 billion people in the developing world (21 per cent of the world population) in extreme poverty, who live on less than US$1 per day.

More than 2.7 billion live on less than US$2 per day. To go further, who are the poorest of the poor and how they can benefit from PPT? It has been pointed out that often the poorest are not subsistence farmers as is often assumed, but rather landless informal agricultural workers and their families. How to include former itinerant sugar workers from Guyana in the new tourism economy of Saint Kitts in the Caribbean is an example of this issue. However, the real meaning of poverty goes beyond just lack of money and its arbitrary measurement.

NET IMPACT

In world (21 per cent of the world population) in extreme poverty, who live on less than US$1 per day. More than 2.7 billion live on less than US$2 per day. To go further, who are the poorest of the poor and how they can benefit from PPT? It has been pointed out that often the poorest are not subsistence farmers as is often assumed, but rather landless informal agricultural workers and their families. How to include former itinerant sugar workers from Guyana in the new tourism economy of Saint Kitts in the Caribbean is an example of this issue. However, the real meaning of poverty goes beyond just lack of money and its arbitrary measurement.

Tourism can have both positive and negative effects on poor people.

There are three:

- *Main ways that tourism can impact on vulnerable people*: through direct effects on the poor, such as tourism jobs and small tourism enterprises;
- Through secondary effects, such as earnings from supply chain industries (for example, food and construction) as well as from tourism workers who spend their earnings in the local economy; and
- Through dynamic effects on the economy such as entrepreneurship, wages and prices, infrastructure development, other export sectors, skill development and the natural environment.

There is no destination where poverty impact has been assessed in all three of these ways. Assessing tourism poverty effects in future needs to look at all three areas of impact. It is most important to be aware that tourism, like any other activity, can have both positive and negative effects on people, especially the poor.

It should not be assumed that PPT strategies will have only positive effects. For example, the introduction of new tourist resorts can benefit the poor through job creation, but may have negative effects through increased prices for land and commodities, or reduced access to beaches and fishing grounds. Strategies that aim to reduce poverty must assess the net impact in order to give a true picture. Future approaches need to consider net effects as well as benefits.

A HOLY COW

There is no unanimity of views on tourism and poverty reduction. For example, according to one critic, most of the effects of tourism on poor people are negative. Anita Pleumarom of the Third World Network says that it is time to stop treating tourism as a "holy cow to be protected and nurtured at all costs".

She observes that:

- The more decision-makers parade tourism policies for poverty elimination, the more the gap widens between the rich and the poor among and within nations, due to aggressive and unfair economic liberalization. While people in rich countries drown in conspicuous consumption thereby destroying their own and others' life bases, communities in less and least developed countries only receive the crumbs from the wealth that capitalist growth produces.

Her paper points to "the financial 'leakage' (due to high import content, repatriation of profits by foreign-owned tourism companies, etc.)" that tourism produces, and "unbalanced and inequitable distribution of income." She writes that "... leakages in the tourism sector total up to 85 per cent in some African least developed countries (LDCs), more than 80 per cent in the Caribbean, 70 per cent in Thailand and 40 per cent in India".

She says that rather than a boon, "... in fact, tourism-related jobs are uncertain, seasonal and part time, with a high turnover of staff". Ms Pleumarom calls for better and well-enforced regulation to tackle these issues. Whether or not one agrees with these views of the tourism industry overall, these are issues that need to be tackled. Donors, governments and the social partners need to address environmental challenges, poor communities do need real benefits from the industry, and financial leakages need to be reduced.

GROWTH VERSUS SHARE

As with broader debates about national and global economies, the issue of absolute growth as against equitable share of that growth is often heard in relation to tourism. The underlying assumption behind this issue is that the two goals are in conflict with each other. However, expanding tourism overall with a bigger share for the poor is achievable.

In destinations where tourism is already pro-poor, studies suggest that the poor will benefit from a combined approach: expanding the overall size of the sector, while simultaneously tackling the bottlenecks that prevent the poor from earning a greater share. The relative value of either one varies by destination. In Da Nang, Viet Nam, for example, removing blockages to growth in upmarket coastal accommodation was the main short-term priority.

This was more effective than the traditional pro-poor policy goal of strengthening local linkages. This was due to the inherent pro-poor characteristics of tourism and extensive existing linkages in the destination, and also to government tourism land supply policy which had held back the expansion of the sector. By contrast, in Ethiopia existing supply chains are disconnected from the local economy. Interventions that enable the poor to participate must be integrated into expansion of the sector for tourism growth to reach the poor.

SCALE

Pro-poor action remains focused at the micro level. PPT should be applicable to all forms of tourism including mainstream tourism, not just a niche product such as eco-tourism or community tourism. The principles of maximizing linkages with the poor can be applied to beach resorts, urban hotels, conferences, wilderness tours, new building projects and on a national and regional scale. However, most tourism for poverty reduction initiatives remain confined to community-based tourism projects, campsites or trekking. They cannot deliver impact at a significant scale.

The significance of scale is underlined by recent academic papers from the University of the South Pacific in Fiji, which argue that the concept of PPT has become too closely associated with community-based tourism. They say it should be reintegrated into mainstream studies of tourism and development, and focus more on the role of mass tourism in alleviating poverty and bringing development.

MARKETS

Often too little attention is paid to market linkages in PPT ventures. Initiatives often concentrate on providing training and infrastructure. Yet products fail to find a market demand, domestic or international, and do not deliver livelihood benefits. In some cases, when tourism development is attempted because there is no alternative, communities are encouraged to invest labour, land and borrowings that have little chance of success.

INSTITUTIONAL FACTORS

Institutional factors can cause market linkage failures and reduce the chances of success for PPT ventures. For example, expanding the tourism sector and increasing the benefits reaching the poor are often made separate tasks for different people. Governments allocate PPT responsibilities to a part-time community tourism staffer, or put them under a separate project. Also, development practitioners who work with communities often know little about commercial tourism markets.

They attempt to implement projects without bringing in business expertise and private sector partners. In the private sector, tourism companies often regard local donations as corporate social responsibility. But fewer seek the commercial and local advantage that can come from doing business differently. In the public sector, a destination level approach to PPT needs complementary policies from tourism, agriculture, transport, enterprise, land, finance and labour departments, plus authority and skills at local government level. But neither integrated government nor strong local authorities are common.

MONITORING

There is a lack of systematic and documented monitoring of changes in poor people's livelihoods due to tourism. Neither the full range of impacts of tourism development on poverty levels, nor the before-and-after impacts of specific pro-poor measures have been rigorously assessed. Despite plenty of literature that suggests various pro poor strategies to adopt, there is little that actually quantifies results. For example, the significant income increases measured for poor people in the Gambia due to a market access initiative in 2001–02, are still frequently quoted because there are so few examples of published action research in this field.

TECHNICAL ASSISTANCE

The level of technical assistance available to help develop pro poor tourism is still less than ideal. However, the international community is beginning to recognize the importance of tourism as a potential driving force in the social and economic development of poor countries. This is because tourism development makes for much better trading opportunities.

Accordingly, it is one of the most effective ways of avoiding marginalization from the global economy. Because it can be a catalyst, tourism is one of the few economic sectors able to guide a number of developing countries to higher levels of prosperity and for some, to leave behind their LDC status. The UNWTO's ST–EP programme began in 2002, and is a good example of how technical assistance to the industry can work.

It provides technical assistance to developing countries on sustainable tourism development. Based on the recommendations resulting from missions, the help it offers can include product development, marketing, strategic planning and skill enhancement for business and national and local government relevant to tourism. Its recommendations can result in funding from international development agencies. ST–EP also facilitates research and identifies models of best practice.

This includes seven mechanisms for poverty reduction through tourism that were identified by the UNWTO after detailed analytical research. These mechanisms have proved to be useful to parties working on development and poverty reduction, including governments, international organizations and NGOs, and community-based organizations. While ST–EP is still relatively new, it builds on work by the increasing number of agencies that have policies linking tourism with poverty alleviation.

These include the Asian Development Bank, the World Bank, the British DFID–ODI, the Netherlands' SNV, UN technical agencies such as the United Nations Conference on Trade and Development (UNCTAD), the United Nations Environment Programme (UNEP), and the World Commission on Environment and Development (WCED), international tourism organizations such as the Pacific Asia Travel Association (PATA) and some international NGOs.

However, tourism development that includes poverty reduction cannot be left to the private sector alone in many developing countries.

This is due to lack of money and weak institutional capacity of the private sector in such destinations. Design and implementation of an effective strategy usually needs strengthening of partnerships between the private sector and national tourism authorities. Help from international agencies is usually needed to achieve objectives.

COMPETITIVENESS

The World Economic Forum (WEF) published an updated travel and tourism report on competitiveness amongst 130 countries in 2008. The travel and tourism competitiveness index (TTCI) measures "the factors and policies that make it attractive to develop the (travel and tourism) sector in different countries". The TTCI is composed of 14 factors of competitiveness.

These factors are grouped into three broad categories:

1. The travel and tourism regulatory framework;
2. The travel and tourism business environment and infrastructure;
3. Travel and tourism human, cultural and natural resources.

All the top ten are developed countries such as Switzerland and the United States, while all of the bottom ten are LDCs such as Bangladesh and Chad. This competitiveness index has generated considerable debate.

For example, the front page of The Jordan Times newspaper related a story about a high-level meeting in Amman during May 2008, during which tourism industry groups criticized the report because Jordan's position on the rankings had dropped from the previous year.

Factors of competitiveness in the travel and tourism industry:

- Policy rules and regulations
- Environmental sustainability
- Safety and security
- Health and hygiene
- Prioritization of travel and tourism
- Air transport infrastructure
- Ground transport infrastructure
- Tourism infrastructure
- Information and communications technology infrastructure
- Price competitiveness
- Human resources
- Affinity for travel and tourism
- Natural resources
- Cultural resources

The index is a useful reference point for analyzing ways to improve economic growth in the industry and to make it more sustainable. While it lacks a strong focus on associated poverty reduction, much of what it recommends is relevant to a future more responsible tourism sector.

Collaboration

The report stresses that the industry should provide value beyond jobs and shareholder returns, as this is of increasing importance to consumers, governments, civil society and even business itself. It says that the industry is in a unique position to make a positive difference to the quality of life, due to its importance as an economic generator and employment provider, as well as because it brings people together.

This means that industry leaders must go beyond traditional day-to-day business. Leaders must also improve individual lives and freedoms by collaborating with governments and civil society to address national and global issues. The competitiveness report says that today's key challenges, such as poverty, climate change, terrorism, disease and corruption, are not part of any one discipline for study, nor can government, business or society solve them on their own. It calls for cross-sector leadership to solve them.

FOREIGN DIRECT INVESTMENT

Whilst tourism is a highly globalized industry, it is not so in terms of foreign direct investment (FDI). This means there is a lot of potential for FDI in poor countries. Conversely, poor countries can take advantage of FDI to improve the industry and benefit development. A recent UN report on this issue cites a growing support from donor and development communities for PPT.

The report points out that much of tourism's development potential results from its links across multiple goods and services activities, as well as from the diversity of enterprises involved. Tourism accounts for no more than one or two per cent of outward FDI from main source countries, such as the United States, United Kingdom, Spain, France and Canada.

Further, much of this FDI is in developed countries. Recently, however, there has been a noticeable increase in FDI for tourism from other sources such as China, Malaysia,

Singapore, United Arab Emirates, Cuba, Poland, South Africa and Mauritius. Most FDI in tourism is in hotels and restaurants.

Local Supply

According to the UNCTAD report, the main advantages of attracting FDI in tourism for poor countries are:

- The attraction of new skills, systems and technologies that international capital can bring;
- Greater product diversity;
- Slightly higher wages than those paid by local enterprises; and, surprisingly,
- Better linkages with local suppliers than local enterprises. In order to take advantage of FDI, UNCTAD advises policies that promote linkages and raise local supply standards.

DECENT WORK

Emphasizing the relationship between decent work and PPT is a significant challenge for the ILO and its constituents. While not specifically focusing on PPT, the ILO has been more closely engaging with the poverty reduction strategy process for several years.

There are three main challenges for the ILO in this:

1. The need for PRSPs to include a more thorough analysis of employment and decent work;
2. The need for labour ministries, employers' and workers' organizations to take greater part in the process; and
3. The need for equity as well as growth to be considered in PRSPs.

The ILO has produced several publications to help in this, including a manual on decent work and poverty reduction strategies. As a result, it has made good progress with 15 PRSP processes, and poverty reduction measures increasingly highlight decent work and equity. But because PRSPs are a "crowded marketplace" for ideas and resources, it needs a sustained effort to make sure that decent work continues to get the attention it deserves. Decent work related to PPT is an even greater challenge.

SOCIAL PARTNERS UNDERVALUED

While the ILO encourages governments to invite trade unions and employers' organizations (the social partners) to be involved in PRSPs, often their views and support are undervalued: According to the ILO, employers' organizations and trade unions often find it hard to get involved in the PRSP process because:

- They normally relate to the labour ministry, which usually has little influence over the PRSP process;
- The process emphasizes the participation of civil society organizations, and unions and employers do not think of themselves as part of such a grouping;
- Established tripartite economic and social councils are often left out of the PRSP process;
- Some governments may fear engaging with the social partners because they are too independent;
- World Bank and IMF staff who advise on the PRSP process are often unfamiliar with the work of the ILO and the social partners;
- Some unions oppose involvement in policies they reject;
- Some employers' organizations decide to concentrate on other aspects of public policy.

Further, in some countries the national law effectively excludes the extremely poor from forming trade unions and therefore they are not represented in PRSP consultations. The ILO and its constituents at the country level will be supported if they campaign more around the central place of decent work in poverty reduction and in relation to the democratic base of their views and expertise. The tourism industry is an ideal sector on which to base this course of action.

AGENDAS

The biggest issue is however, getting PPT and decent work onto development agendas. Whether the PPT becomes part of

PRSPs, or other forms of development assistance, it first needs more networking and advocacy in order to be heard and understood.

MAINSTREAMING POVERTY REDUCTION THROUGH TOURISM

This part outlines some of the factors that should be considered when devising measures to advance PPT, particularly through PRSPs and related means. Mainstreaming in this context means that sustainable tourism development should be included in wider poverty elimination programmes. Conversely, mainstreaming means that poverty reduction measures should be part of the sustainable development of tourism. It also implies that PPT should be on a big scale rather than a piecemeal microenterprise approach. All forms of decent work should be considered in assessing value chain benefits to the poor.

PARTICIPATION

A country's poverty reduction strategy paper is the centre of development action, and it is where the ILO and its constituents need to take part. A PRSP should be created through wide participation and the process should encourage governments to answer to their own people, rather than to external donors. The World Bank sourcebook on PRSPs sets out the process and how it should involve different stakeholders. A stakeholder is any organization or group with an interest in the PRSP process, and may include government ministries, including NGOs, religious bodies and donors. Employers' and union organizations are recognized stakeholders who have a right to be involved.

Opportunities

A PRSP is an evolving document that must be regularly reviewed. How often it is reviewed depends on local conditions, but a PRSP must be implemented, monitored and evaluated. At each stage in the PRSP cycle, there are opportunities for stakeholders, including employer and union bodies, to provide input. It is important to see the PRSP as a long-term, ongoing process. Often one cycle lasts three–five years. Wherever the country is in the cycle, organizations can still be usefully involved. Even if issues do not get picked up in the first cycle, organizations can still push for them in a later cycle by lobbying for their priorities to be included.

Aim

For the ILO and its constituents, getting involved in the PRSP process in relation to PPT means being clear about the aim of their participation. The central aim of an involvement strategy is to get the priorities of the organization in the PRSP action summary. This is the summary table listing what measures are to be taken by whom and by when, usually in the latter part of the document. If this does not happen, then there is little chance of wide-scale coordinated interventions in the industry to benefit the poor.

Coordination

It is important that there is coordination and cooperation within and between the ILO and its constituents to maximize resources and effectiveness. Union and employers' organizations, (the social partners) are partners with the government in the social and economic development of the nation. In many countries, there is more than one union or employers' organization at the national level. There may be more than one national union federation, and more than one union directly involved in tourism.

Also, there are often different types of organizations for employers. There may be an employers' federation, a chamber of commerce, foreign investor associations and sector-based organizations, like a chamber of tourism. There needs to be coordination within constituents as well so that advocacy for PPT in development plans is clear and united.

BENEFITS

Aside from benefits to the poor and to the industry, there are also considerable wider benefits for the social partners to get involved in PRSPs.

Direct Effects

A PRSP is the key to many policy and programme decisions in a country. It sets the framework for decision-making for years to come on economic and other government policy, programme and spending priorities. It will cover things like sectoral trade and private sector development, as well as social justice initiatives. These decisions will directly affect employers and workers. This especially applies to tourism, which is usually the main source of economic growth in poor countries.

Best Strategies

Creating decent work is central to reducing poverty. Employers' and union organizations have knowledge and experience in this field, which they can use to help develop the best strategies for the industry and the sectors it links with.

Building Networks

A PRSP process involves many different organizations and people working to combat the problem of poverty. Through their involvement, union and employers' organizations are able to extend their networks to other groups and individuals who share common concerns. Any organization gains from a broader pool of people with whom it can work.

The Bigger Picture

Governments often consult employers' and union organizations on industrial relations, and labour matters, but not on the broader issues. Being part of a PRSP process is a way to uncover the bigger picture and have a say. Where the tourism industry fits in the bigger picture in the future is a central part of this.

Organizational Planning

Employers' and union organizations need to plan for their own future and growth, and it helps to know what the policy and programme environment is likely to be. This makes it easier to predict potential opportunities and threats. Within the tourism industry, advance knowledge of proposed developments and policy measures can help synchronize employer development planning, and help bring about decent working conditions through union recruitment and social dialogue.

New Skills

Getting involved in a PRSP will give new and better skills for union and employers' organizations in areas like advocacy, planning, consultation, policy development, programming, monitoring and evaluation. These are all important skills for the social partners.

ACTION PRINCIPLES

When determining the kinds of measures needed to implement PPT, some guidance is available. Based on significant research on PPT, several action principles have been identified that can be used to guide mainstreaming approaches in tourism and its related sectors. These principles should be borne in mind when designing measures to increase benefits to the poor. They provide for growth as well as for more equitable distribution of economic benefits.

Partnerships

Develop partnerships between international, government, non-government and private sector organizations that have the common aim of reducing poverty through tourism. In developing countries, it is especially unlikely that any one organization will have the capacity to implement programmes alone.

Linkages

Build linkages from the local economy to tourism supply chains. In this way, industries related to tourism can grow, become more competitive and contribute to a more dynamic economy.

Markets

Reduce leakages from supply chains based on genuine

market opportunities. Leakages can be identified and measured by assessing supplies and services that are imported to fill market needs.

Integration

Integrate approaches with other sectors so there is not an overdependence on tourism. Other sectors such as agriculture, fishing and construction can also be developed to fit with seasonal patterns of tourism demand.

Equity and Growth

Include both equity and economic growth in tourism development strategies. One need not be at the expense of the other. Rather, if the right policy mix is implemented, they can support each other.

Local

Focus specific action at the destination level. These actions should be supported by national policy, resources and a strong relationship between national and local government.

Remove Barriers

Remove discrimination, exploitation and barriers that may apply to poor people seeking to work in the tourism and related supply-chain industries. Decent jobs that can be accessed by the poor are key to reducing poverty.

Access

Ensure that poor people have access to relevant information, influence and are able to make their own decisions. This requires good government at all levels, as well as access to mobile phones and the Internet.

Measurement

Develop valid indicators and systems to measure before and after impact of tourism on poverty. Impact measurement is one of the most neglected areas of PPT. Measurement helps determine what does not work as well as what does.

OTHER SECTORS

One of the characteristics of tourism is its extensive links with other sectors. The more these linkages can be strengthened through deliberate interventions, the greater the benefit to wider economic development and poverty reduction. At the same time, there should be greater efficiencies and other benefits for the tourism industry itself. The main sectors related to tourism are construction, agriculture, fishing, food processing, furniture manufacturing, transport, utilities and services. The provision of infrastructure can also be significant for poor people as well as for general economic growth. The informal sector, including the manufacture and sale of craftwork, as well as microfinance and entertainment and cultural activities also has potential strong relationships with the industry.

Agriculture

In agriculture, it is still common for major tourist facilities to get food supplies from other countries. They do so due to poor quality, limited variety and unreliable local supply. Yet much poverty is associated with subsistence-level agriculture. Often local farmers may simply lack knowledge of what major hotels require, or they may suffer from equipment, water, seed and transport shortages.

Where programmes have been set up (often with government support) to overcome these issues, the results have benefited the industry, the tourists and the farmers involved. The Sandals resort chain in several Caribbean destinations is one example where this has occurred. This luxury resort chain now engages local farmers to supply much of its fresh food needs. Explaining the standards and nature of supplies required was central to the programme's success.

Often ensuring facilities for produce display–such as in markets–can be a significant step in maintaining communication between buyers and suppliers. In 2008, some developing countries began export bans on certain staple food items such as rice due to production downturns and rapidly increasing prices. This is a further factor that points to the need to secure local supplies by the industry, as well as by the wider national economy.

Construction

The construction of tourism facilities and infrastructure can benefit the poor significantly. The destination will usually be able to supply significant quantities of unskilled and semi-skilled labour. Where there is minimum wage legislation, or where workers are paid at decent levels, short-term returns to the poor are maximized. Benefits can be extended by getting materials from sustainable local sources and by helping upgrade skills and methods. Wider and more long-term dynamic benefits are also possible.

There are already many examples where unique local skills have been used to build or restore tourist accommodation that combines local styles with upgraded amenities. The Haciendas project in Mexico is one example where local workers have restored abandoned historic buildings in high poverty areas. This project was financed by the Starwood hotel chain and a Mexican company. It combines economic profit and close integration with the local community.

Another successful example is the construction of a series of several lodges and other facilities in traditional style in the Siwa oasis region of Egypt for tourism. The Canadian International Development Agency (CIDA) partly funded the project, which has won several international awards. Often such projects need to train more people with the necessary skills than are immediately available. This can help to support future construction in other sectors and help provide economic opportunity for those trained.

Fishing

Inclusive tourism businesses more often benefit themselves and local people through sourcing fish and crustacean supplies locally. Local catches are often more highly valued by international tourists than expensive frozen supplies, because of freshness, price and because they are connected with the destination. Industry support for the development of fish farming can enhance reliability of supply and increased value added in this sector. Fish stocks worldwide are under increasing pressure and any support to make the sector more sustainable is a good thing.

The downside is that fishing for supply to tourist ventures can compete with local subsistence supply–either directly or by effecting price increases. On the other hand, the tourist industry can help sustain fish supplies, especially with government support for industry regulation. Such regulation can help prevent overexploitation of particular species, and also ensure that waste is not released untreated into catchment areas.

As with agriculture, it is important for the industry to communicate with suppliers on their needs, such as price, quantity, quality, timing and species. The industry also needs to discuss with suppliers on the issues they face, such as accessibility, competition, seasonality, pollution and poaching. Provision of market facilities can maintain and extend benefits to the wider community.

Food Processing

Food processing will often be very limited in many destination countries. The production of basic international items such as meat products, milk and fruit juices may not even exist or be of poor standard. An inclusive tourism sector can help improve the supply of such products by detailing the standards, quantities and prices they need to supplement or replace imported items. Early discussions between the tourism and potential food industry representatives are needed to begin this. Government and international support may be needed. Implementation plans should include dialogue involving the social partners.

Furniture Manufacturing

As with construction, the supply of furniture and its repair to tourism enterprises can often be undertaken locally. Some countries (such as Kenya and Thailand) have developed export markets that were originally based on supplying furniture to the local tourism industry. Despite this, many international tourism enterprises fail to consider or work towards such sourcing. If orders are sufficient, it is also possible for the industry to help develop local skill training in what can be a highly valuable and diverse industry. Textile manufacturing for furniture finishing, soft furnishing and bed linen also links here.

Infrastructure

Major tourism developments are often in otherwise remote parts of developing countries. Developers base these on natural attractions such as sun and sand, or link them to cultural sites such as ancient monuments. In many cases, the viability of such developments depends on upgrading or creating entirely new infrastructure.

The construction of airports, bridges, power and telecommunication links and the upgrading of roads, waterways and port facilities that the development requires can significantly benefit the local poor. Better public transport infrastructure means that the poor can more easily access markets and jobs. It means they can better deliver supplies and services–to the wider economy as well as to tourist developments. Telecommunication links such as mobile phone facilities and Internet coverage benefit the poor because they give access to information.

Services

The tourism industry supports local services (such as guides, haircuts, laundry, massage, and entertainment) since they are supplied only at the point of consumption. However, larger industry developments can be more pro-poor if they make information available on local services available, make services more accessible, and help ensure higher standards. The Starwood Haciendas project in Mexico trains local people in traditional massage techniques, for example. While there was some cultural reluctance initially in supplying this as a service to tourists, it has become popular amongst guests and with workers for the income it generates.

In Fiji, only one tribe traditionally undertakes fire-walking. This cultural exhibition is now popular with tourists and the families of the fire-walkers benefit significantly from the revenue generated. Generally, the communication of standards required is just as important in the provision of services as it is for supplies. So is skill training which can significantly help economic opportunity and mobility. The downside of tourism in some developing countries is often sex tourism. The industry should disavow links with exploitative sex enterprises. It must also work with governments to enforce local laws aimed at preventing exploitation, particularly of women and children, in what has become a form of modern slavery.

Transport

As well as international and domestic air transport, tourism is also associated with most other modes of travel. This can range from taxi and hire cars, motorized and pedalpowered vehicles, buses, boats, rail, and even hot air ballooning. Integration with local transport modes, rather than offering completely separate and expensive hotel-run modes can work best here. Visitors can benefit from the choice of options available to them.

Tour operators often use minibuses and other local forms of transport for tourists. Both can help support employment directly, as well as by using transport support services such as garages for fuel and maintenance. If the industry supports safe driver training for its staff and local people, it can make a further contribution to the welfare of the poor and at the same time help protect visitors from what is a major hazard of travel in developing countries.

Utilities

The tourism industry–especially hotels and restaurants–requires reliable utilities such as electricity, gas and water. These necessities are often in short supply in developing countries. Yet too often major luxury hotels at night will be ablaze with light often from their own generators while nearby poor settlements make do with battery power and candles. Too often luxury hotels secure fresh water supplies from adjacent catchment areas, fresh water that also supports green lawns and golf courses, while surrounding poor communities make do with communal taps or wells of dubious quality. If major tourism developments also help make reliable electricity and water available to the communities they are associated with, then the poor also benefit, even if no longterm employment is generated directly as a result.

VALUE CHAIN ANALYSIS

If tourism's potential to improve the livelihoods of poor people is to be fulfilled, then we need to understand and measure how much of tourism benefits reach the poor. This can help determine how the poor can better access the tourism value chain–whether from employment or from other means. There have been few studies on this. Conventional tourist analysis focused on tourist arrivals, foreign exchange receipts and investments, with little emphasis on measuring benefits to the poor. Because of this, much PPT analysis used a micro-level approach that looked at the livelihood effects on poor people involved with specific niche tourism enterprises.

A limited geographical scale, descriptive nature and niche focus meant these studies did not make any recommendations for boosting PPT benefits in most mainstream tourist destinations. However, some development researchers are starting to close this information gap by using value chain analysis (VCA) to map the tourism economy, its revenue streams and beneficiaries. This form of analysis can be used to address questions for policy makers who want to improve the pro-poor impact of tourism. While there are several factors that affect the degree of pro-poor benefit, some results are becoming clearer.

Although it must be remembered that the information on which it is based remains quite limited, the analysis should be taken into account when planning pro-poor interventions. The domestic sourcing of supplies for the tourism industry can be an especially important factor in its contribution to poverty reduction. The Cambodia PRSP, for example, states: "Estimates show that for every tourist dollar, 75 cents are returned to Thailand to import fresh vegetables, fruit, flowers, handicrafts and furniture." If such leakages are reduced, there are benefits for both industry profitability and the local poor.

BARRIERS

There will always be particular barriers that need to be overcome if poor people are to significantly benefit from tourism. The ODI lists 15 different types of barriers to consider in this regard. Policies, programmes or projects that attempt to incorporate pro-poor dimensions in tourism and other sectors can use this as checklist to ensure that potential barriers are identified, evaluated and addressed.

While some of these possible barriers to the poor benefiting need government intervention to be overcome (for example regulation and red tape, lack of pro-active government support) others can be overcome by those directly involved in the tourism industry. The industry can help overcome skill deficiencies by in-house training, it can help provide access to tourism markets and it can give information on product specifications and help link with local suppliers.

VOLATILITY

Hunger is neither seasonal nor temporary. Decent work depends on regular employment throughout the year, over a long period. However, in many destinations there is marked variation in tourist demand. This variation affects industry profit, job security and the tourist expenditure on which many poor people depend. Variation in demand is due to two main factors: seasonality and external shock.

Seasonality

Seasonal changes in tourist demand can be offset by marketing the destination in areas of the country where there are less extreme micro-climates. If the peak tourist period can be extended only a few weeks at either end through pricing and marketing, it can make a big difference to the destination's economy. Cooler mountain resorts can offset extreme heat in tropical countries during the dry season. Also, the seasonal downturn can be used for preparation and maintenance activities including staff recruitment and training, in appropriate segments of the industry.

External Shock

Tourism in particular destinations has suffered external shocks such as tsunamis, severe acute respiratory syndrome (SARS) and the threat of bird flu, as well as the wider effects of terrorist attacks, climate change and air travel fuel cost increases.

However, it is remarkable how quickly tourism can regain lost ground after catastrophe. Infrastructure and accommodation may need to be repaired and improved. Security may need to be tightened. New marketing strategies may need to be developed.

If these things are wellplanned, and if local labour is used where possible, the harm to the industry and to the poor can be reduced to a minimum. The Indonesian island of Bali is an example of one destination that has recovered quickly from recent external shock. Low-lying islands that risk being submerged as a result of climate change are a much more difficult problem whether or not they depend on tourism. This issue requires global as well as regional action.

Indicators

When intervening in the tourism industry to produce better results for poor people, it is critical that concrete outcomes are demonstrated so that further interventions can evolve. The way to demonstrate outcomes is by selecting good indicators before the intervention begins. Indicators are also important to show where policies may not have had the desired effects, and what mix of measures work best for the local industry.

Four Types

The World Bank identifies four different types of

indicators. Under the source column, the "survey data" it refers to is usually the sample household surveys that support census information between census years. "Facility" and "community surveys" are usually undertaken by the institution or project concerned.

Selecting Indicators

- Selecting the right indicators–especially of outcomes and impact–needs a lot of thought. A good indicator: Is easy to understand and easy to measure. Indicators that are easy to understand are better for programme focus. If large surveys are needed, monitoring is more costly and requires more time.
- Is a direct and clear measure of progress. For example, immunization coverage is clearer than household expenditure on health, because an increase in health expenditure could be a good thing if it means that households have more resources to get healthcare. Or it could be a bad thing if it means that disease incidence or the cost of care has increased.
- Is relevant. It should directly relate to the measures undertaken. For instance, hotel operating costs depend on energy prices, and also on many other factors such as labour costs, marketing costs and occupancy rates. It might therefore not be a good indicator for progress on energy efficiency.
- Varies across areas, groups, over time and is sensitive to changes in policies and programmes. For instance, child malnutrition is more likely to vary quickly over time than life expectancy. Employment levels will be more sensitive than incidence of poverty.
- Is reliable and not easy to manipulate. Objective indicators are more reliable than indicators that depend on the interpretation of the user.
- Is gender disaggregated. Almost all changes affect men and women differently. Therefore the indicator should show both sexes separately as well as the total.

Pro-poor Tourism Indicators

The kinds of indicators that can be used to assess PPT outcomes and impacts depend on the interventions made. However, the following areas should be considered. The indicator measurements should be made both before and after the intervention has continued for a reasonable time. Often more reliable data can be obtained if confidentiality of the information can be guaranteed.

- *Movement from informal to formal employment*: This measures the number of people formally employed by the tourism sector (or enterprise) full-time and part time, before the intervention, compared with similar categories after the intervention. Of these, the number who previously worked in the formal economy, the informal economy, or who were unemployed prior to the intervention should be measured. A should be completed before the intervention and at 12-month intervals later to minimize seasonal variations. The data would be best collected through face-to-face interview questions matched with payroll totals to ensure complete coverage. For larger populations, samples rather than complete coverage could be used.

The example shows a 31.25 per cent ((75 ÷ 240) x 100) total movement from the informal to the formal economy, as indicated by the data in bold. If the intervention is designed to increase the number of people moving from informal to formal employment in the industry, then its success would tend to be demonstrated by a higher number than 75 at the bottom of column 4 in the later survey. Also note the different situation for men and women in the example.

- Income from formal employment. This measures total income from formal employment in the sector, before and after. A related indicator could measure average income per person formally employed (men, women, total). Data for such indicators may be more difficult to collect than for the informal-formal employment indicator above. This is because it involves questioning personal income as well as possibly payroll data. Confidentiality would have to be guaranteed.

- Earning from selling goods, service or labour, linked with other economic sectors. This measures income from tourism-related activities in other sectors, before and after and sex-disaggregated. For example, it would include profits made from craft and produce sales to the tourism industry, income from transport services, and income from work on infrastructure related to the industry.
- Profits arising from locally-owned enterprises with links to the tourism industry. This would require an estimation of the amount and proportion of profits accruing from the tourism linkage. Again confidentiality guarantees would be critical to its raw collection.
- Collective income from community enterprises, land rental or joint ventures. A starting point for accessing some of this data could often be local government who should be aware enterprise development in their area.
- Improvement of living and working conditions in the tourism sector, plus improvements in living and working conditions in linked sectors. Much of this information would have to be subjective or qualitative. For example respondents might be asked to rate their living and working conditions on 10-point scales relative to several criteria. Working conditions criteria could be based on core international labour standards and also include wage rates, hours worked and non-wage benefits.– Infrastructure. This measures (before and after) the value or quantity of infrastructure created or repaired, such as kilometres of roads, capacity of water reservoirs, number of homes linked to electricity, bridges constructed or extent of mobile telephone coverage. Some of this information may

be available from planning or infrastructure ministries and agencies such as the World Bank may in involved in funding the provision of major infrastructure development.

A lot of information is available from household surveys conducted by planning ministries and used in poverty assessments between each national census. If programmes can use some of this information to support impact measurement, then the results may be more rigorous. Lastly, if indicators are consistent with those already established by the World Bank and the ILO, then they are likely to be more successful.

DECENT WORK AND THE MILLENNIUM DEVELOPMENT GOALS

The future of development programmes in any industry lies in closer integration of United Nations and other agencies at the national level. When developing programmes and projects, including those related to PPT, the ILO and its constituents must express proposals in a more integrated framework. Decent work programmes at the country level should be integrated into the PRSP process (and with the MDGs) to have the best impact. This is quite feasible in relation to both poverty reduction and the wider list of MDGs.

Poverty Reduction

The ILO's Decent Work Agenda directly relates to poverty reduction. The ILO itself summarized this relationship in 2005:

- Rights enable the empowerment of men and women to escape poverty;
- Employment involving productive work is the principal route out of poverty;
- Social protection safeguards against poverty;
- Dialogue, or employers' and workers' organizations participating in shaping government policy is key to poverty reduction.

Millennium Development Goals

The relationship between decent work and the full list of

MDGs is more complicated. However, the Decent Work Agenda does contribute to all eight MDGs. Goal 1 (halving those with incomes of less than one dollar a day) and goal 8 (building a global partnership for development) are overarching goals towards poverty reduction. They both rely on decent work for their attainment. So does goal 7 on sustainable development. Goal 3 on gender equality is a condition for meeting all the MDGs, and gender mainstreaming is part of all ILO programmes. Decent work for parents and the elimination of child labour are essential to universal primary education. Social protection contributes directly to the health-related MDGs. Effective dialogue between government, employers' and workers' organizations supports inclusive policy reform. Institutions that foster social dialogue help good governance and social stability which are needed to achieve all of the MDGs.

Tourism Framework

Because PRSPs relate to the MDG framework, it is useful to outline how decent work fits with the MDGs in the particular context of tourism industry policy. The suggests how they all relate. The four decent work pillars head columns 2–5, while the eight MDGs head rows 3–10. The matrix outlines how examples of pro-poor measures in the tourism industry can fit within the two frameworks.

POVERTY REDUCTION STRATEGY PAPER CONTENT

Typically, PRSPs consist of an overall analysis of the economic development situation in the country, followed by several parts on measures planned by each sector. An example of such a PRSP part on tourism. At the end of the PRSP, there is usually a summary action plan in table form that outlines the measures to be taken, the resources devoted to them and the responsibility for their implementation. This summary action plan is the most important part of the document.

USES OF POVERTY REDUCTION STRATEGY PAPERS

PRSPs are not only the central document that determines

key development measures; they also have several related uses.

PRSPs can be used:

- By the national government as a planning and budgetary framework;
- For World Bank and IMF loans and funding;
- For United National Development Assistance Framework (UNDAF) funding for a country;
- By international donors and non-government agencies as a framework for their own aid activities;
- As a monitoring and evaluation tool;
- As a framework for public consultation and discussion on priorities for poverty reduction.

For all these reasons, the ILO and its constituents need to get their PPT issues on the PRSP agenda if their proposals are to be taken seriously.

Lobbying

Lobbying can be useful to ensure national tourism administrations are involved in the PRSP process and also that poverty reduction is mentioned in national tourism policies and strategies. Lobbying can also help build support for PPT measures at all stages of the PRSP process.

Getting Issues Included

To ensure that an organization's issues are included in the PRSP, it is essential that it is clear about what measures it wants taken. In other words, organizations must first identify their priorities and strategies to achieve them.

Identify Priorities

Organizations can identify issues, priorities and strategies through workshops, possibly using input from studies like the Tanzanian example in the concept note part of this booklet. Priorities for PPT can be determined by identifying those that are both urgent and important. Priority issues identified (major problems) can be changed into priority objectives (positive objectives) by inversion. For example, a priority problem such as child labour is widespread in the industry can be inverted to the priority objective eliminate child labour in the industry.

Develop Strategies

Developing strategies to achieve priority objectives is best done in small groups that report back to the wider workshop. Ideas for strategies should be specific, practical and cost-effective.

It is also important to review the strategies selected to ensure men and women benefit equally. Select the best ideas to include in the summary.

For example, ideas to eliminate child labour in the industry might include:

- Set up a special labour inspectorate taskforce for the industry;
- Develop posters on the objective;
- Market the goal of eliminating child labour in tourist brochures;
- Set up discussions between schools, employers and unions in the industry.

Include Indicators

Where possible, the indicators to assess the net benefits to the industry and the poor should also be identified. Following the child labour example, an industry indicator could be based on the marketing of the campaign to tourists– by promoting the destination as one free of child labour, where instead children go to school. Tourists could be surveyed to find out of the industry campaign affected their decision to holiday at the destination.

Unacceptable work indicators include both:

- Children not in school by employment status (percentage by age);
- Children in wage employment activity rate (percentage by age). Child labour also relates to:
- MDG indicator No. 45 (youth unemployment rate);
- *Target 3*: Ensure that all boys and girls complete a full course of primary schooling.

Get Endorsement

The next step is getting the organization's plan endorsed. At this point, you have a draft list of objectives, strategies and indicators that your organization would like to see in the PRSP. Before any formal consultation on the list, get it endorsed by your organization's representative body. A trade union centre would put it before a meeting of delegates for endorsement. An employers' organization would go to its board of directors. Modify the list according to any substantial changes the representative body wants made before it proceeds through the PRSP process, so it truly represents the views of your organization.

Contact

Despite the intention that PRSPs should be locally owned and developed, often key staff from the World Bank write the final document, or are closely involved in its development. It is therefore most important for ILO staff and the social partners to identify, make contact with such people and discuss how to ensure that the measures they want to see for PPT are included in the summary action plan.

Securing Support

The final step before input to the PRSP process is securing support from other organizations that relate to the ILO (employer, worker, ministry and NGOs), and also from those external to the ILO that have most influence over the process. These latter groups will usually include the World Bank, the planning, commerce and tourism ministries, and the UNDP, especially if it is part of the "One UN" system in the country concerned. This networking and lobbying is a significant task that ideally should build on established relationships. However, it can be time and effort well-spent if it means that the PPT concept delivers the results intended.

8

Eco-tourism and Planning in Tourism

ECO-TOURISM AND THE TOURISM INDUSTRY

Fundamentally, eco-tourism means making as little environmental impact as possible and helping to sustain the indigenous populace, thereby encouraging the preservation of wildlife and habitats when visiting a place. This is responsible form of tourism and tourism development, which encourages going back to natural products in every aspect of life. It is also the key to sustainable ecological development.

The International Eco-tourism Society defines eco-tourism as "responsible travel to natural areas that conserves the environment and improves the well-being of local people." This means that those who implement and participate in Eco-tourism activities should follow the following principles:

- Minimize impact,
- Build environmental and cultural awareness and respect,
- Provide positive experiences for both visitors and hosts,
- Provide direct financial benefits for conservation,
- Provide financial benefits and empowerment for local people,
- Raise sensitivity to host countries' political, environmental, and social climate,
- Support international human rights and labour agreements.

Aware of the Environment-Today the "Green Laws" of conservation are making people aware of how man and the environment can live symbiotically for more time to come and eco-tourism is the only way to maximize the economic, environmental and social benefits of tourism. Everyone is a stakeholder in the process and we clearly need to avoid our past shortcomings and negative impact that they have had.

Of all the participants in the Eco-tourism activity, the tourism industry is perhaps the most important and the least appreciated by conservationists. Many conservationists dislike having to deal with the corporate, profit-motivated entrepreneurs that they characterize as comprising the tourism industry.

Nevertheless, these entrepreneurs are essential to achieving conservation goals via Eco-tourism. They can, and indeed some of them must, become allies and partners with NGOs, protected area managers and communities if Eco-tourism is to become more than an abstract concept. Increasingly, the tourism industry becomes the most powerful advocate for supporting protected areas, and this dynamic should be encouraged by establishing adequate mechanisms for communication and collaboration between protected area managers and tour operators.

The mechanics of international and even national, level tourism require that a complex set of arrangements (transportation, lodging, guides, etc.) exists to facilitate the movement of tourists from their home to the tourism destination. Each arrangement necessitates a specific set of activities and corresponding set of employees, infrastructure and costs. Few tour operators specialize in Eco-tourism. There are, however, many adventure and nature tour operators, most of whom do not fully comply with Eco-tourism standards. Conventional tourism practices still predominate in the tourism industry, just as conventional practices still dominate in every other aspect of our lives, in spite of initiatives for them to become more sustainable. Nevertheless, the tourism industry is "greening" at an ever-accelerating pace as tourists demand more environmentally-sound services. For example, many hotels now recycle cans and bottles and encourage guests to reuse towels in order to save on water use.

The number of Eco-tourism businesses is also growing as new companies are established. Many of these have developed from the outset with an understanding of and commitment to the principles of sustainability, whereas many of the older, more established nature tourism companies have been slow to integrate all the principles of Eco-tourism into their activities.

- Conservation NGOs working in partnership with private tour operators are ideally placed to provide the Ecotourist technical guidelines which upgrade a nature tourism operation into an Eco-tourism operation. They will be located in the eco travellers country of origin. They produce brochures annually with a series of fixed departures for each tour Programmes, and they often have a loyal clientele who return to purchase trips on a regular basis. They will put together a complete package for the tourist including air tickets, and may provide a tour leader to accompany their client groups but will typically contract with an inbound operator to provide services in the destination country.
- *The Inbound Operator*: Located in the destination country, they provide complete packages of services from arrival in the country to departure. They may have their own facilities (vehicles, lodges) or they may subcontract others in the cities and regions the tourists will visit. Outbound operators contract with them to provide all "on-the-ground" services. With the advent of the internet, they are increasingly competing directly with the outbound operators for clients.
- *Local Service Providers*: Outside the big cities, near the natural attractions; these may be local lodge and hotel owners, local transport providers, community-based Eco-tourism enterprises and local guides. These are where local communities typically join the tourism chain.

Implementing Eco-tourism can be a very challenging and costly venture. If the tourism industry is part of this process from the beginning, costs can be greatly reduced and success made more likely. Including the experience of a private tour operator in the Eco-tourism planning and design process would be invaluable and could not be duplicated by conservation NGO.

Essential inputs by various segments of the tourism industry could include:

- Providing information about the potential market for Eco-tourism activities.
- Providing advice concerning visitor preferences in terms of attractions, accommodations, food and transportation services.
- Marketing an Eco-tourism activity or Programmes.
- Providing one or more of the services needed to facilitate visitor access to and appreciation of the Eco-tourism site.
- Providing training of local guides and entrepreneurs.
- Investing in an Eco-tourism operation. The investment will likely be contingent upon an expectation of a certain level of financial return.
- Operating an Eco-tourism operation. Within a protected area situation, these operators would be considered concessionaires. As such, they would be subject to strict guidelines covering everything from the energy sources used to operators who identified this as one of their primary destinations to the utilization of local supplies and labour. They would also be required to pay a concession fee to the protected area administration.

Eco-tourism is more than a catch phrase for nature loving travel and recreation. Eco-tourism is consecrated for preserving and sustaining the diversity of the world's natural and cultural environments. It accommodates and entertains visitors in a way that is minimally intrusive or destructive to the environment and sustains and supports the native cultures in the locations it is operating in. Responsibility of both travellers and service providers is the genuine meaning for eco-tourism. Eco-tourism also endeavours to encourage and support the diversity of local economies for which the tourism-related income is important. With support from tourists, local services and producers can compete with larger, foreign companies and local families can support themselves. Besides all these, the revenue produced from tourism helps and encourages governments to fund conservation projects and training Programmes.

Saving the environment around you and preserving the natural luxuries and forest life, that's what eco-tourism is all about. Whether it's about a nature camp or organizing trekking trips towards the unspoilt and inaccessible regions, one should always keep in mind not to create any mishap or disturbance in the life cycle of nature. Eco-tourism focuses on local cultures, wilderness adventures, volunteering, personal growth and learning new ways to live on our vulnerable planet. It is typically defined as travel to destinations where the flora, fauna, and cultural heritage are the primary attractions. Responsible Eco-tourism includes Programmes that minimize the adverse effects of traditional tourism on the natural environment, and enhance the cultural integrity of local people. Therefore, in addition to evaluating environmental and cultural factors, initiatives by hospitality providers to promote recycling, energy efficiency, water reuse, and the creation of economic opportunities for local communities are an integral part of Eco-tourism.

Historical, biological and cultural conservation, preservation, sustainable development etc. are some of the fields closely related to Eco-Tourism. Many professionals have been involved in formulating and developing eco-tourism policies. They come from the fields of Geographic Information Systems, Wildlife Management, Wildlife Photography, Marine Biology and Oceanography, National and State Park Management, Environmental Sciences, Women in Development, Historians and Archaeologists, etc.

In India too the movement is gathering momentum with more and more travel and travel related organisation's are addressing the needs of the eco-tourists and promoting eco-tourism in the country.

Some basic do's and don'ts of eco-tourism are listed below:

Do's

- Carry back all non-degradable litter such as empty bottles, tins, plastic bags etc. These must not litter the environment or be buried. They must be disposed in municipal dustbins only.
- Observe the sanctity of holy sites, temples and local cultures.
- Cut noise pollution. Do not blare aloud radios, tape recorders or other electronic entertainment equipment in nature resorts, sanctuaries and wildlife parks.
- In case temporary toilets are set-up near campsites, after defecation, cover with mud or sand. Make sure that the spot is at least 30 meters away from the water source.
- Respect people's privacy while taking photographs. Ask for prior permission before taking a photograph.

Don'ts

- Do not take away flora and fauna in the forms of cuttings, seeds or roots. It is illegal, especially in the Himalayas. The environment is really delicate in this region and the bio-diversity of the region has to be protected at all costs.
- Do not use pollutants such as detergent, in streams or springs while washing and bathing.
- Do not use wood as fuel to cook food at the campsite.
- Do not leave cigarettes butts or make open fires in the forests.
- Do not consume aerated drinks, alcohol, drugs or any other intoxicant and throw bottles in the wild.
- Do not tempt the locals, especially children by offering them foodstuff or sweets. Respect local traditions.
- Polythene and plastics are non biodegradable and unhealthy for the environment and must not be used and littered. As a traveller, you will have an impact on the environment and culture of the place you are

visiting. Here are some rules of thumb to make this impact positive.

GOLDEN RULES FOR TRAVEL

- Learn about your destination before you get there. Read guidebooks, travel rticles, istories, and/or novels by local authors and pay particular attention to customs such as greetings, appropriate dress, eating behaviours, etc. Being sensitive to these customs will increase local acceptance of you as a tourist and enrich your trip.
- Follow established guidelines. Ask your eco-tour operator, guide and/or the local authorities what their guidelines are for limiting tourism's impact on the environment and local culture. Staying on trails, packing up your trash, and remaining set distances away from wildlife are a few ways to minimize your impact in sensitive areas.
- Seek out and support locally owned businesses. Support local businesses during your eco-travels to ensure maximum community and conservation benefit from your spending. Eco-Tourism in India is still at a very nascent stage, but there are for sure conscious efforts to save the fragile Himalayan Eco System and culture and heritage of the indigenous people, which is probably the largest concentration in the world.

ECO-TOURISM IN INDIA

KERALA ECO-TOURISM

The naturally beautiful and exquisite Kerala landscape is one of the greenest destinations in India and is the perfect place to go on eco-tourism vacations. The clean and tranquil Kerala backwaters, the soothing velvety Kerala hills and a riotous explosion of greens in the intoxicating Kerala wilds offers countless opportunities for eco-tourism and nature vacations. The entire Kerala landscape is generously covered with coconut palms, pineapple groves, banana trees, Pandanus plants, thick leafy plants, dense forests and neatly clipped tea bushes. Acres of submerged paddy fields located in perfect harmony with the winding Kerala backwaters and the gentle rolling Kerala hills are heavenly paradisiacal eco-tourism vacation destinations.

Regale the verdant Kerala beauty on your eco-tourism vacations to Kerala, South India with Kerala India Vacations. Visit the fascinating Kerala wildlife destinations and spot rare wild animals lazing in their natural habitat and enjoy the magic of nature. Eco-tourism in Kerala, South India is a fast developing sector and the state government is making extra efforts to promote eco-tourism. Among the manifold advantages of promoting eco-tourism in Kerala, South India one very important aspect is revenue generation and environment conservation at the same time. The concept of eco-tourism basically means that you get to visit the exotic nature rich tour destinations but at the same time you must take care not to soil the beauty of the region by not using polythene bags and other materials or things such as tin cans, wrappers etc. that adversely affect the environment.

Kerala India Vacations guides you through the lush green paths within acres of rubber plantations so that you can experience first hand the incomparable natural beauty of green Kerala, South India on your eco-tourism vacations. Kerala, South India happens to be one of the leading producers of rubber in India though rubber is not a native Indian plant and was introduced by the Dutch colonialists, in fact Kerala accounts for 92 per cent of the rubber produced in India. Stay at a luxury resort or a farmhouse near a Kerala rubber plantation and enjoy the warm hospitality of the Kerala rubber plantations during your eco-tourism vacations to Kerala, South India and be fascinated by the rural Kerala lifestyle while you observe busy twittering birds, brightly coloured butterflies and squirrels scurrying here and there. Admire the thick shapely leaves on straight trunks that glisten in the bright sun.

Botanically known as Havea brasiliensis, a single rubber plant takes about 7 years to mature and can be harvested for latex (processed for natural rubber) for almost 20 years. The local rubber tappers who stay close to these lush rubber plantations harvest latex from these trees. Pineapple is planted as an intercrop in most of the Kerala rubber plantations so you get to taste the juicy Mauritius pineapple variety while on your eco-tourism vacations to the scenic Kerala rubber plantations. Kottayam in Kerala, South India is an important Centre of commercial rubber plantations set on the picturesque banks of the serene palm fringed Kerala backwaters. Extensive rubber plantations cover the hillocks wrapped by silver ribbons of the fascinating Kerala backwaters, not a sight you would like to miss while on your eco-tourism tours to Kerala, South India.

Acres of tea plantations interspersed with shade fruit trees wrap the gentle Kerala hill slopes in a warm embrace and create soothing and striking vistas for you to visit on your Kerala eco-tourism vacations. Rows of neatly clipped tea bushes carpet the Kerala hills on the Western Ghats in Kerala, south India and offer you ample opportunity to gaze at the naturally enthralling Kerala beauty at its beatific best while on your Kerala India eco-tourism vacations.

The Britishers introduced the tradition of tea plantations in India. Tea bushes have the potential to grow to tree heights though they are kept neatly trimmed to waist height to make it feasible for the plantation workers to pluck tea leaves without much difficulty. Gaze at the lovely Kerala tea plantations while on your eco-tourism vacations and mark the fact that each tea bush is planted at a distance of 1 to 1.5 meter from each other along the contours of the landscape. Stay at the resorts and clean home-like accommodations on the Kerala tea plantations and spend your eco-tourism vacations in Kerala, South India in the midst of pure undulating greens. Watch the plantation workers plucking tea leaves and filling the baskets slung on their backs while you enjoy nature treks.

Usually it's the women who are employed for plucking tea leaves on these tea plantations in Kerala, South India. These women work in unison and sing peppy songs while plucking tea leaves and move along the rows of tea bushes in perfect rhythm. Kerala, South India has some of the highest tea estates located in India. Munnar is one of the most popular Kerala hill stations, which is known for its sweeping tea plantations. Some of the popular tea plantations in Kerala, South India are located at Peerumadu that is situated at a height of 914-meters above the sea level, Anayirankal that has acrès of tea plantations located in the midst of dense evergreen forests and a few other Kerala hill stations that are definitely worth visiting on your Kerala eco-tourism tours to Kerala, South India.

Wander at leisure on the aromatic Kerala spice plantations during your Kerala India eco-tourism Vacations. Stay at the spice plantation farmhouses with the plantation owners and experience the magical charm of staying in the midst of luxuriant plantations laden heavily with a combination of scents of the various spices that are grown on these extensive plantations.

Though you can visit spice plantations almost all over beautiful Kerala, Periyar is one of the most popular spice districts in Kerala, South India. This absolutely beautiful hill district is covered with a variety of spice plantations that lie close to the famous Periyar wildlife sanctuary.

Shop for rare spices at the local Kerala spice markets and inhale the intoxicating aroma of cinnamon, cardamom, pepper, ginger, turmeric, curry leaves and other spices. Besides the cultivation of these traditional Kerala spices the Kerala plantation owners have also taken to growing spices such as rosemary, oregano, mint, vanilla, bay leaves, basil, thyme and others. Discover the secret of the mouthwatering Kerala cuisine as you visit the acres of Kerala spice plantations on your eco-tourism vacations with Kerala India Vacations. Spices are basically fragrant substances of vegetable origin with distinct flavours used in selective combinations to give a special flavour to the exotic Indian cuisine.

Enjoy bird watching tours and nature treks to the lovely Kerala spice plantations with Kerala India Vacations and experience the Kerala natural beauty at its aromatic best. Watch the locals work on the extensive spice plantations and observe closely the way of life in these Kerala spice plantations and enjoy your eco-tourism vacations thoroughly.

ORISSA ECO-TOURISM

Organized by Tourism of Orissa offers you the best seats in the house to attend what is essentially a spectacular show of competing colours, cacophony of voices, a jumble of animal instincts and raw emotions. No, we aren't talking about a Broadway show or a Hollywood musical production. Eco-tourism in Orissa is what concerns us at Tourism of Orissa. With Eco-tourism in Orissa tour package, offered by Tourism of Orissa, you get to see all the shades of the diverse ecological system that reside within the state of Orissa. Eco-tourism in Orissa may revolve around water bodies or beaches or national parks and wildlife sanctuaries alone or, it can be a combination of all these features that make Orissa such as enticing choice as a destination for eco travel and tours.

While hot springs (Atri and Tarabalo), lakes (Chilika), waterfalls (Badaghagra, Khandadhar) and reservoirs (Hirakud, Indravati) in Orissa have tourists lining up, the beaches of Orissa (Puri, Chandrabhaga, Gopalpur, Chandipur) have dazzled international and national tourist for centuries with their pristine beauty and positive vibes. Orissa's varying topography-from the wooded Eastern Ghats to the fertile river basin-has proven ideal for evolution of compact and unique ecosystems. Thereby creating such treasure troves of flora and fauna that even seem inviting to many migratory species of birds and reptiles.

Bhitar Kanika National Park is famous for its second largest mangrove ecosystem. The bird sanctuary in Chilika (Asia's biggest brackish water lake) and the tiger reserve and waterfalls in Simlipal National Park are integral part of any eco tours in Orissa, arranged by Tourism of Orissa. The Gharial Sanctuary at Tikarpada and the Olive Ridley Sea Turtles in Gahirmatha turtle sanctuary also feature on the list of avid nature watchers.

The city wildlife sanctuaries of Chandaka and Nandan Kanan are a must visit for the lessons they teach is conservation and revitalization of species from the brink of extinction. Since Orissa is so rich in culture-history, traditions and people, Tourism of Orissa can even have your eco tour clubbed with other tours in Orissa so that you get the best of al te worlds at a single destination called Orissa.

ECO-TOURISM IN CHHATTISGARH

Chhattisgarh, the 26th state of the Indian Union, is located in the central part of India. The newly formed Indian state of Chhattisgarh is famous for its enchantingly beautiful natural landscapes, rich cultural heritage and unique tribal populations. With over 44 per cent of its total area under forests, Chhattisgarh is also amongst the greenest states of India. The Chhattisgarh region is known as a great repository of biological diversity. The unique combination of rich cultural heritage and biological diversity makes Chhattisgarh an ideal eco-tourism destination with immense potentials for the growth eco-tourism the region. The Indian Govt. is actively collaborating with the local officials of the state to realise the full potential of Eco-tourism growth of the region in order to make Chhattisgarh as one of the most important eco-tourism destinations in India.

Chhattisgarh is one of the greenest states of India with over 44 per cent of its total area under lush forests. The forests of Chhattisgarh are not only known for their diverse flora and fauna but also contain about 88 species of medicinal plants. In addition, Chhattisgarh has also formulated several ecological plans and working in the direction to become the country's first bio-fuel self-reliant state by 2015. And to achieve this goal the green state has devised a plan to plant over 100 million saplings of Jatropa Carcus. Chhattisgarh is also unique in its wildlife population and has 3 National Parks and 11 Wildlife Sanctuaries, housing some of the rare wildlife and bird species. With so much of variety for Eco-tourism, Chhattisgarh promises to be an ideal holiday destination for nature lovers, wildlife enthusiasts and also for those who want to discover the unique tribal life of the region.

Chhattisgarh has identified some regions with a very high potentiality for eco-tourism. The green state has launched an eco-tourism project covering three potential tourist tracks-Raipur-Turtiria-Sirpur, Bilaspur-Achanakmar and Jagdalpur-

Kanger Valley National Park. In addition, a number of herbal gardens and natural health resorts have been created with increased local participation. The use of ethno-medicine, which has been practiced by aboriginal tribes since centuries, predating even Ayurveda, is also being promoted in Chhattisgarh. The major eco-tourism attractions, which are getting prime attention in Chhattisgarh, include the protection and development of the wildlife areas, camping grounds and trekking facilities. With so many initiatives, Chhattisgarh is destined to become the most Favourite eco-tourism destination in India and few among best in the world.

RAJASTHAN ECO-TOURISM

The Cultures of the Rajasthan Desert are some of the most well preserved in India. We, at Marwar Eco-Cultural Tours and Travels, are passionate about this land, its cultures and its people and we want to share this passion with you. The Desert and its people will captivate you.

Because we are able to provide you with in-depth cultural information that you would not receive on other Tours. If you have an adventurous spirit or a cultural thirst to quench, we have a Tour that should surpass all of your expectations. We also offer opportunities to get involved with the people and assist in ongoing, non-profit projects. As an NGO, we have assistance projects in most villages we will visit. All of our guides are from Rajasthan, and most are village natives or indigenous people.

They have a great knowledge of local and regional history and are great storytellers. They will keep your attention for hours next to a fire, counting tales of kings and warlords; castles, forts and Havelis (mansions); rituals and traditions. You will see the camel herds, observe villagers' craftsmanship, and gain insight into indigenous nomadic lifestyles. We will show you the best of Rajasthan, and we are very flexible and can modify our tours according to the group's needs. You can also design your own tour. You dream it up; we'll do the rest. We will organize the tour and guide you according to your wishes. Among other things, we can arrange a visit to a marriage ceremony, a farming or agricultural tour, Handicraft and Jewelry making, a stay in an Ayurvedic (traditional Indian Medicine) clinic, and more.

MADHYA PRADESH ECO-TOURISM

Eco-tourism signifies to save the environment around us and preserving the natural luxuries and forest life. Whether it's about a nature camp or organizing trekking trips towards the unspoilt and inaccessible regions, one should always keep in mind not to create any mishap or disturbance in the life cycle of nature. A destination enveloped in magic, Madhya Pradesh is one of the most popular tourist destination in India. It's many tourist destinations are, by far, some of the most magical locales in the world.

With the highest mountains, beautiful wildlife, a cosmopolitan heritage from different civilizations, it is so rightly called tourist paradise. It has lot to offer from breathtaking natural vistas, amazing architecture, rich culture, and a warm hearted society of people living in virtual harmony.

HIMACHAL PRADESH ECO-TOURISM

The majestic coniferous trees from an enchanting backdrop to the mountains with broad-leafed species like the Oaks, Maples, Birdcherry, Hazelnut, Walnut, Horsechestnut and Rhododendrons adding grandeur to the landscape. Whereas the ivies clinging to the trunks of stately Cedars appear to veil secrets of Nature, the vines flowing from atop the trees seem to invite the visitors with open arms. The violas popping up from under the forest floor and the riot of colours provided by the anemones, primulas, buttercups and many other herbs in the alpine meadows lay a colourful feast before eyes of the beholder.

Besides plants. the State also provides a very congenial habitat to a wide variety of Himalayan fauna. The Himalyan Tahar and the Ibex can be spotted as silhouettes on the high ridges in the trans-Himalayas. The Brown Bear and Musk Deer roam happily in the temperate forests, in the company of colourful pheasants including the Monal, the Western Hornes Tragopan, the Koklas and the Kalij. The lucky ones can even be traeted to rare sight of critically endangered species like the Snow Leopard and Snow Cock. Also known as the 'Abode of Gods', the State conjures up visions of ancient temples, with exquisitely carved wooden panels, occupying almost every hilltop and the festivities associated with these religious places. Even a casual glimpse at the traditionally attired local deities being carried in meticulously decorated palanquins, devotees dancing to the rhythmic play of traditional drums and clarions, leaves a lasting imptint on one's mind. This natural and cultural richness of the State coupled with its simple peace loving people and traditional hospitality makes the State a most favoured tourist destination. Anybody with a zest for life, a spirit of adventure and a love for nature will find all that his heart desires amongest the pristine environs of Himachal Pradesh.

UTTARANCHAL ECO-TOURISM

Uttaranchal blessed with magnificent glaciers, majestic snow-clad mountains, gigantic and ecstatic peaks, valley of flowers, skiing slopes and dense forests, this Abode of Gods includes many shrines and places of pilgrimage. Char-dhams, the four most sacred and revered Hindu temples: Badrinath, Kedarnath, Gangotri and Yamunotri are nestled in the Mighty Mountains. A picturesque state, with a breathtaking panoramic view of Himalayas, Uttaranchal promises its tourists a visit full of fun and unforgettable moments.

Uttaranchal blessed with magnificent glaciers, majestic snow-clad mountains, gigantic and ecstatic peaks, valley of flowers, skiing slopes and dense forests, this Abode of Gods includes many shrines and places of pilgrimage.

India's first National Park is cradled in the foothills of the Himalayas and spreads over an area of 520 sq. kms., along the bankds of the Ramganga river. The dense Sal forests of the Himalayan foothils and the tall grassy neadows make it one of the richest areas of northern India for the habitation of the big mammals.

ECOSYSTEM IN INDIA

The Himalayan region is a particularly fragile ecosystem. The interconnections between the different types of vegetation, between plant life and the soil, between the soil, vegetation and water are so close and so precariously balanced that the slightest change in one plunges the entire system into jeopardy. Ecosystems on seismic belts, for example, are literally 'at the mercy of the land'. Nature plays havoc in other ways too: the monsoon pattern often spells drought in the dry season, and terrible floods during rainfall.

DEFORESTATION

Growing Population

Way back in 326 B.C., when Alexander the Great came to India, his advance was checked by almost impenetrable forests along the Indus. By the time Emperor Ashoka ascended the throne, stretches of forests had already been cleared to make roads. Ashoka realised the importance of conserving forests, and even appointed an officer for the purpose. Sher Shah Suri was also farsighted, and planted trees all along the route from Delhi to his capital Patna. However, the Mughals' interest in forests was sadly limited to a rather hedonistic passion for big game. Under the British rule, deforestation became rampant in order to procure timber to build furniture, railway sleepers and ships for the British navy. However, the British soon realised that forests had to be spared the ordeal. After Independence, forests were cleared whenever wood was needed either for timber or agriculture, or for setting up townships. Forests were razed to the ground mindlessly till the eastern hill people decided to say a collective 'Stop'.

Forest Distructions Through Fire

Forest fires have largely contributed to deforestation. Forests in India are very susceptible to fires, especially in summer. All it takes is one little spark and a forest fire could reduce considerable green stretches to ashes in a matter of a few hours. Earlier the Bishnois of Jodhpur (Rajasthan) even laid down their lives to save trees. The Bishnois are a religious community, famous for their loyalty towards animals and trees. In fact, they are known to worship the blackbuck as a sacred animal. Various measures are being taken to curb the felling of trees. Clearing forests is now an offence under Indian law, unless approved by the concerned authorities. However, deforestation has acquired alarming proportions in India. The country's total forest cover today has fallen to a little more than approximately 10 per cent–a dismal situation for a country with a population of over a billion.

Land Degradation

Every year, valuable topsoil is swept away by floods in the rainy season. and deforestation contributes to the problem of soil erosion. Man may well have compounded the problem.

Chemical Farming

To sustain the country's enormous population, intensive chemical farming was introduced in the 1960s, ushering in the 'Green Revolution'. Chemical fertilizers and high yield grains were used on an unprecedented scale. Although production tripled, the quality of the land took a battering. Chemicals and toxic substances too have taken their own toll on the land. Desertification (cultivable land turning barren) is a serious problem in some parts of the country, especially in Rajasthan.

Water Conditions

Despite high rainfall, water levels have dropped alarmingly in many places in the country. Obviously this is due to the demands of a burgeoning population. In any case, the monsoon cannot always be relied upon; it is not uncommon for a region like Rajasthan to be stricken by drought once every two to three years. While hydroelectric projects are a partial solution to the problem, their overall 'efficiency' is not beyond interrogation. The Narmada Valley Project–a vast project of several dams aimed at providing water and power for Gujarat, Rajasthan, Madhya Pradesh and Maharashtra–when completed, is projected to submerge an estimated 350,000 hectares of forest and 200,000 hectares of cultivated fields, and displace nearly 400,000 people. Spearheaded by the environmentalist Baba Amte, Medha Patkar, and more recently Arundhati Roy, a vigourous campaign is in progress against the building of the dams. Another controversial project is the Tehri Dam in Uttar Pradesh. Besides the displacement and loss it is projected to cause, another dread is that the dam may burst as it is being constructed on an earthquake-prone zone. The distinguished man in white, Sunderlal Bahuguna has once again spared no effort at raising public consciousness about the issue at hand.

Pollution

Despite having some of the strictest laws in the world against pollution, India is one of the most environmentally polluted countries in the world. Air pollution is so grave in cities like Delhi, Calcutta, Kanpur and some others, that simply breathing the air is equivalent to smoking 10-20 cigarettes a day! Recently, Delhi acquired the dubious distinction of being one of the five most polluted cities in the world. The rivers in the country have not been spared either. Industrial waste and a combination of other factors have contributed to the plight of these 'dying' rivers. In some places, safe drinking water, is a rare commodity. Lakes and river habitats too have been polluted. The Yamuna Action Plan was a project undertaken at a tentative cost of ₹20,000 crore to cleanse the river of pollutants. A similar project was undertaken for the mighty Ganga River.

Conservation

Ancient texts including the epics, the Buddhist Jatakas, the Panchatantra or the more recent Jain scriptures, all preach non-violence towards even the lowest forms of animal and plant life, a philosophy that the Indian Maharajas and their British guests chose to overlooked for a while. The Indian Government has an uphill task to perform. It has been able to protect only about 4 per cent of the total forest cover in the form of National Parks and similar reserves. Underhand activities like poaching are not entirely unheard of even in these restricted areas. Currently there are about 80 National Parks and 441 sanctuaries in the country. Massive tree plantation Programmes are also being undertaken. The Vana Mahotsava, first started in 1950, is an annual tree-planting festival celebrated across the nation.

Individual Efforts

Vishweshwar Dutt Saklani of Garhwal, in Uttar Pradesh, is a small time farmer who started planting trees to seek solace after the death of his brother (who had initiated the practice) in 1948. In the last 50 years, Vishweshwar has overlaid 100 hectares of land with oak, cedar, walnut and rhododendron. People were dismissive of him until they saw the sea change that his work had brought about in the village. Denuded hills became green, land became more fertile and dry streambeds filled up.

Fodder and fuel were in plenty and everyone was happy.Vishweshwar received the Indira Priyadarshini Vrikshamitra Award in 1986. Bikkalu Chikkaiah and Thimmakka were a childless couple who worked in a quarry close to Bangalore. They decided to raise banyan trees in lieu of the children they were unable to have.

So they chose a barren piece of land en route to their quarry. The couple planted saplings and put protective barriers around them. In the evenings, they lugged water from a well a kilometre away. 40 years later, 284 banyan trees provided shade to a 3km stretch. Thimmakka received the National Citizen's Award in 1996. Abdul Karim of Kasargod, Kerala too did something similar. He turned a dry piece of land into a veritable forest after 19 years of hard labour. His deciduous trees brought water back into the soil. Karim went a step ahead and got some animals in this forest, to successfully replicate a healthy ecosystem.

ECO-TOURISM POLICY

The Draft Tourism Policy 1997 states that "in the context of economic liberalisation and globalisation being pursued by the country, the development policies of no sector can remain static. "The policy further states that" the emergence of tourism as an important instrument for sustainable human development including poverty alleviation, employment generation, environmental regeneration and advancement of women and other disadvantaged groups in the country" requires support to realise these goals. India's tourism resources have always been considered immense, in a tourism audit. The geographical features are diverse, colourful and varied. The coastline offers opportunities for developing the best beaches in the world. There are a wealth of eco-systems including bio-sphere reserves, mangroves, coral reefs, deserts, mountains and forests as well as an equally wide range of flora and fauna. The Policy further states that "international tourists visiting interiors of the country for reasons of purity of the environment and nature contributes to the development of these areas particularly backward regions". Thus Tourism "should also become a reason for better preservation and protection of our natural resources, environment and ecology". The policy recognises that sustained growth of tourism can give rise to conflicts.

To ensure that the growth of tourism takes place along desired lines, certain guidelines have been framed:

- To remove the constraint of the information gap.
- To create a tourist product that is desirable and supported by an integrated infrastructure.
- To involve all agencies, public, private and government, in tourism development.
- To create synergy between departments and agencies that have to deliver the composite tourist product.
- To use both the circuit and scheme approach so that peoples participation through panchayats, local bodies, NGO's, and youth organisations will create a greater awareness of tourism. The Central Government can thus concentrate on larger investment oriented projects.
- To create direct access for destinations off the beaten track.

- To diversify the product with new options like beach tourism, forests, wild life, landscapes and adventure tourism, farm and health tourism.
- To ensure that the development does not exceed sustainable levels.
- To develop the seven north-eastern states, the Himalayan region and Islands for tourism.
- To maintain a balance between the negative and positive impacts of tourism through planning restrictions and through education of the people for conservation and development.

DEVELOPMENT PLAN

The strategy for development should take into consideration the carrying capacity, local aspirations and benefits likely to accrue to the community. In particular specific policies and guidelines for eco-tourism development and adventure tourism are to be formulated, primarily through a regulatory framework. The Draft Guidelines have been approved at a State Ministers Conference and have been circulated to various trade and industry bodies. The guidelines draw a distinction between mass or resort tourism and nature or Eco-tourism, as the kind of tourism that has a lower impact on the environment and requires less infrastructural development. The Ministry hopes that the environment conscious international tourist will be made aware that India is taking steps to protect its ecology and environment.

Apart from the do's and don'ts, the guidelines are governed by a tourism management plan, the key elements of which are the protection of natural resources and a positive involvement of local communities, along with an optimum number of environmentally conscious visitors. The principles of management are scientific planning, effective control and continuous monitoring, development of physical infrastructure, zoning and a Management plan for public use of natural sites. The management plan should establish standards for resort development, style and location of structures, waste disposal, treatment of sewage, control of litter, use of public spaces and fragile areas. The operational guidelines rely on sensitisation of all the role players and this Programmes is based on a self-regulated environmental code.

Area specific rather than universal development plans keeping in mind the unique character of the location and its economic and social environment are important. This would help the State Government to coordinate with the industry in managing visitors and their activities. NGO's working on socio-economic Programmes in forest and remote areas could have a closer coordination with tourism service operators to transfer economic benefits, particularly the handicraft production and marketing sector. The guidelines are only a beginning, and it is hoped that with increasing awareness of the visitor the industry will regulate its practices.

TOURISM ADVISORY COMMITTEE

There is an emphasis on the needs and perceptions of the international tourist running through the discussion on the guide lines although the data from the National Parks makes it evident that the domestic tourists outnumber international visitors, although they do not pay the same amount as the foreign visitor either in entry fees or for board and lodging and transport facilities. They do however demand a much higher per capita use of resources like water, fuel for heating and cooking and transport. They also make the same intensive use of time and try to maximize their stay by the number of animals and birds they can view in the 24-hour period.

It is interesting to note that no democratic participation has been called for in the policy formulation process, and all the amendments to the policy have come from trade associations and government think tanks. The tourism Advisory Committee also consists of eminent persons and community representation has been ignored.

The policy clearly recognises the debate on the tourism issue which has surfaced wherever tourism development, particularly in the case of tourism projects relating to the "gifts of nature" like beaches, rivers, mountains and forests, have already been developed. However, mere recognition of the hostility of people to tourism development is not enough to change the nature of tourism development or the resistance to tourism or what many have termed a poor tourism culture.

Perhaps to understand this in a better perspective, we should look at the issue of sustainable development in a critical way. Perhaps we can question the impact of sustainable development on the environment and sift through the jargon of development planners, international agencies, and environmental activists to see how sustainable development can be achieved without all the contradictions that are apparent as in the case of the tourism sector.

DEVELOPMENT IN TOURISM

The concept of sustainability originated in the context of renewable resources like forests and fisheries and was subsequently adopted by the environmental movement. In most cases it is understood to mean "the existence of the ecological conditions necessary to support human life at a specific level of well being through future generations." However, in addition to ecological conditions there are social conditions that influence ecological sustainability in a nature-people interaction. The social connotations have been described by Barbier (1987) who has defined social sustainability as "the ability to maintain desired social values, traditions, institutions, cultures or other social characteristics." The term sustainability came into usage in 1980 when the IUCN presented the World Conservation Strategy where sustainable development was linked to conservation of living resources. However, the fundamental goals have often been lost sight of because of operational goals (*e.g.* food, water, shelter, health are fundamental goals to be realised through self reliance, cost effectiveness, appropriate technology, people centred-ness etc.)

Consequently, the WCED made its definition brief: Social Development is development that meets the needs of the present without compromising the ability of future generations to meet their own needs. They did not make any assumptions on the direction in which changes in demand would take place.

(*e.g.* equity, social justice, self-determination, or cultural diversity).

India's tourism policy follows the mainstream SD (Sustainable Development) thinking by adopting all the critical objectives: revive growth change the quality of growth meet essential needs for jobs, food, energy, water and sanitation ensure sustainable levels of population conserve and enhance the resource base reorient technology and management risk merge environment and economics in decision making reorient international economic relations make development more participatory.

These objectives are responsible for building a very broad consensus on the issue of sustainable development, yet the debate at the operational level continues. Most participants in the debate now accept that many human activities are reducing the long-term ability of the natural environment to provide goods and services, which will eventually affect human health and well being.

ENVIROMENTAL DEGRADATION

Many also accept that poverty is devastating the lives of millions in the Third World since there is no consensus between what is environmentally necessary and what is economically and developmentally feasible. The level of inter-dependence between the two insights is yet to be incorporated in the concept of Social Development.

Some problem areas are: Environmental degradation, already affecting millions in the Third World, is likely to reduce human well being across the globe. Who is responsible for this rapid degeneration? Is it the poor or the rich? The poor have no option but to exploit resources for short-term survival.

If we take the example of forests and their resources, which have been traditionally outside the market system and in the sphere of tribal or indigenous peoples rights, they are today seen as exploiters of the forests as against tourists, with all their demand for infrastructure and superstructure, who are seen to be conservationists.

The inter-linked nature of the problem of sustainability

is such that the impact of degradation will be quicker on the poor than on the rich. Can Sustainable Development be the metafix it claims to be in reconciling increasing industrial, agricultural and resource use productivity with environmental needs. The weakness of the Social Development argument lies in the techno-economic approach to solutions with regard to common property resource management, through know how transfers, resource pricing, subsidy policies and building management capabilities.

World Bank, 1987 Deeper processes such as land reforms, industrial demands on raw materials, over consumption, changing legal and political structures are either ignored or looked at in a cursory manner.

For instance how can we claim a consensus between those who are concerned for the survival of future generations with those who are concerned with the survival of wild life, or human health and subsistence?

Unless we can identify the trade-offs necessary for each specific objective of sustainability, we will not have clarity in the discussion. We will also fail to understand why, even when there is a broad consensus, projects on the ground result in conflicts.

Suggested refinements could be:

- A distinction between ecological and social sustainability and in the process an identification of the inter-linkages a distinction between renewable and non-renewable resources, between environmental processes crucial to human life and crucial to other forms of life dependent on the resources. a distinction between the techno-economic aspects of social sustainability (infrastructure, services, government) with political and cultural sustainability.
- A distinction between equitable development and local participation, and decentralisation, what many have called NGOisation of sustainable development. This is because no rigorous testing of local participation leading to social equity or to sustainable resource use have been reported.

ENVIRONMENTAL IMPACT

Case studies reflect personal, organisational or political preferences. Tourism is one of the activities which have caused concern because of the effects of increasing human traffic on fragile environments. Countries which are looking towards Tourism as a means of economic growth, like India, have limited resources and cultural restraints and they have the greatest need to pay heed to the possible negative impacts of tourism. The environmental impact of tourism is a basic issue, whether we are looking at a developed or an underdeveloped area, region or country.

The costs of tourism for a country like India include extensive investment in fixed assets with a low rate of return for infrastructure, transportation, accommodation, cultural institutions, exhibition centres, and park facilities. To this maybe added the social and cultural costs like additional demands on infrastructure like land, water, health services; the creation of new jobs for displaced people; the cost of positive community relationships; the disparity between the lifestyle of visitors and those who serve them; the possible friction between local residents and new users of valued local resources; the perception of local residents of the spending of scarce capital resources on what they consider low priority areas like tourism; cultural cost of alterations in local ceremonial or traditional values; loss of privacy for local communities as tourists come to gape at their living conditions and rituals.

Tourism also causes increasing congestion and pollution as thousands of visitors flock to parks and sanctuaries in motorised vehicles; there are changes in accessibility, landscape and the ecological balance between man and nature; there is the cost, both monetary and human, of creating conservation zones (core/buffer) with unforeseen or undesirable side effects; which have been observed in the Eco-tourism movement.

The benefit of revenue from tourism does not always redress these problems but goes towards the cost of administering the project. The tourism industry is generally self-centred and not given to educational, cultural or exchange Programmes on a philanthropic basis. The natural environment, with the best will in the world, cannot escape damage with the volume of visitors. As more and more tourists, both domestic and international seek the exotic and remote destinations around the world, the likelihood of the environment suffering as a result become greater.

Forests can suffer from trampling, fires, tree felling for facilities and waste. Wildlife, despite the protection in national parks, has suffered a loss of habitat, hunting and poaching, viewing and photographing, leading to an interruption of feeding and breeding patterns or hunting for food undisturbed. These are the prized moments for the viewer. The trade in wild life trophies or tourist souvenirs is the more deliberately destructive aspect of such tourism.

SANCTUARIES

The building of tourist lodges in materials that are not integrated with the environment and the pressure they put on the land and water bodies is also wilfully destructive. Management techniques that include being less user friendly or control of numbers by closing access or by multiplying the number of attractions and areas or charging higher admission fees are generally not popular with the tourist or the tour operator and are also difficult to implement because of high administrative costs.

Equations, through its involvement in the field have had a variety of experiences relating to the debate on Eco-tourism and sustainable development. The major issues that have emerged after the policy of notification of wild life sanctuaries and their management by the Forest Departments are quite disturbing. Wherever notification has led to displacement of people the experience of rehabilitation has not been successful and the conservation aims have not been met. Several sanctuaries have witnessed militant action by displaced communities against the developers of tourism. In many cases the tourism aims have also not been met in making the sanctuary accessible to viewers, naturalists, wild life photographers. Tourism has not been able to counteract poaching and the most extensive and the oldest conservation project, Project Tiger has not been able to save the tiger population.

The commercialisation of the experience, like the privileging of one species, for example the tiger, has led to congestion and noise pollution and this has put a pressure on the management of the sanctuary to organise tiger shows which are putting a pressure on the feeding and mating habits of the tiger. These are very invasive techniques of experiencing the wild. On the plus side, the concept of beneficiary led development has helped indigenous people to organise against their displacement and exploitation as well as to fight for the retention of their traditional rights and life styles.

Environmentalists have not only been involved in such organisations and movements but have done valuable documentation. This has influenced many urban visitors to be more sensitive to the wild and to follow the rules when participating in eco-tourism. This has also led to the development of a code of conduct for the tourist, the industry and the administrator. These attempts are in a very nascent stage. The kind of co-ordination that is required between the environmentalist and economist is just beginning to emerge and have still to counter the myths of neo-classical economists in the field of tourism. But a beginning has been made.

COASTAL ISSUES

The Coastal Regulation Zone (CRZ) came into existence on February 19, 1991, with the gazetting of the notification by the Union Ministry of Environment and Forests (MoEF) under Sec. 3(1) and Sec. 3(2)(v) of the Environment Protection Act, 1986, and Rule 5(3)(d) of the Environment Protection Rules, 1986. Through the Notification the Central Government declared the coastal stretches of seas, bays, estuaries, creeks, rivers and backwaters, which are influenced by tidal action (in the land ward side), up to 500m. from the high tide line (HTL) and the land between the low tide line (LTL) and HTL as CRZ. In the case of rivers, creeks and backwaters, the

Notification stated that the CRZ could be modified on a case by case basis, on the basis of reasons to be recorded during the preparation of the coastal zone management plan (CZMP). However, the width of the CRZ from each bank could not be less than 100 m., or the width of the water body, whichever was less.

Activities Prohibited in the CRZ:

- Setting up of new industries and expansion of existing ones, except those directly related to waterfront or requiring foreshore facilities.
- Manufacture, handling, storage or disposal of hazardous substances.
- Setting up and expansion of fish processing units including warehousing (excluding hatchery and natural fish drying in permitted areas).
- Discharge of untreated wastes and effluents from industries, cities, towns or other human settlements. The existing practices would have to be phased out by the concerned authorities within three years.
- Dumping of ash or any waste from thermal power plants.
- Land reclamation, bunding or disturbing the natural course of sea water with similar obstructions. Exceptions are made for activities required for the control of coastal erosion, the maintenance of water ways to ports; clearing sand bars; and for the construction of regulators, storm water drains and structures for the prevention of salinity ingress.
- Mining of sand, rocks and other substrata materials, except those raw minerals not available outside the CRZ areas.
- Drawing or harvesting of groundwater and construction of mechanism within 200 m. of the HTL. Between 200 and 500 m. it will be permissible only if done manually through ordinary wells for drinking, horticulture, agriculture and fisheries.
- Construction activity in ecologically sensitive areas.
- Any construction activity between LTL and HTL

except facilities for carrying treated effluents and waste water discharge into the sea, facilities for carrying sea water for cooling purposes, oil, gas and similar pipelines and facilities essential for facilities permitted under the notification.

- Dressing or altering of sand dunes, hill, natural features including landscape changes for beautification, recreation and other such purposes, except as permitted under the notification.

Regulated activities (requiring environmental clearance from MoEF):

- Construction activities related to Defence requirements for which foreshore facilities are essential. Residential office, hospital, workshops will not normally be permitted in the CRZ, except in very special cases.
- Operational construction for ports and harbors and light house.
- Foreshore facilities of thermal power plants for transport of raw materials, in-take of cooling water and out fall for discharge of treated wastewater or cooling water.
- All other activities with investment exceeding. 5 crores.

Coastal Zone Management Plan (CZMP)

All the coastal states have to prepare, within one year, CZMPs identifying and classifying CRZ areas as per the Notification guidelines. These plans have to be approved by MoEF All further development activities should be within the framework of these plans.

In the interim period, before the approval of the plans, development activities should not violate the provisions of the Notification.

Violations are punishable under the provisions of the Environment Protection Act of 1986. For regulating developmental activities, the coastal stretches within 500m of the HTL are classified into CRZ-1, CRZ-11 and CRZ-III.

CRZ-I: Areas that are ecologically sensitive and important (national parks, coral reefs, mangroves, areas close to the breeding and spawning grounds of fishes, areas of high natural beauty, historical heritage, high genetic diversity, and those likely to be inundated by global warming, 'etc.); and areas within the LTL and HTL.

Regulations in CRZ-I

- No new construction shall be permitted within 500 m of the HTL.
- No construction activity except for facility for carrying treated effluents and waste water into the sea or carrying sea water for cooling, oil, gas or similar pipelines will be permitted between the LTL and the HTL.

CRZ-II

- Areas that have already been developed up to or close to the shore-line. 'Developed areas' that come within municipal limits or other legally designated urban areas which have been substantially built up and which have been provided with infrastructural facilities like drainage, approach road, water supply and sewage mains.

Regulations in CRZ-III

- Buildings will not be permitted in the seaward side of existing roads (or those proposed in the CZMP) nor on the seaward side of the existing authorised structures.
- Reconstruction of authorised buildings to be permitted subject to the existing floor space and without change in existing use CRZ III Areas that are relatively undisturbed and do not belong to either CRZ-I or CRZ-II. This will include coastal zones in the rural areas and also areas within municipal limits or urban areas that are not substantially built up.
- Areas up to 200 m. from the HTL earmarked as no development zone (NDZ). No construction will be permitted within this zone except for repairs of existing authorised structures not exceeding the

existing plinth area and covered apace. Raising of horticultural crops, gardens, pastures, parks, play fields, forestry and salt manufacture from sea water permitted in this zone.

- Development of vacant plots between 200 m. 500 m. from the HTL, in designated areas with prior approval of MoEF, permitted for hotels and beach resorts.
- Construction or reconstruction of dwellind units between the 200m and 500m of the HTL permitted so long as it is within the ambit of traditional rights and customary uses such as existing fishing villages and gouthans.

  Building conditions would be based on the conditions that the total number of dwelling units does not increase more than double of the existing units; the total covered area is not more than 33 per cent of the plot area; the overall height is not more than two floors and 9 m. Guidelines for development of beach resorts in the designated areas of CRZ-III · No construction within 200 m. from the HTL and in the area between LTL and HTL.
- The total plot size should not be less than 0.4 hectare and the covered area should not be more than 33 per cent. · The total height of the construction should not be more than 9 m. and the building should not be more than two floors. Groundwater cannot be tapped within 200m of the HTL. Between 200 and 500 m. it can be tapped with the concurrence of the State or Central Groundwater Board.
- Extraction of sand, leveling or digging of sandy stretches, except for the structural foundation will not be permitted within 500 M. of the HTL.
- The quality of treated effluents, solid wastes, emissions and noise levels etc. must be within the standards laid down by the central or state pollution control boards. Untreated effluents and solid wastes should not be discharged into the water or beach.

- To allow public access there should be a gap of 20m. width between two hotels. Two consecutive gaps should not be more than 500 m. apart.

THE WORLD SCENARIO OF TOURISM

In recent years tourism has emerged as a major economic activity that is employment oriented and earns foreign exchange. Its share in the worlds GDP in 1994-95 was 10 per cent which is more than the world military budgets put together. In global terms, the investment in tourism industry and travel trade accounts for 7 per cent of the total capital investment. Today 21.2 crore people around the globe are employed in travel trade and tourism. In future, this industry is likely to see unprecedented growth. According to the World Tourism Council at Brussels, the revenues from travel and tourism in Asia Pacific region will grow at the rate of 7.8 per cent annually over the next decade.

Amongst the economic sectors, the tourism sector is highly labour intensive. A survey by the Government of India notes that the rate of employment generation (direct and indirect) in tourism is 52 persons employed per ₹10 lakh investment (based on 1992-93 Consumer Price Index). This is much higher than the rates of employment generation in most other economic sectors.

Indian tourism industry has also recorded phenomenal growth. The rate of international arrivals in India in recent years has been to the tune of about 19 lakh arrivals per year. The unprecedented growth in tourism in India has made it the third largest foreign exchange earner after gem and jewellery and ready-made garments. This is not surprising since India possesses a whole range of attractive normally sought by tourists and which includes natural attractions like landscapes, scenic beauty, mountains, wildlife, beaches, major rivers and manmade attractions such as monuments, forts, palaces and havelis.

However, in global terms, in spite of such attractions, tourist arrivals in India are a mere 0.30 per cent of the world arrivals. Receipts are similarly low, just a 0.50 per cent of the world receipts. We are still quite far from the target of 50 lakh tourist arrivals per year.

Travel and Tourism is the world's largest industry and creator of jobs across national and regional economies. WTTC/WEFA research show that in 2000, Travel and Tourism will generate, directly and indirectly, 11.7 per cent of GDP and nearly 200 million jobs in the world-wide economy. Jobs generated by Travel and Tourism are spread across the economy-in retail, construction, manufacturing and telecommunications, as well as directly in Travel and Tourism companies.

These jobs employ a large proportion of women, minorities and young people; are predominantly in small and medium sized companies; and offer good training and transferability. Tourism can also be one of the most effective drivers for the development of regional economies. These patterns apply to both developed and emerging economies.

CONTRIBUTING TO SUSTAINABLE DEVELOPMENT

The 1992 United Nations Conference on Environment and Development (UNCED), the Rio Earth Summit, identified Travel and Tourism as one of the key sectors of the economy which could make a positive contribution to achieving sustainable development. The Earth Summit lead to the adoption of Agenda 21, a comprehensive Programmes of action adopted by 182 governments to provide a global blueprint for achieving sustainable development. Travel and Tourism is the first industry sector to have launched an industry-specific action plan based on Agenda 21.

Travel and Tourism is able to contribute to development which is economically, ecologically and socially sustainable, because it:

- Has less impact on natural resources and the environment than most other industries;
- Is based on enjoyment and appreciation of local culture, built heritage, and natural environment, as such that the industry has a direct and powerful motivation to protect these assets;

- Can play a positive part in increasing consumer commitment to sustainable development principles through its unparalleled consumer distribution channels; and
- Provides an economic incentive to conserve natural environments and habitats which might otherwise be allocated to more environmentally damaging land uses, thereby, helping to maintain bio-diversity.

There are numerous good examples of where Travel and Tourism is acting as a catalyst for conservation and improvement of the environment and maintenance of local diversity and culture. (Some of these are set out in Section B of this paper and a fuller illustration of the range of industry action can be found on the World Travel and Tourism Council's Of course, there are also examples where development has not been sustainable. (Some of the lessons learnt from these poor practices are illustrated in Section C of this paper.)

PROVIDING INFRASTRUCTURE

To a greater degree than most activities, Travel and Tourism depends on a wide range of infrastructure services-airports, air navigation, roads, railheads and ports, as well as basic infrastructure services required by hotels, restaurants, shops, and recreation facilities (*e.g.* telecommunications and utilities). It is the combination of tourism and good infrastructure that underpins the economic, environmental and social benefits. It is important to balance any decision to develop an area for tourism against the need to preserve fragile or threatened environments and cultures. However, once a decision has been taken where an area is appropriate for new tourism development, or that an existing tourist site should be developed further, then good infrastructure will be essential to sustain the quality, economic viability and growth of Travel and Tourism. Good infrastructure will also be a key factor in the industry's ability to manage visitor flows in ways that do not affect the natural or built heritage, nor counteract against local interests.

CHALLENGE FOR THE FUTURE

Travel and Tourism creates jobs and wealth and has tremendous potential to contribute to economically, environmentally and socially sustainable development in both developed countries and emerging nations. It has a comparative advantage in that its start up and running costs can be low compared to many other forms of industry development.

It is also often one of the few realistic options for development in many areas. Therefore, there is a strong likelihood that the Travel and Tourism industry will continue to grow globally over the short to medium term.

Of course, if Travel and Tourism is managed badly, it can have a detrimental effect-it can damage fragile environments and destroy local cultures.

The challenge is to manage the future growth of the industry so as to minimise its negative impacts on the environment and host communities whilst maximising the benefits it brings in terms of jobs, wealth and support for local culture and industry, and protection of the built and natural environment.

OBJECTIVES

The main objective of the States Tourism Policy will be to undertake intensive development of tourism in the State and thereby increase employment opportunities.

The following related objectives are dovetailed with main objectives:

- Identify and develop tourist destinations and related activities.
- Diversifications of tourism products in order to attract more tourists through a varied consumer choice.
- Comprehensive development of pilgrimage centres as tourist destinations.
- Create adequate facilities for budget tourists.
- Strengthen the existing infrastructure and develop new ones where necessary.

- Creation of tourism infrastructure so as to preserve handicrafts, folk arts and culture of the state and thereby attract more tourists.

APPROACH AND STRATEGY

In addition to the facilitation role assigned to itself by the Government in the development of tourism, the Government will adopt the following strategy towards the private sector with the objective of securing its active involvement in leading the development of tourism in the State.

- The tourism will be given the status of industry in order that the facilities and benefits available to the industry are also made available to tourism projects.
- A special incentives package will be made available for encouraging new tourism projects as well as expansion of existing tourism units.
- Infrastructural facilities will be strengthened and developed within the State, particularly in Special Tourism Areas which will be notified latter and which will be developed by adopting an integrated-area.
- Effective mechanisms will be set up to build meaningful co-ordination with the Central Government and the State Governments agencies, the local self-government bodies and the NGOs.
- Government will encourage building effective linkages with the relevant economic agents and agencies such as the national and international tour operators and travel agents of repute, hotel chains and global institutions connected with tourism such as WTO.

So far, the lending from the State Financial Institutions has been largely confined to hotels only. In reality, the range of activities for tourism projects is far larger than just hotels as can be seen from the following illustrative list

TEN COMMANDMENTS

1. Respect the frailty of the earth. Realise that unless

all are willing to help in its preservation, unique and beautiful destinations may not be here for future generations to enjoy.

2. Leave only footprints. Take only photographs. No graffiti! No litter! Do not take away souvenirs from historical sites and natural areas.
3. To make your travels more meaningful, educate yourself about the geography, customs, manners and cultures of the region you visit. Take time to listen to the people. Encourage local conservation efforts.
4. Respect the privacy and dignity of others. Inquire before photographing people.
5. Do not buy products made from endangered plants or animals, such as ivory, tortoise shell, animal skins, and feathers. Read Know Before You Go, the U. S. Customs list of products which cannot be imported.
6. Always follow designated trails. Do not disturb animals, plants or their natural habitats.
7. Learn about and support conservation-oriented Programmes and organizations working to preserve the environment.
8. Whenever possible, walk or use environmentally-sound methods of transportation. Encourage drivers of public vehicles to stop engines when parked.
9. Patronize those (hotels, airlines, resorts, cruise lines, tour operators and suppliers) who advance energy and environmental conservation; water and air quality; recycling; safe management of waste and toxic materials; noise abatement, community involvement; and which provide experienced, well-trained staff dedicated to strong principles of conservation.
10. Encourage organizations to subscribe to environmental guidelines. ASTA urges organizations to adopt their own environmental codes to cover special sties and ecosystems.

Travel is a natural right of all people and is a crucial ingredient of world.

TOURISM PLANNING

Tourism is one of many activities in a community or region that requires planning and coordination. This bulletin provides a simple structure and basic guidelines for comprehensive tourism planning at a community or regional level. Planning is the process of identifying objectives and defining and evaluating methods of achieving them. By comprehensive planning we mean planning which considers all of the tourism resources, organizations, markets, and Programme within a region. Comprehensive planning also considers economic, environmental, social, and institutional aspects of tourism development.

TWO SIDES OF PLANNING

Tourism planning has evolved from two related but distinct sets of planning philosophies and methods. On the one hand, tourism is one of many activities in an area that must be considered as part of physical, environmental, social, and economic planning.

Therefore, it is common to find tourism addressed, at least partially, in a regional land use, transportation, recreation, economic development, or comprehensive plan. The degree to which tourism is addressed in such plans depends upon the relative importance of tourism to the community or region and how sensitive the planning authority is to tourism activities.

Tourism may also be viewed as a business in which a community or region chooses to engage. Individual tourism businesses conduct a variety of planning activities including feasibility, marketing, product development, promotion, forecasting, and strategic planning. If tourism is a significant component of an area's economy or development plans, regional or community-wide marketing plans are needed to coordinate the development and marketing activities of different tourism interests in the community.

A comprehensive approach integrates a strategic marketing plan with more traditional public planning activities. This ensures a balance between serving the needs and wants of the tourists versus the needs and wants of local residents. A formal tourism plan provides a vehicle for the various interests within a community to coordinate their activities and work towards common goals. It also is a means of coordinating tourism with other community activitiès.

STEPS IN THE PLANNING PROCESS

Like any planning, tourism planning is goal-oriented, striving to achieve certain objectives by matching available resources and Programme with the needs and wants of people. Comprehensive planning requires a systematic approach, usually involving a series of steps. The process is best viewed as an iterative and on-going one, with each step subject to modification and refinement at any stage of the planning process.

There are six steps in the planning process:

1. Define goals and objectives.
2. Identify the tourism system.
    - Resources
    - Organizations
    - Markets
3. Generate alternatives.
4. Evaluate alternatives.
5. Select and implement.
6. Monitor and evaluate.

Step one: Defining Goals and objectives. Obtaining clear statements of goals and objectives is difficult, but important. Ideally, tourism development goals should flow from more general community goals and objectives. It is important to understand how a tourism plan serves these broader purposes. Is the community seeking a broader tax base, increased employment opportunities, expanded recreation facilities, better educational Programme, a higher quality of life? How can tourism contribute to these objectives?

If tourism is identified as a means of serving broader community goals, it makes sense to develop plans with more specific tourism development objectives. These are generally defined through a continuing process in which various groups and organizations in a community work together towards common goals. A local planning authority, chamber of commerce, visitor's bureau, or similar group should assume a leadership role to develop an initial plan and obtain broad involvement of tourism interests in the community. Public support for the planning process and plan is also important.

Having a good understanding of tourism and the tourism system in your community is the first step towards defining goals and objectives for tourism development. The types of goals that are appropriate and the precision with which you are able to define them will depend upon how long your community has been involved in tourism and tourism planning.

In the early stages of tourism development, goals may involve establishing organizational structures and collecting information to better identify the tourism system in the community. Later, more precise objectives can be formulated and more specific development and marketing strategies evaluated.

Step two: Identifying Your Tourism System When planning for any type of activity, it is important to first define its scope and characteristics. Be clear about exactly what your plan encompasses. A good initial question is, "What do you mean by tourism?" Tourism is defined in many ways. Generally, tourism involves people traveling outside of their community for pleasure. Definitions differ on the specifics of how far people must travel, whether or not they must stay overnight, for how long, and what exactly is included under traveling for "pleasure". Do you want your tourism plan to include day visitors, conventioneers, business travellers, people visiting friends and relatives, people passing through, or seasonal residents?

Which community resources and organizations serve tourists or could serve tourists? Generally, tourists share community resources with local residents and businesses. Many organizations serve both tourists and locals. This complicates tourism planning and argues for a clear idea of what your tourism plan entails.

You can begin to clarify the tourism system by breaking it down into three subsystems:

1. Tourism resources,
2. Tourism organizations, and
3. Tourism markets.

An initial task in developing a tourism plan is to identify, inventory, and classify the objects within each of these subsystems.

Tourism Resources are any:

- Natural,
- Cultural,
- Human, or
- Capital resources that either are used or can be used to attract or serve tourists.

A tourism resource inventory identifies and classifies the resources available that provide opportunities for tourism development. Conduct an objective and realistic assessment of the quality and quantity of resources you have to work with.

Tourism organizations combine resources in various proportions to provide products and services for the tourist. It is important to recognize the diverse array of public and private organizations involved with tourism. The most difficult part of tourism planning is to get these groups to work towards common goals. You should develop a list of these organizations within your own community and obtain their input and cooperation in your tourism planning efforts. Setting up appropriate communication systems and institutional arrangements is a key part of community tourism planning.

TOURISM MARKETS

Tourists makeup the third, and perhaps most important subsystem. Successful tourism Programme require a strong market orientation. The needs and wants of the tourists you choose to attract and serve must be the focus of much of your marketing and development activity. Therefore, it is important to clearly understand which tourism market segments you wish to attract and serve. Tourists fall into a very diverse set of categories with quite distinct needs and wants. You should identify the different types of tourists, or market segments that you presently serve or would like to serve. This may involve one or more tourism market surveys.

A visitor survey identifies the size and nature of the existing market and asks the following questions:

- What are the primary market segments you presently attract?
- Where do they come from?
- What local businesses and facilities do they use?
- What attracted them to the community?
- How did they find out about your community?
- How satisfied are they with your offerings?

A market survey (usually a telephone survey) also can be conducted among households in regions from which you wish to attract tourists. This type of study helps identify potential markets, and means of attracting tourists to your area.

TOURISM MARKET SEGMENTS

In a general tourism plan, some clear target tourism market segments should be identified. You might begin by defining the market area from which you will draw most of your visitors. The size of your market area depends upon the uniqueness and quality of your "product", transportation systems, tastes and preferences of surrounding populations, and your competition. Identifying the market area will help target information and promotion and define transportation routes and modes, competition, and characteristics of your market.

Next, divide your travel market into the following trip length categories:

- Day trips from a 50 mile radius,
- Day trips from 50 to 200 miles away,
- Pass-through travellers,
- Overnight trips of 1 or 2 nights (most likely weekends), and
- Extended overnight vacation trips.

After you have an idea of your market area and kinds of trips you will be serving, begin defining more specific market segments like vehicle campers, downhill skiers, sightseers, family vacationers, single weekenders, and the like. These segments can be more clearly tied to particular resources, businesses, and facilities in your community.

What kinds of products and services are likely to attract each of these groups? Tourist needs as well as their impact on the local community are quite different for day tourists versus overnight tourists. Areas catering primarily to weekend traffic will experience large fluctuations in use. In deciding the relative importance of these different segments, communities need to assess both their ability to provide required services (do you have enough rooms?), as well as the demand for different types of trips relative to the supply and your competition.

The Environment

A tourism plan is significantly affected by many factors in the broader environment. Indeed, one of the complexities of tourism planning is the number of variables that are outside of the control of an individual tourism business or community. These include such things as tourism offerings and prices at competing destinations, federal and state policy and legislation, currency exchange rates, the state of the economy, and weather. These factors are discussed more fully in Extension bulletin E-1959 as part of the market environment analysis.

Local populations also must be considered in tourism planning. As they compete with tourists for resources, they can be significantly affected by tourism activity, and they are an important source of support in getting tourism plans implemented. A survey of local residents can be conducted to assess community attitudes towards tourism development, identify impacts of tourism on the community, and obtain local input into tourism plans. Public hearings, workshops, and advisory boards are other ways to obtain public involvement in tourism planning. Local support and cooperation is important to the success of tourism Programme and should not be overlooked.

Step three: Generating Alternatives. Generating alternative development and marketing options to meet your goals requires some creative thinking and brainstorming. The errors made at this stage are usually thinking too narrowly or screening out alternatives prematurely. It is wise to solicit a wide range of options from a diverse group of people. If tourism expertise is lacking in your community, seek help and advice outside the community. Tourism planning involves a wide range of interrelated development and marketing decisions.

The following development questions will get you started:

- How much importance should be assigned to tourism within a community or region?
- Which general community goals is tourism development designed to serve?
- Which organization(s) will provide the leadership and coordination necessary for community tourism planning? What are the relative roles of public and private sectors?

Tourism Marketing Decision Questions Include

- *Segments*: Which market segments should be pursued; geographic markets, trip types, activity or demographic subgroups?
- *Product*: What kinds of tourism products and services should be provided? Who should provide what?
- *Place*: Where should tourism facilities be located?
- *Promotion*: What kinds of promotion should be used, by whom, in which media, how much, when? What community tourism theme or image should be established?
- *Price*: What prices should be charged for which products and services. Who should capture the revenue?

Step four: Evaluating Alternatives. Tourism development and marketing options are evaluated by assessing the degree to which each option will be able to meet the stated goals and objectives.

There are usually two parts to a systematic evaluation of tourism development and marketing alternatives:

- Feasibility analysis, and
- Impact assessment.

These two tasks are interrelated, but think of them as trying to answer two basic questions:

1. Can it be done?, and
2. What are the consequences?

A decision to take a specific action must be based both on feasibility and desirability.

FEASIBILITY ANALYSIS

First, screen alternatives and eliminate those that are not feasible due to economic, environmental, political, legal, or other factors. Evaluate the remaining set of alternatives in more detail, paying particular attention to the market potential and financial plan. Make a realistic assessment of your community's ability to attract and serve a market segment or segments. This requires a clear understanding of the tourism market in your area and how this market is changing. Also carefully identify your competition and evaluate your advantages and disadvantages compared to the competition. Plan towards the future because it takes time to implement decisions and for your actions to take effect. Therefore, look at the likely market and competition for several years to come. Review forecasts for the travel market in your area, if available. Careful tracking of tourism trends in your own community can help identify changes in the market that you will have to adapt to.

IMPACT ASSESSMENT

When evaluating alternative development and marketing strategies it is important to understand the impacts, both positive and negative, of proposed actions. The types of impacts and their importance vary across different communities and proposed actions.

Generally, the size, extent, and nature of tourism impacts depend upon:

- Volume of tourist activity relative to local activity

- Length and nature of tourist contacts with the community
- Degree of concentration/dispersal of tourist activity in the area
- Similarities or differences between local populations and tourists
- Stability/sensitivity of local economy, environment, and social structure
- How well tourism is planned, controlled, and managed.

Look at both the benefits and costs of any proposed actions. While tourism development can increase income, revenues, and employment, it also involves costs. Evaluate benefits and costs of tourism development from the perspectives of local government, businesses, and residents.

IMPACTS ON LOCAL GOVERNMENT

Local government provides most of the infrastructure and many of the services essential to tourism development, including highways, public parks, law enforcement, water and sewer, garbage collection and disposal. Evaluate tourism decisions with a clear understanding of the capacity of the local infrastructure and services relative to anticipated needs, and take into account both the needs of local populations and tourists.

A fiscal impact analysis evaluates the impact of tourism on the community's tax base and local government costs. It entails predicting the additional infrastructure and service requirements of tourism development, estimating their costs, deciding who will pay for/provide them, and how. Will tourism generate increased local government revenue through fees and charges, local sales or use taxes, increased property values or property tax rates, or larger local shares of federal and state tax revenues?

IMPACTS ON BUSINESS AND INDUSTRY

Businesses that are directly serving tourists benefit from sales to tourists. Through secondary impacts, tourism activity also benefits a wide range of businesses in a community. For example, a local textile industry may sell to a linen supply firm that serves hotels and motels catering primarily to tourists. A local forest products industry sells to a lumberyard where local woodcarvers or furniture makers buy their supplies. They in turn sell to tourists through various retail outlets. All of these businesses benefit from tourism.

If most products and services for tourists are bought outside of the local area, much of the tourist spending "leaks" out of the local economy. The more a community is "self-sufficient" in serving tourists, the larger the local impact.

IMPACTS ON RESIDENTS

Local residents may experience a broad range of both positive and negative impacts from tourism development. Tourism development may provide increased employment and income for the community. Although tourism jobs are primarily in the service sectors and are often seasonal, part time, and low-paying, these characteristics, are neither universal nor always undesirable. Residents may value opportunities for part time and seasonal work. In particular, employment opportunities and work experiences for students or retirees may be desired.

Residents may also benefit from local services that otherwise would not be available. Tourism development may mean a wider variety of retailers and restaurants, or a better community library. It may also mean more traffic, higher prices, and increases in property values and local taxes. The general quality of the environment and life in the community may go up or down due to tourism development. This depends on the nature of tourism development, the preferences and desires of local residents, and how well tourism is planned and managed.

Steps five and six: Implementation, and Monitoring and Evaluation. We will not attempt a complete discussion of decisionmaking, plan implementation, and monitoring, but these are critical steps in the success of a tourism plan. A set of specific actions should be prescribed with clearly defined responsibilities and timetables. Monitor progress in implementing the plan and evaluate the success of the plan in meeting its goals and objectives on a regular basis. Plans generally need to be adjusted over time due to changing goals, changing market conditions, and unanticipated impacts. It is a good idea to build monitoring and evaluation systems into your planning efforts.

Successful tourism planning and development means serving both tourists and local residents. The bulletins in this series stress the importance of a market orientation for attracting and serving tourists. This market orientation must be balanced with a clear view of how tourism serves the broader community interest and an understanding of the positive and negative impacts of tourism development. Remember, tourism should serve the community first and the tourist second. Tourism development must be compatible with other activities in the area and be supported by the local population. Therefore, the tourism plan should be closely coordinated with other local and regional planning efforts, if not an integral part of them.

TERRITORIAL PLANNING IN TOURISM

Environmental quality is often a key success factor for tourism. At the same time, tourism makes extensive use of natural resources thereby jeopardizing its long-term viability. To address such a dilemma, from the general notion of sustainable development (SD) tourism scholars have coined the term 'sustainable tourism' (ST) that encompasses a set of principles, business methods and policy prescriptions relevant to the tourist industry (Sinclair and Stabler, 1997). However, recent research has advocated the need to reconcile the concept of ST with that of SD, by making the concerns of the former adhere more strictly to the tenets of the latter (Collins, 1999; Hunter, 1997). This paper looks at the issues of tourism development and environmental conservation through the lens of SD principles and assesses the pivotal role that local governments can play in designing policies that make the two perspectives compatible.

A common denominator in the literature on SD is the Bruntland Commission's definition that "SD is development that meets the need of the present without compromising the ability of future generations to meet their own needs". Such a mandate affirms the importance of intragenerational and intergenerational equity issues. As far as the former is concerned, "SD places emphasis on providing for the needs of the least advantaged in society". This is particularly relevant in developing countries, where the need to generate income is more likely to lead to a rapid exploitation of the resource base and an uneven distribution of the related profits between foreign investors and host populations. To prevent this, it is generally recommended that local populations and governments be directly involved in the shaping of development activities in association with foreign developers, because locals can better assess the short and the long-term effects of growth.

As far as the latter is concerned, intergenerational fairness implies that future generations should receive a fair share of the net benefits generated by the development. The fact that development is sustainable only as long as future generations are fairly treated led to the view that "...we in the present generation are but the present tenants of the earth, not its absolute owners. As present tenants we have the right to make use of its productivity, but not the right to impair its productivity for its later tenants the future generations".

In theory, future generations are entitled to just compensation for the current generation's actions that lead to a depletion of natural resource. In practice, doing so requires making difficult judgments about the substitutability of natural capital with physical capital. This is a crucial point in the case of tourism, whose activity relies extensively on the transformation of natural capital into accommodation and service facilities. Thus, the tourism industry faces the particularly difficult challenge to "develop tourism capacity and the quality of its products without adversely affecting the physical and human environment that sustains and nurtures them".

It is argued, however, that the WCED definition is too vague to use as a working tool, and often results in ambiguous admonition for policymakers (Norton and Toman 1997). Indeed, the requirement that the needs of the present generation be met without compromising the ability of future generations to meet their needs, could be satisfied simply by allowing constant consumption over time at no more than a subsistence level. Although such a policy would achieve equity among different generations, it could hardly be accepted as a reasonable target for public policy, as it may fail to incorporate a notion of dynamic efficiency. In the following analysis, efficiency implies a notion of "non-wastefulness", that is, the possibility that inputs are transformed in a way that leads to an increase in individuals' well-being in a sustainable manner, *e.g.*, consumption above the subsistence level for every generation.

Such an increase in individuals' welfare entails a decision on the optimal allocation of scarce resources (*e.g.* natural assets) among alternative uses (*e.g.*, development or preservation). Because tourism can never be totally without environmental impacts, the real challenge is to indicate sustainable policies that combine intra-generational and intergenerational equity with efficiency considerations in a mutually compatible manner. As far as intergenerational equity and efficiency considerations are concerned, assessing under what circumstances turning natural resources into capital stock (*e.g.* a hotel) leads to an increase in the well-being of the present and future generations, is central.

Furthermore, the notion of efficiency is closely linked with that of intragenerational equity when the local populations of the tourist areas are allowed to appropriate a fair share of the net benefits generated by tourism. The theoretical analysis in this article presents a policy measure that enables local governments to retain the surplus from tourism activities when these are run by foreign organizations. The existing literature has refined the definition of sustainable development-from very weak to very strong depending on the importance given to such notions as reversibility and substitutability between physical and natural capital. Unfortunately, the interpretation of such concepts varies, depending on the disciplinary approach being adopted. For instance, economists and ecologists assign different meanings to the notions of substitutability and reversibility. For economists, substitutability refers to the possibility of maintaining a desired level of production using different combinations of inputs, while reversibility indicates the extent to which a given resource becomes scarce as a consequence of human actions. For ecologists, these two factors determine such ecosystems' physical properties as, for instance, resilience. In this sense, a more resilient ecosystem is one that is more likely to revert to its original condition after a perturbation and/or to find other substitutes in the event that one of the ecosystem attributes is diminished.

Applying the notion of weak sustainability is possible if we assume that natural and physical capitals are substitutable, or when changes to the natural asset base are reversible. This implies that under the weak sustainability paradigm, intra-generational equity is obtained through the distribution of the efficiency gains arising from the implementation of development projects, while future generations are compensated for the loss of natural assets by inheriting a greater stock of physical capital.

However, even advocates of weak sustainability acknowledge that under certain circumstances, *e.g.* when physical capital is a poor substitute for the natural resource, efficiency considerations ought not to occupy a central role. For instance, it has been argued that one generation might set aside special places and features such as the Grand Canyon or the Reef Barrier for future generations because of their intrinsic qualities.

The uncertainty surrounding both the effects of human intervention on the environment and the likelihood of finding feasible technological solutions to environmental problems provides an important argument for strong sustainability. By this it is meant that the opportunities of future generations can be secured only if natural resources and environmental quality are specifically conserved for their benefit. Thus, within the strong sustainability paradigm, conservation concerns are paramount.

COMBINING CONSERVATION AND EFFICIENCY

The foregoing discussion has illustrated that intragenerational/efficiency and intergenerational equity goals are less likely to be in conflict when considered from within a weak sustainability perspective, while supporters of strong sustainability are inclined to reject any trade-off between conservation and efficiency. In line with the latter view, it has become abundantly clear that tourism cannot continue to be the killer of the "goose laying golden eggs".

However, it has been argued that strong sustainability, with its emphasis on intergenerational fairness, can conflict with the efficient use of resources that may engender beneficial effects for both the present and the future generations. That is, the strong sustainability approach is often associated with an anti-economic growth position that appears to deny the world's poor the opportunity of meeting basic needs, both in the short and the long run.

Therefore, this article takes the Centre ground stance indicated in Hunter (1997) by arguing that the essential role of ecological conservation in the implementation of sustainable tourism strategies should, depending on the circumstances, be complemented by efficiency considerations. This is in line with many methodological contributions aimed at bringing together efficiency and intergenerational equity.

The combination of a conservation criterion with an efficiency criterion constitutes the central element of the two-tier method advocated by Page (1977). Using this approach, problems are categorized as being intragenerational or intergenerational in their effects, in the sense specified above. That is, when intergenerational issues figure prominently, more attention is given to conservation, with possible applications of the 'safe minimum standard of conservation principle', which places the burden of proof on today's resource allocators to demonstrate that their behaviour is consistent with intergenerational fairness (Howarth, 1997). In practice, this approach recognizes the fundamental right of future generations to inherit an intact stock of natural resources, unless the costs of foregoing the resource exploitation, that is, the loss of the efficiency gains from development, are unbearably high.

Page (1997) provides a list of inter-related issues that need to be addressed to achieve a satisfactory combination of efficiency and equity. First, instruments need to be identified. He suggests that "shifting the tax base towards virgin material taxes and taxes on environmental harms would work towards sustainability". Second, intergenerational equity should always come first when the resource is essential. He cites the U.S. Drinking Water Regulation as an example of public intervention based on equity grounds, as future generations are entitled to a safe supply of drinking water.

The example that comes to mind in the case of tourism, is the establishment of parks or natural reserves, where regulatory measures are taken towards environmental protection so that the functional integrity of essential, and possibly unique, natural ecosystems is preserved as far as is possible, for the benefit of future generations. Indeed, once a law attributes the status of park or of natural reserve to a given geographical area, heavy restrictions are imposed on the possibility to develop the area, that curtail or impede tourist activity.

More importantly, to guarantee that the resource base remains intact, and can be bequeathed to future generations, the status of park cannot be abolished and remains associated with the area indefinitely. Third, and related to the latter point, the role of the legal framework in which the decision-makers operate is crucial. Practically, this entails that the environmental decisions associated with important equity and efficiency considerations should be dealt with in a manner similar to that used to preserve a system of constitutional law.

This is because the "framers of a constitution are expected to abstract themselves from their own narrow self-interest and establish the rules of the game that are sustainable indefinitely".It is essential for modern societal institutions to maintain the constitutional system: to protect it from myopic opportunism triggered by short-term benefits, it is commonplace to have special procedures to modify constitutional dictates.

By the same token, environmental problems with important intergenerational equity aspects should be dealt with like constitutional issues whereby the future generations' entitlement to an intact resource base has paramount importance.

Three points that are central in this study may be inferred from the previous discussion:

1. The importance of natural resources,
2. The identification of appropriate policy instruments and
3. The legislative framework. This article aims to clarify some of the relationships among these issues. At the same time it develops a conceptual framework encompassing all the basic elements that are taken into account in the public assessment of tourism development projects. To this purpose, a theoretical economic model of land taxation is illustrated. Its results show the crucial role played by a tax on land development for the joint achievement of conservation and economic efficiency goals. In addition, its cost-benefit approach clearly indicates that in environmentally sensitive areas-where the resource is essential-the tax should be set at a level that deters development. This result is thus equivalent to the creation of a park or a reserve that remains as close to its original form as possible.

The importance of the legislative framework is investigated using the case study of the so-called "Master Plan" in North Sardinia (Italy). The evidence presented, together with considerations from the theoretical model, are used to shed light on the Sardinian government's refusal to grant a developer special exemptions from existing territorial planning legislation. Indeed, the Sardinian government decided to forego the short-term benefits of a large tourism development because the development allowed the possibility of construction within 300 meters of the coastline, a practice that is prohibited by Sardinian law.

The local government recognized that the Defence of the conservation principle embodied in the regional law could not be a matter of bargaining, even though this would have entailed, as it actually did, the withdrawal of the project by the developer. Regardless of the merit of the specific project and the good reputation of the developer for quality tourism, the Sardinian government's stance on the project aimed to ensure that other developments might not be created unless sustainable principles were applied.

Sustainability and Public Intervention

To our knowledge, there is no formal economic model explicitly linking tourism and sustainable development. There exists, however, a growing literature aimed at integrating sustainability and formal economic analysis.

Faucheux et al. (1996) classified the existing analytical approaches to sustainability using four categories of models:

- Neoclassical,
- Evolutionary,
- Ecological economic and
- Neo-ricardian.

The model presented in the next subsection falls within the first category but departs from existing models by adopting a game theoretic approach where different incentives faced by public and private institutions are taken into account. For a technical presentation of the model, the reader is referred to Piga (1999). The emphasis here will be the description of the assumptions used in this model, and the policy recommendations that can be drawn. The second part of the section consists of a case study that complements and supports the theoretical analysis.

SUSTAINABILITY AND TAXATION

The model under analysis is dynamic; that is, it considers a sequence of time periods and how decisions taken in early periods influence the outcomes of subsequent periods. A dynamic approach allows a better identification of the development's long-term effects, notably on land, which is the natural resource under study.

This is particularly relevant for tourism because territorial planning, environmental design and land use, are crucial factors that create and sustain a tourist resort competitive advantage. This is because tourists increasingly expect a picturesque landscape to be integral to the holiday experience. Moreover, land development is associated with various forms of environmental costs. Both these aspects are captured in the following analysis.

The first economic agent taken into account is a private tourism developer who owns a territory of size L For instance; L could represent the size of an island. The developer chooses the rate of land exploitation, that is, the portion of the site on which tourist facilities will be erected. Denoting with B(t) the stock of developed land at time t and with the size of territory on which the developer decides to build in period t, we postulate that these two variables are linked by this simple law of variation over time. t). Such an expression indicates that in every period t a portion of land sð(t) is used to build accommodations. Thus, what is built this year is added to what was built in previous years, thereby increasing the stock of buildings that constitute the site's capacity.

The discussion so far highlights the well known impact of tourism development on environmental quality: "In reality, it is impossible to imagine any kind of tourism activity being developed and then operating without in some way reducing the quantity and/or quality of natural resources somewhere". In this particular case, for tourism activity to take place, it is impossible to maintain the resource base intact (*i.e.,* not to exploit land). It follows that a satisfactory combination of efficiency and conservation hinges around the identification of both the private and public benefits engendered by the development, of its environmental costs and of the appropriate policy instruments that induce an optimal level of use of the natural resource.

The first type of private benefit that we consider is the revenue deriving from selling to tourists. Revenues depend on the price of the holiday and on the site's capacity, B (t). In turn, it is assumed that the tourists' willingness to pay for a holiday (which represents the highest price they would pay for a holiday) is positively influenced by the environmental quality of the site, which is measured by the amount of land that is left unused.

More importantly, the previous analytical expression indicates that the more the place is developed (*i.e.*, the greater B (t) relative to L), the lower the price the developer can charge for a holiday. Therefore, the developer, when deciding to expand (*i.e.*, increase the size of B(t) through the choice of ó(t)), has to take into account that the revenue increase, due to the possibility of accommodating more tourists, may be more than offset by the reduction in price that is triggered by the deterioration in the environmental quality.

Such a novel representation of the links between tourists' demand and environmental quality captures a peculiar feature of the tourist industry that is supported by empirical evidence. Font (2000) presents evidence supporting the notion that environmental considerations are important drivers of tourism demand. Huybers and Bennett (2000) reach a similar conclusion in an analysis of changes in environmental quality and other features that affect demand.

The local government is the second economic agent taken into consideration. The instrument used to achieve sustainability is a tax on each unit of newly built territory. This clarifies the crucial role of the public sector: the tax is a cost to the developer and can be used by the government to appropriate some of the profits generated by the development. As discussed below, the tax guarantees the achievement of intragenerational equity objectives, as the tax revenues in each year can be deployed to ameliorate the local public infrastructure which is then inherited by future generations.

In line with the real-world situation where the legislative framework and the taxing policy is often a given for the developers, the economic model assumes that the local government has a first-mover advantage, that is, the government sets the tax level before the developer decides the expansion size. In the economic literature the player that moves first is defined as a "Stackelberg leader". In each period, the local government obtains tax receipts given by the tax multiplied by the size of the expanded capacity.

The second part of the government's objective function consists of the net value derivable from the use of the land. Such a value is the net outcome of the government's evaluation of the public benefits from development against its environmental costs. On the one hand, public benefits are generated by tourism development through a multiplier effect on the local economy arising because a local workforce is used in construction, in operating the tourist facilities and because tourists consume local products.

For more examples of the relationship between tourism and the local multiplier. On the other hand, land development engenders environmental costs for the local population both in terms of congestion and exhaustion of the natural resource and in the form of loss of non-market benefits such as bequest, option and existence values. The bequest value is the willingness to pay to preserve the environment for the benefit of future generations.

The option value identifies an expression of preference for the preservation of an environment against some probability that a community will make use of it at a later date. The existence value is represented by the utility that individuals enjoy when the risk to an endangered species has been reduced. Development implies the loss of all these values for the local population, the sum of which constitutes the non-market environmental costs.

These are particularly high in areas where the ecosystem is less resilient, that is, less likely to fully recover from exogenous shocks, and where, therefore, development may engender irreversible degradation to the environment. Finally, land development engenders another form of environmental costs to the local population, that is, the lack of access to natural resources (*e.g.*, beaches) due to congestion arising from having an intensively developed destination occupied by tourists. The foregoing analysis of the local government's pay-off function has highlighted that the development engenders benefits in the form of private profits and public income multiplier effects, and environmental costs whose size depends on the characteristics of the area's ecosystem. The difference between these benefits and costs gives rise to a net value function, W(B(t)), that depends on the size of the development. A realistic analytical expression for the net value function W(B(t)) is one that allows, at an early stage of development, growth benefits, and the related efficiency gains, to be greater than environmental costs, which become predominant as the development increases in size.

A quadratic function such as $W(t)=B(t)-\tilde{a}B^2(t)$, exhibits this property: the minus sign attached to the quadratic value of the total development size, denoted by B(t), implies that the environmental costs associated with development, increase at a faster rate than growth benefits, captured by the linear part of B(t). Furthermore, this effect is reinforced depending on the value of ã, that is, the larger ã, the larger the environmental costs relative to the growth benefits. Note, however, that when ã is sufficiently large (*e.g.*, when the loss of existence, option and bequest values is conspicuous) W(t) may be negative even for small levels of development.

This is made up of the pecuniary tax take and of the external effects of the development, namely the growth benefits and the environmental costs. When ã is large enough, environmental costs exceed the monetary value of tax receipts and income multiplier effects even for small values of B(t) that correspond to an early stage of development. In this case, given that $E\,(t)<0$, the local government should not allow any development in the territory. However, in more general cases, the tax receipts may be used to improve the site's infrastructures-schools, hospitals, roads etc.-whose creation thus compensates future generations for inheriting a smaller stock of natural rescurce.

The foregoing discussion highlights the different objectives pursued by the developer and the local government, because the taxation policy creates a benefit for the latter and a cost for the former. However, without the tax, the external (*i.e.*, income multiplier and non-market environmental) effects that the tourist development engenders do not affect the developer's pay-off. Thus, the tax constitutes an instrument that induces the internalization of these external effects in the developer's decision concerning the amount of land to develop.

Furthermore, we have noted that the local government can use taxation to appropriate some of the private profits. This guarantees the participation of the local population in the sharing of the tourist development's benefits and, hence, intragenerational equity. It has also been argued that tourism developments are unable to transfer an intact stock of natural resources to future generations. It follows that the analysis of intergenerational equity, and the related issues of conservation and efficiency, should be carried out by studying how the development tax presented above should be set depending on the environmental characteristics of the territory.

Results: The following results are derived assuming that both the developer and the government choose, respectively, the size of newly developed land and the land tax in each period so as to maximize the discounted flow of profits over an infinite time horizon. The optimal tax is such that the local government's inter-temporal pay-off E(t) is maximized. The technical analysis used to derive the solution to this maximization problem is beyond the scope of this article.

To analyse how the tax affects the equilibrium value of land use, it is customary to derive the socially optimal result and use it as a benchmark against which the model's results are compared. The best outcome, from a social viewpoint, is one in which both parties mutually agree on the size of the territory that is developed in every period. Such a decision entails that all types of benefits and costs identified above are taken into account. Hence, there is no need for the tax, as both parties understand the impact of development on the environment, to the extent that no development is carried out if the environmental costs are greater than the private and public benefits. If development is undertaken, then a lump-sum transfer from the developer to the local government is sufficient to obtain intragenerational equity.

We denote such a benchmark case as the "cooperative case", to emphasize the fact that the parties behave as a single entity: this implies that all the external effects associated with the development are internalized and properly accounted for in the decision regarding the project's size. In the remainder of the paper, the equilibrium level of land use in the perfectly cooperative scenario is denoted as B (t). Such a case is equivalent to the partnerships model advocated in Middleton (1998: 128-9), where a collaborative process is established between the private and the public institutions for dealing with tourism planning and management for a destination.

However, it is very unlikely that the developer and the government have perfectly aligned objectives. While the cooperative case can be used as a benchmark, in a more realistic case the government and the developer behave non-cooperatively as two distinct entities pursuing conflicting goals. Indeed, it is reasonable to expect that the developer wants to maximize the development's private benefits without considering the social costs that it entails, while the government may be particularly concerned with its social costs and the loss of environmental values.

From a strategic viewpoint, the government can exploit its 'first-mover advantage' by imposing a development tax, in order to induce the optimal level of land use which is equivalent to that in the cooperative case. Indeed, if the developer were left free to operate without any form of public intervention, the development size would exceed that in the cooperative case, as the environmental costs would not be taken into account. However, even in the non-cooperative scenario, obtaining.the socially optimal level of land use is possible when the government behaves like a Stackelberg leader.

Another advantage of the non-cooperative scenario is that it allows analyzing the effects that different weights used by the parties to discount future benefits and costs have on the resource use. Such weights are represented by the discount factors that capture the extent to which different individuals presently value a gain or a loss that will occur in the future. Those who prefer to make a lower gain today rather than a higher gain tomorrow have a greater discount factor. The length of the planning horizon over which investments are evaluated also influences the discount factor. Traditionally, private developers are more concerned about the short-term implications of their strategies, and therefore discount the future more heavily. When evaluating the impacts of human activity on the environment, governments are, at least in theory, more likely to consider the related long-term costs.

Hence, more concern by the government for the intergenerational effects of development is represented by a lower discount rate. The results from the theoretical model reported below are obtained assuming that the developer's discount rate is greater than the government's rate. However, the results are reversed if the local government discounts the future more than the developer, a situation that is more likely to occur in a certain phase of the political cycle, namely before an election. Having defined the model's components, we now describe the qualitative features characterizing the model's solution.

First, a result common to the cooperative and the non-cooperative setting is that the largest portion of space is developed at the beginning of the development. The rationale behind such a choice is clear: it is optimal to build as much capacity as possible at the beginning of a project because an extra unit of capacity generates revenues forever. Thereby, the developer can more quickly recoup the large initial capital investment used to finance the high start-up costs associated with the development.

It would therefore seem that the two settings generate the same outcome with regard to the conservation issue. However, in the non-cooperative setting the two institutions usually value future benefits and costs differently. This has profound bearings on the development size in equilibrium. Indeed, as assumed before, if the private developer is fewer patients, then the model clearly shows that in the non-cooperative case less land will be used in total relative to the benchmark. The rationale of such a result is intuitive. A government that places a great weight on the environmental costs that future generations will incur.

It can be shown that the rate of exploitation of the natural resource occurs at a slower pace in the non-cooperative case, that is, less land is used in every period. It follows that less environmental costs are also incurred. The results that in the non-cooperative case less land is used in total and that the development occurs at a slower pace, cast some doubts on the recommendation that the private and the public sector should seek more collaborative forms of organization of the tourism activity.

While it can be argued that the same outcome could be achieved without the tax by having the government setting the limits of development, and the developer agreeing to comply with these limits, such a command-and-control arrangement presents, relative to the market instrument of taxation, at least two drawbacks.

First, it carries high bureaucratic costs for monitoring and enforcement. Second, and most importantly, it may be easier for the parties to renegotiate the terms of the initial agreement because of changes in socio-economic and/or political conditions, while changes in the tax legislation have to undergo a lengthy parliamentary scrutiny. We then conclude that a better outcome is obtained when the local government regulates the activity of the private developer by imposing a development tax, relative to a situation where a mutual agreement between the parties is created.

The model indicates how public policy adjusts according to the relative size of environmental costs and public benefits in the cost-benefit analysis. First of all, regardless of whether the environmental costs are greater than the benefits from development or not, it is always optimal for the local government to impose a positive tax on the use of the natural resource at the outset of planning. Obviously, the tax remains positive whenever the environmental costs are greater than the public benefits due to endogenous growth and income multiplier effects.

However, when the public benefits are larger than the environmental costs at any level of development, the optimal tax's time profile exhibits an interesting behaviour: at the outset of planning, the tax is positive but at some point in time it is turned into a subsidy, which corresponds to a negative tax. Traditional economic literature suggests the use of a subsidy to attract investments that determine beneficial effects for the host community (*e.g.*, jobs creation, higher local firms' birth rate etc). An important difference in the present case is that it is optimal for the policymaker to introduce the subsidy only after an appropriate time period, and not at the outset. The rationale can be found in the ability of the tax to extract some of private benefits engendered by the development which otherwise would be totally appropriated by the firm.

Finally, the analysis implicitly allows geographic areas to be taxed differently depending on the sensitiveness of the natural environment. Low environmental costs are associated with non-sensitive areas. The government therefore initially imposes a low tax for development in such areas, which may then become a subsidy if public benefits are greater than environmental negative effects.

On the other hand, when concerns for the resilience of the natural environment exist, the tax is set at such a high level that no development is economically profitable for the developer. This is tantamount to one of the four sustainable tourism approaches proposed by Hunter, that of "Neotenous Tourism", which corresponds to a "very strong sustainability approach predicated upon the belief that there are circumstances in which tourism should be actively and continuously discouraged on ecological grounds".

Furthermore, Hunter (1997: 862) argues that "In some places, including national reserves of national or international importance, tourism growth should be sacrificed for the greater good". Such a recommendation is equivalent to the case of no development due to the high tax that arises as an equilibrium outcome in the model.

To summarize, the results from the economic model of taxation show that it is possible to pursue conservation objectives without hindering the implementation of viable economic projects that impact the environment. The results crucially hinge on the assumption that the government has a concern for conservation, which in practice is identified by the government's willingness to give proper weight to environmental damages that may occur in the distant future. As argued in the Introduction, such willingness can be expressed by the creation of a legislation that has constitutional value. The following case study illustrates the crucial role that regional planning legislation plays for the establishment of a government's stance towards conservation.

An Application: The Case of Costa Smeralda in Sardinia

The previous analysis is based on the properties of a normative model that encompasses a set of economic issues. We now test its predictions by considering a case study involving a local government and a tourist developer. The evidence presented suggests that the recommendations derivable from the model's results provide a set of principles that local governments apply-or should begin to apply-in their evaluation of tourist projects.

In 1997 a multinational company, Ciga Immobiliare, prepared a development scheme for a part of Costa Smeralda on the Northeast coast of Sardinia in the Mediterranean Sea. The project was literally called Master Plan in the Sardinian and national press, and this is how it will be referred to in the remainder of this article. The following are taken from the executive summary released by the developer when the project was presented to the press. The entire project was to cover an area of 24 km^2, 85 per cent of which is located in the territory of the Arzachena municipality and the remainder 15 per cent in the Olbia municipality territory.

The total volume of the 11 hotels, 2,000 villas and 1,900 apartments included in the project was estimated to be 2,550,000 m^3 (14 per cent in hotels, 9 per cent in ancillary services and 77 per cent in residential dwellings). The planned capacity of hotels and residential dwellings was, respectively, 4,000 and 16,000 beds. The cost of the total investment was calculated to be US$1.45 billion and the related increase in local income to be $2.375 billion, with an investment multiplier of 1.72. Although the project was to cover a time span of 25 years, most construction would be completed within the first 5-10 years. The yearly demand, measured in bednights, was evaluated at 504,000 units in hotels and 960,000 units in residential dwellings, the total being almost three times higher than the average of 560,000 units recorded during the 1990's in the already existing hotels owned by the developer in Costa Smeralda. The expenditure by tourists in hotel accommodation and dwellings was expected to total, respectively, $151 and $240 millions and generate an increase in local production of around $500 millions. Finally, the developer's study estimated the overall increment in employment in Sardinia to be 12,200 jobs: 4,800 new jobs in hotels and restaurants, 2,000 in trade and retailing, 4,200 in the services and 1,200 in manufacturing.

Given these figures, the project should certainly have appeared enticing to a local government operating in a region characterized by an extremely high unemployment rate and a much lower per capita income than the Italian average. How was it, then, that the parties did not find a satisfactory agreement and eventually the developer withdrew the project? An answer can be found by analyzing the political stance of the Sardinian government with respect to the magnitude of the social and environmental costs associated with the project.

The Sardinian government had made it clear that the "safeguard of the environmental quality is a factor for economic development". Moreover, as far as the Master Plan was concerned, the position of the Sardinian government was that "a better balance between the use of the territory, the socio-economic effects and the developer's profit has to be found".

The Sardinian government seemed inclined to grant the building permission, subject to a few changes in the project, including:

- A significant reduction in the number of residential dwellings, and possibly an increase in the number of hotels;

- Priority to the building of hotels and tourism facilities; and
- Respect for the norm that prohibits the construction of any building within 300 metres of the coastline.

Finally, the local government expressed concern about the number of "scattered dwellings" presumably villas-which "consume land and make access to the sea more difficult". The Sardinian government's preference for hotels, as expressed by requirement (b) and the request to increase the number of hotels can be found in the regional government's belief that hotels and related facilities would extend the tourist season well beyond the peak months of July and August. The Sardinian government's remark that villas and apartment use more land than hotels is consistent with the theoretical approach and indicate the government's awareness of the environmental costs associated with the development.

The first part of requirement (a) is directly linked to the theoretical analysis. The number of dwellings increased sharply thereby suggesting that intensive building activity took place during the decade in the municipalities of Olbia and Arzachena. A similar phenomenon occurred also in the remaining part of the North Sardinian Province, which includes many other seaside resorts. A first consideration is the obvious positive correlation between the change in the number of resident population and the increase in the number of occupied dwellings. However, more relevant to the present analysis is the drastic increase in the number of holiday dwellings, whose number more than doubled in Arzachena and almost doubled in Olbia.

Row (5) reports the ratio of holiday dwellings over occupied dwellings. It shows that, relative to the rest of the province, the two municipalities are characterized to a great extent by the so-called "second homes" phenomenon (*i.e.*, holiday houses which are left unoccupied for most of the year). In terms of the theoretical analysis, the extensive use of land associated with this type of accommodation entails high environmental costs, deriving for example, from loss of flora and fauna, beach erosion, and degradation of water quality.

Other environmental problems relate to the fact that second homes are used mainly during the period of peak demand. Moreover, self-catering accommodations, such as second homes, do not generate as high multiplier effects as hotels. The Master Plan might have exacerbated the overcrowding and congestion.

Indeed, the dwelling density for the Master Plan–3900/ 24=162.5 dwellings per Km^2 (3900 is the sum of 2000 villas plus 1900 apartments, 24 Km^2 is the size of the territory)—is well above the averages of the territories concerned. This is indicative of how intensively some parts of the space would have been used by the developer. As many of the Master Plan's buildings would have occupied areas characterized by high environmental sensitivity, it can be inferred that the social costs deriving from the loss of the "hidden environmental values" would have been conspicuous.

The variables are the volumes built for residential and non-residential purposes, the number of new residential dwellings and the related number of rooms. Volumes are used in the following analysis for various reasons. First, in Italy planning regulations dictate the maximum allowable volume of a building erected in a territory of given size. Statistics are collected accordingly. Second, volume is a good indicator of building activity because territorial planning imposes restrictions on the total height of buildings. Therefore, volumes are highly correlated with the size of the territory occupied by buildings.

First, notice that the volume of residential buildings completed over the period in the two municipalities is less than the amount planned by the Master Plan's developer (row

The comparison and the size is made even more striking by the consideration that only 15 per cent of the project was planned in the Olbia municipality. This implies that 85 per cent of the residential volumes intended in the Master Plan (totaling 1668975 m^3) would have been built in the Arzachena's territory. This exceeds the total volumes built there for residential and non-residential purposes over the period 1982-1996.

Second, an inspection of rows (4) and (5) reveals that the number of residential dwellings and rooms intended in the Master Plan is greater than the number of residential dwellings and rooms actually built in each single municipality over the period 1982-1996. Hence, had the project been allowed to progress as originally planned, many future development options in the area would have been foreclosed, thereby engendering further social costs in territories where building activity for tourism has been particularly intensive over the last two decades.

The rationale for condition (c) (*i.e.*, respect for the norm that prohibits construction with 300 meters of the coastline) lends support to the choice in the theoretical model of considering the local government as endowed with a first-mover advantage enabling them to pursue long-term conservationist policies. By stating in the law that no building permit would be granted within 300 meters from the coastline, the Sardinian government had declared its commitment towards the safeguarding of the coastal environmental quality. The exception granted to the Master Plan's developer could easily have become the rule, and led to greater environmental costs from over-exploitation. When it became clear that the project had to be changed substantially in its residential component and that condition (c) was not negotiable, the developer decided not to exercise the option to buy the territories from the current owner (the American multinational Starwood) and abandoned the project.

To summarize, the analysis of the case study highlighted the following points that are consistent with the theoretical predictions from the model discussed in the previous section. Firstly, the concern of a local government for the preservation of environmental quality may lead to no development. Secondly, the local government's behaviour emphasizes the importance of maintaining existing legislation aimed at conservation, thereby giving it the status of constitutional dictate. Finally, and more generally, the study also shows how the variables considered in the theoretical analysis are normally taken into account in the blueprint of any investment project in the tourism industry. This study argues that a limitation of the strong sustainability approach is the lack of emphasis given to efficiency considerations. It suggests the application of the two-tier approach outlined in Page (1997) as a conceptual framework to tackle the issues of intergenerational equity and economic efficiency simultaneously. Such a two-tier method conceives the importance of the natural resource, the identification of the appropriate instruments and the legislative framework as crucial elements. To provide further support to Page's recommendations for the case of tourism, this study has presented a theoretical economic model of taxation and a case study involving a local government and a private developer.

When economic efficiency considerations are paramount, the theoretical model suggests the use of a land tax at the beginning of the development followed by the possible introduction of a subsidy at a later stage. The tax guarantees that local communities can extract some of the rents created by the development that otherwise would entirely accrue to the developer. At the other extreme, when the development endangers the existence of an essential resource or ecosystem, the theoretical model suggests the prevention of any form of development. In intermediate cases, the tax on land use combines efficiency and conservation goals, as the tax curtails, but does not prevent, the development. This situation is represented in the case study where emphasis is given to the crucial role of territorial planning legislation for the reduction of negative impacts of tourism development.

Indeed, in the two municipalities of Arzachena and Olbia the number of holiday homes has grown dramatically over the last two decades, thus suggesting the economic viability of such developments. At the same time, the norm prohibiting constructions within 300 meters of the coastline has prevented the irreversible damage that building on the coast entails, and has forced developers to locate their sites in less sensitive areas. The fact that the Sardinian government chose not to create a precedent by allowing special treatment for the Master Plan's developer, suggests that the norm regulates issues that deserve to be treated within a constitutional framework, in line with Page's recommendations. Unfortunately, the norm above does not have a legal constitutional status, and could therefore be changed using the process applicable to any ordinary law. This is indeed the intention of the new Sardinian government elected in the year 2000, that is, to modify legislation on territorial planning to accommodate the possibility of buildings near the coastline.

Both the model of taxation and the Sardinian case study provide support for the argument in Middleton (1998) that governments do not need to introduce new policy instruments but rather, they should gear the existing ones towards the achievement of sustainable objectives.

Thus territorial planning, building regulation, provision of.infrastructure, fiscal incentives and disincentives, ecological labeling assessment and management of carrying capacity information and education of tourists can all be used effectively and play a central role in a public strategy for sustainable tourism.

However, the view advocated by Middleton (1998) that the public and the private sector should seek more integrated forms of organization in the management of tourism does not necessarily follow. The theoretical analysis of taxation clearly indicates that the best outcome, both in terms of conservation and overall efficiency, is obtained when the public sector takes advantage of its ability to set the rules of the game.

The "Master Plan" example shows that negotiations with the private sector may turn out to be unbeneficial in the long run, especially if the private developer requests special exemptions from the existing legislation, which is aimed at limiting the environmental impact of development. Whenever the government and the private developer have conflicting views regarding the development of an environmentally sensitive area, the analysis of the theoretical model, and the support it has received from the case study, suggest that the government should exploit its first-mover advantage, which is incompatible with Middleton's bargaining approach. As a corollary to the analysis, we may conclude that private-public partnership may be Favoured whenever intergenerational equity issues are not a crucial concern.

CITIES AND TOURISM

CITIES TO ABSORB GROWTH IN WORLD TOURISM

International tourist arrivals in 1995 were 563 million and are expected to reach 1.6 billion by the year 2020. These forecasts use a conservative growth rate of 4.3 per cent and 6.7 per cent respectively; less than the current growth rate. They do not include any domestic tourism which can readily be anticipated to equal the international. It is obvious that most of this increase will have to be absorbed by cities.

—*World Tourism Organisation*

The most recent trends and forecasting studies by the World Tourism Organisation indicate that cities will continue to be in high demand by tourists of all sorts, and the problems associated with the handling of these tourists will have to be more systematically tackled by all parties concerned.

Cities face, therefore, a double challenge. Firstly, they have to be able to respond to the expectations and needs of the growing numbers of tourists who are attracted to their rich and varied array of cultural, business, entertainment, shopping, sports and other attractions; furthermore, they need to continuously renovate and improve such facilities in order to maintain their share in the competitive tourism market and the benefits resulting from it.

Secondly, cities have to ensure that tourism is developed and managed in such a way that it benefits the resident population, does not contribute to the deterioration of the urban environment but rather to its enhancement, and does not become a financial burden to the local authority.

Some of the key stakeholders in urban tourism include: Private Sector *i.e.* airlines, hotel chain operators and owners, tour operators, credit card companies, tourist attraction operators (theme parks, events etc.), real estate agencies;

- Public Sector *i.e.* city managers (from the historic city to the seaside resort), transportation planners, bus and train operators, information departments, economic development agencies, national parks, national tourist organisations;

- Touristic Institutions *i.e.* museums, art galleries, historic facilities (*e.g.* the national trust) and educational organisations.

There are three key dimensions of tourism in cities and urban areas:

- *Products*: The anticipated changes necessary from tourist attraction providers; theme parks, operators of events (sports, shows, fairs), museums and hotels. What are their plans, how do they respond to the anticipated growth?
- *Information*: How does a city make itself more tourist friendly? What are the information systems available to tourists? How do tour operators deal with this growing demand? How to accumulate information on customer preferences and requirement, seasonal changes, age groups etc.? How to develop enduring attractions which will provide sustainable development? What information does the city provide in order to attract tourist attraction providers?
- *Impacts*: Economic and development opportunities as well as the impact of tourism growth on sustainable development, transportation, cultural and environmental, social and economic aspects.

9

Human Resource Management in Tourism

Most of the tourism activity also involves economic costs, including the direct costs incurred by tourism businesses, government costs for infrastructure to better serve tourists, as well as congestion and related costs borne by individuals in the community. Community decisions over tourism often involve debates between industry proponents touting tourism's economic impacts (benefits) and detractors emphasizing tourism's costs.

Sound decisions rest on a balanced and objective assessment of both benefits and costs and an understanding of who benefits from tourism and who pays for it. Businesses and public organizations are increasingly interested in the economic impacts of tourism at national, state, and local levels. One regularly hears claims that tourism supports X jobs in an area or that a festival or special event generated Y million dollars in sales or income in a community. "Multiplier effects" are often cited to capture secondary effects of tourism spending and show the wide range of sectors in a community that may benefit from tourism. Tourism's economic benefits are touted by the industry for a variety of reasons. Claims of tourism's economic significance give the industry greater respect among the business community, public officials, and the public in general. This often translates into decisions or public policies that are favourable to tourism.

Community support is important for tourism, as it is an activity that affects the entire community. Tourism businesses depend extensively on each other as well as on other businesses, government and residents of the local community. Economic benefits and costs of tourism reach virtually everyone in the region in one way or another. Economic impact analyses provide tangible estimates of these economic interdependencies and a better understanding of the role and importance of tourism in a region's economy.

Tourism's economic impacts are therefore an important consideration in state, regional and community planning and economic development. Economic impacts are also important factors in marketing and management decisions. Communities therefore need to understand the relative importance of tourism to their region, including tourism's contribution to economic activity in the area.

A variety of methods, ranging from pure guesswork to complex mathematical models, are used to estimate tourism's economic impacts. Studies vary extensively in quality and accuracy, as well as which aspects of tourism are included. Technical reports often are filled with economic terms and methods that non-economists do not understand. On the other hand, media coverage of these studies tend to oversimplify and frequently misinterpret the results, leaving decision makers and the general public with a sometimes distorted and incomplete understanding of tourism's economic effects.

How can the average person understand these studies sufficiently to separate good studies from bad ones and make informed choices? The purpose of this bulletin is to present a systematic introduction to economic impact concepts and methods. The presentation is written for tourism industry analysts and public officials, who would like to better understand, evaluate, or possibly conduct an economic impact assessment. The bulletin is organized around ten basic questions that either are asked or should be asked about the economic impacts of tourism.

ECONOMIC IMPACT ANALYSIS

A variety of economic analyses are carried out to support tourism decisions. As these different kinds of economic analysis are frequently confused, let's begin by positioning economic impact studies within the broader set of economic problems and techniques relevant to tourism. These same techniques may be applied to any policy or action, but we will define them here in the context of tourism. Each type of analysis is identified by the basic question(s) it answers and the types of methods and models that are appropriate. Benefit cost analysis and economic impact analysis are frequently confused as both discuss economic "benefits".

There are two clear distinctions between the two techniques. B/C analysis addresses the benefits from economic efficiency while economic impact analysis focuses on the regional distribution of economic activity. The income received from tourism by a destination region is largely off-set by corresponding losses in the origin regions, yielding only modest contributions to net social welfare and efficiency. B/C analysis includes market and non-market values (consumer surplus), while economic impact analysis is restricted to actual flows of money from market transactions.

While each type of economic analysis is somewhat distinct, a given problem often calls for several different kinds of economic analysis. An economic impact study will frequently involve a demand analysis to project levels of tourism activity. In other cases demand is treated as exogenous and the analysis simply estimates impacts if a given number of visitors are attracted to the area. A comprehensive impact assessment will also examine fiscal impacts, as well as social and environmental impacts. Be aware that an economic impact analysis, by itself, provides a rather narrow and often one-sided perspective on the impacts of tourism.

Studies of the economic impacts of tourism tend to emphasize the positive benefits of tourism. On the other hand environmental, social, cultural and fiscal impact studies tend to focus more on negative impacts of tourism. This is in spite of the fact that there are negative economic impacts of tourism (*e.g.*, seasonality and lower wage jobs) and in many cases positive environmental and social impacts (*e.g.*, protection of natural and cultural resources in the area and education of both tourists and local residents). An economic impact assessment (EIA) traces changes in economic activity resulting from some action.

An EIA will identify which economic sectors benefit from tourism and estimate resulting changes in income and employment in the region. Economic impact assessment procedures do not assess economic efficiency and also do not generally produce estimates of the fiscal costs of an action. For many problems economic impact analysis will be part of a broader analysis. Environmental, social, and fiscal impacts are often equally important concerns in a balanced assessment of impacts. An economic impact analysis will assess the contribution of tourism activity to a region's economy.

The basic questions an economic impact study usually addresses are:

- How many jobs in the area does tourism support?
- How much tax revenue is generated from tourism?
- How much do tourists spend in the area?
- What portion of sales by local businesses is due to tourism?
- How much income does tourism generate for households and businesses in the area?

An economic impact analysis also reveals the interrelationships among economic sectors and provides estimates of the changes that take place in an economy due to some existing or proposed action.

The most common applications of economic impact analysis to tourism are:

1. To evaluate the economic impacts of changes in the supply of recreation and tourism opportunities. Supply changes may involve a change in quantity, such as the opening of new facilities, closing of existing ones, or expansions and contraction in capacity. Supply changes may also involve changes in quality, including changes in,
   - The quality of the environment,
   - The local infrastructure and public services to support tourism, or

- The nature of the tourism products and services that are provided in an area.

2. To evaluate the economic impacts of changes in tourism demand. Population changes, changes in the competitive position of the region, marketing activity or changing consumer tastes and preferences can alter levels of tourism activity, spending, and associated economic activity. An economic impact study can estimate the magnitude and nature of these impacts.
3. To evaluate the effects of policies and actions which affect tourism activity either directly or indirectly. Tourism depends on many factors at both origins and destinations that are frequently outside the direct control of the tourism industry itself. Economic impact studies provide information to help decision makers better understand the consequences of various actions on the tourism industry as well as on other sectors of the economy. For example, increased air pollution standards have been opposed in some regions due to the predicted economic consequences of the closing of plants that cannot meet the new standards. Tourism interests counter these arguments with estimates of the potential gains in income and jobs in tourism industries that depend on good air quality and visibility.
4. To understand the economic structure and interdependencies of different sectors of the economy. Economic studies help us better understand the size and structure of the tourism industry in a given region and its linkages to other sectors of the economy. Such understandings are helpful in identifying potential partners for the tourism industry as well as in targeting industries as part of regional economic development strategies. Issues such as economic growth, stability, and seasonality may be addressed as part of these studies.
5. To argue for favourable treatment in allocation of resources or local tax, zoning or other policy

decisions. By showing that tourism has significant economic impacts, tourism interests can often convince decision-makers to allocate more resources for tourism or to establish policies that encourage tourism. Tax abatements and other incentives frequently given to manufacturing firms have also been granted to hotels, marinas and other tourism businesses based on demonstrated economic impacts in the local area.

6. To compare the economic impacts of alternative resource allocation, policy, management or development proposals. Economic impact analyses are commonly used to assess the relative merits of distinct alternatives. The economic contribution of expanded tourism offerings may be compared for example with alternatives such as resource extraction activities (mining, timber harvesting) or manufacturing. Impacts of alternative tourism development proposals may also be evaluated, *e.g.*, tourism strategies that emphasize outdoor recreation, camping development, a convention facility, or a factory outlet mall.

Tourism has a variety of economic impacts. Tourists contribute to sales, profits, jobs, tax revenues, and income in an area. The most direct effects occur within the primary tourism sectors—lodging, restaurants, transportation, amusements, and retail trade. Through secondary effects, tourism affects most sectors of the economy. An economic impact analysis of tourism activity normally focuses on changes in sales, income, and employment in a region resulting from tourism activity.

A simple tourism impact scenario illustrates. Let's say a region attracts an additional 100 tourists, each spending $100 per day. That's $10,000 in new spending per day in the area. If sustained over a 100 day season, the region would accumulate a million dollars in new sales. The million dollars in spending would be distributed to lodging, restaurant, amusement and retail trade sectors in proportion to how the visitor spends the $100. Perhaps 30% of the million dollars would leak out of the region immediately to cover the costs of goods purchased by tourists that are not made in the local area (only the retail margins for such items should normally be included as direct sales effects). The remaining $700,000 in direct sales might yield $350,000 in income within tourism industries and support 20 direct tourism jobs. Tourism industries are labour and income intensive, translating a high proportion of sales into income and corresponding jobs.

The tourism industry, in turn, buys goods and services from other businesses in the area, and pays out most of the $350,000 in income as wages and salaries to its employees. This creates secondary economic effects in the region. The study might use a sales multiplier of 2.0 to indicate that each dollar of direct sales generates another dollar in secondary sales in this region. Through multiplier effects, the $700,000 in direct sales produces $1.4 million in total sales. These secondary sales create additional income and employment, resulting in a total impact on the region of $1.4 million in sales, $650,000 in income and 35 jobs.

While hypothetical, the numbers used here are fairly typical of what one might find in a tourism economic impact study. A more complete study might identify which sectors receive the direct and secondary effects and possibly identify differences in spending and impacts of distinct subgroups of tourists (market segments). One can also estimate the tax effects of this spending by applying local tax rates to the appropriate changes in sales or income. Instead of focusing on visitor spending, one could also estimate impacts of construction or government activity associated with tourism. There are several other categories of economic impacts that are not typically covered in economic impact assessments, at least not directly.

For example:

- *Changes in prices*: Tourism can sometimes inflate the cost of housing and retail prices in the area, frequently on a seasonal basis.
- *Changes in the quality and quantity of goods and services*:

Tourism may lead to a wider array of goods and services available in an area (of either higher or lower quality than without tourism).

- *Changes in property and other taxes*: Taxes to cover the cost of local services may be higher or lower in the presence of tourism activity. In some cases, taxes collected directly or indirectly from tourists may yield reduced local taxes for schools, roads, etc. In other cases, locals may be taxed more heavily to cover the added infrastructure and service costs. The impacts of tourism on local government costs and revenues are addressed more fully in a fiscal impact analysis.
- *Economic dimensions of "social" and "environmental" impacts*: There are also economic consequences of most social and environmental impacts that are not usually addressed in an economic impact analysis. These can be positive or negative. For example, traffic congestion will increase costs of moving around for both households and businesses. Improved amenities that attract tourists may also encourage retirees or other kinds of businesses to locate in the area.

INDUCED EFFECTS

A standard economic impact analysis traces flows of money from tourism spending, first to businesses and government agencies where tourists spend their money and then to:

- *Other businesses*: Supplying goods and services to tourist businesses,
- *Households*: Earning income by working in tourism or supporting industries, and
- *Government*: Through various taxes and charges on tourists, businesses and households

Formally, regional economists distinguish direct, indirect, and induced economic effects. Indirect and induced effects are sometimes collectively called secondary effects. The total economic impact of tourism is the sum of direct, indirect, and induced effects within a region. Any of these impacts may be measured as gross output or sales, income, employment, or value added. Direct effects are production changes associated with the immediate effects of changes in tourism expenditures.

For example, an increase in the number of tourists staying overnight in hotels would directly yield increased sales in the hotel sector. The additional hotel sales and associated changes in hotel payments for wages and salaries, taxes, and supplies and services are direct effects of the tourist spending.

Indirect effects are the production changes resulting from various rounds of re-spending of the hotel industry's receipts in other backward-linked industries (*i.e.*, industries supplying products and services to hotels). Changes in sales, jobs, and income in the linen supply industry, for example, represent indirect effects of changes in hotel sales. Businesses supplying products and services to the linen supply industry represent another round of indirect effects, eventually linking hotels to varying degrees to many other economic sectors in the region. Induced effects are the changes in economic activity resulting from household spending of income earned directly or indirectly as a result of tourism spending. For example, hotel and linen supply employees supported directly or indirectly by tourism, spend their income in the local region for housing, food, transportation, and the usual array of household product and service needs. The sales, income, and jobs that result from household spending of added wage, salary, or proprietor's income are induced effects.

By means of indirect and induced effects, changes in tourist spending can impact virtually every sector of the economy in one way or another. The magnitude of secondary effects depends on the propensity of businesses and households in the region to purchase goods and services from local suppliers. Induced effects are particularly noticed when a large employer in a region closes a plant. Not only are supporting industries (indirect effects) hurt, but the entire local economy suffers due to the reduction in household income within the region. Retail stores close and leakages of money from the region increase as consumers go outside the region for more and more goods and services. Similar effects in the opposite direction are observed when there is a significant increase in jobs and household income. Final demand is the term used by economists for sales to the final consumers of goods and services. In almost all cases, the final consumers of tourism goods and services are households. Government spending is also considered as final demand. The same methods for estimating impacts of visitor spending can be applied to estimate the economic impacts of government spending, for example, to operate and maintain a park or visitor centre.

REGIONAL MODELS

An input-output model (I-O model) is a mathematical model that describes the flows of money between sectors within a region's economy. Flows are predicted by knowing what each industry must buy from every other industry to produce a dollar's worth of output. Using each industry's production function, I-O models also determine the proportions of sales that go to wage and salary income, proprietor's income, and taxes. Multipliers can be estimated from input-output models based on the estimated re-circulation of spending within the region. Exports and imports are determined based upon estimates of the propensity of households and firms within the region to purchase goods and services from local sources (often called RPC's or regional purchase coefficients). The more a region is self-sufficient and purchases goods and services from within the region, the higher the multipliers for the region. Input-output models make a number of assumptions.

The basic ones are that:

- All firms in a given industry employ the same production technology (usually assumed to be the national average for that industry), and produce identical products.
- There are no economies or diseconomies of scale in production or factor substitution. I-O models are essentially linear—double the level of tourism

activity/production and you double all of the inputs, the number of jobs, etc.

- The model doesn't explicitly keep track of time, but analysts generally report the impact estimates as if they represent activity within a single year.
- One must assume that the various model parameters are accurate and represent the current year.

I-O models are firmly grounded in the national system of accounts, which relies on a standard industrial classification system (SIC codes) and various federal government economic censuses, in which individual firms report sales, wage and salary payments and employment. I-O models will generally be at least a few years out-of-date, although this isn't usually a major problem unless the region's economy has changed significantly. An I-O model represents the region's economy at a particular point in time. Tourist spending estimates are generally price adjusted to the year of the model.

Multiplier computations for induced effects generally assume that jobs created by additional spending are new jobs, involving new households in the area. Induced effects are computed assuming linear changes in household spending with changes in income. Estimates of induced effects may be inflated due to the violation of these assumptions. Induced effects tend to account for the vast majority of the secondary effects of tourism, and therefore should be used with caution.

MULTIPLIERS EFFECTS OF TOURISM

Multipliers capture the secondary economic effects (indirect and induced) of tourism activity. Multipliers have been frequently misused and misinterpreted in tourism studies and are a considerable source of confusion among non-economists. Multipliers represent the economic interdependencies between sectors within a particular region's economy. They vary considerably from region to region and sector to sector. There are many different kinds of multipliers reflecting which secondary effects are included and which measure of economic activity is used (sales, income, or employment).

For example,

- The Type I sales multiplier = direct sales + indirect sales direct sales.
- The Type II or III sales multiplier[1] = direct sales + indirect sales + induced sales direct sales.

Multiplying a Type I sales multiplier times the direct sales gives direct plus indirect sales. Multiplying a Type II or III sales multiplier times the direct sales gives total sales impacts including direct, indirect and induced effects. The multipliers defined above are called ratio type multipliers as they measure the ratio of a total impact measure to the corresponding direct impact. Comparable income and employment ratio type multipliers may be defined by replacing sales with measures of income or employment in the above equations. Ratio multipliers should be used with caution.

A common error is to multiply a sales multiplier times tourist spending to get total sales effects. This will generate an inflated estimate of tourism impacts. The problem is that tourism spending or sales is not exactly the same as the "direct effects", appearing in the multiplier formula. Tourist purchases of goods (vs. services) are the primary source of the problem. To properly apply tourist purchases of goods to an input-output model (or corresponding multipliers), various margins (retail, wholesale and transportation) must be deducted from the "purchaser price" of the good to separate out the "producer price".

In an I-O model, retail margins accrue to the retail trade sector, wholesale margins to wholesale trade, transportation margins to transportation sectors (trucking, rail, air etc.) and the producer prices of goods are assigned to the sector that produces the good. In most cases the factory that produces the good bought by a tourist lies outside of the local region, creating an immediate "leakage" in the first round of spending and therefore no local impact from production of the good. Before applying a multiplier to tourist spending, one must first deduct the producer prices of all imported goods that tourists buy (*i.e.* only include the local retail margins and possibly wholesale and transportation margins if these firms lie within the region). Generally, only 60 to 70% of tourist spending appears as final demand in a local region. While all tourist purchases of services will accrue to the local region as final demand, only the margins on goods purchased at retail stores should be counted as local final demand. The ratio of local final demand to tourist spending is called the capture rate.

Capture rate = local final demand/tourism spending in local area. Capture rates, like multipliers, will vary with the size and nature of the region as well as the kind of tourist spending included. One must therefore be cautious in taking a multiplier or capture rate cited in one study and using it in another. Another way of calculating a multiplier (generally the preferred approach among economists) is as a ratio of income or employment to sales. This kind of multiplier is sometimes called a Keynesian multiplier or response coefficient.

- Type III Income multiplier = Total direct, indirect, and induced income direct sales
- Type III Employment multiplier = Total direct, indirect, and induced employment direct sales

This income (employment) multiplier produces total income (employment) impacts when multiplied by the direct sales. One must still be careful in distinguishing between tourism spending/sales and direct sales effects. Some studies may embed the capture rate in the multiplier, expressing the ratio in terms of tourism spending rather than direct sales.

The economic impacts of tourism are typically estimated by some variation of the following simple formula:

Economic Impact of Tourism = Number of Tourists × Average Spending per Visitor × Multiplier

The formula suggests three distinct steps and corresponding measurements or models:

1. Estimate the change in the number and types of tourists to the region due to the proposed policy or action. Estimates or projections of tourist activity generally come from a demand model or some system for measuring levels of tourism activity in an area. Economic impact estimates will rest heavily on good estimates of the numbers and types of visitors.

These must come from carefully designed measurements of tourist activity, a good demand model, or good judgement. This step is usually the weakest link in most tourism impact studies, as few regions have accurate counts of tourists, let alone good models for predicting changes in tourism activity or separating local visitors from visitors from outside the region.

2. Estimate average levels of spending (often within specific market segments) of tourists in the local area. Spending averages come from sample surveys or are sometimes borrowed or adapted from other studies. Spending estimates must be based on a representative sample of the population of tourists taking into account variations across seasons, types of tourists, and locations within the study area. As spending can vary widely across different kinds of tourists, we recommend estimating average spending for a set of key tourist segments based on samples of at least 50-100 visitors within each tourism segment. Segments should be defined to capture differences in spending between local residents vs. tourists, day users vs. overnight visitors, type of accommodation (motel, campground, seasonal home, with friends and relatives), and type of transportation (car, RV, air, rail, etc.). In broadly based tourism impact studies, it is useful to identify unique spending patterns of important activity segments such as downhill skiers, boaters, and convention and business travellers. Multiplying the number of tourists by the average spending per visitor (be careful the units are consistent) gives an estimate of total tourist spending in the area. Estimates of tourist spending will generally be more accurate if distinct spending profiles and use estimates are made for key tourism segments. The use and spending estimates are the two most important parts of an economic impact assessment. When combined, they capture the

amount of money brought into the region by tourists. Multipliers are needed only if one is interested in the secondary effects of tourism spending.

3. Apply the change in spending to a regional economic model or set of multipliers to determine secondary effects. Secondary effects of tourism are estimated using multipliers or a model of the region's economy. Multipliers generally come from an economic base or input-output model of the region's economy. In many cases multipliers are borrowed (often improperly) or adjusted from published multipliers or other studies. One should not take a multiplier estimated for one region and apply it in a region with a quite different economic structure. Generally, multipliers are higher for larger regions with more diversified economies and lower for smaller regions with more limited economic development. A common error is to apply a statewide multiplier (since these are more widely published) to a local region. This will yield inflated estimates of local multiplier effects. Multipliers can also be used to convert estimates of spending or sales to income and employment. Simple ratios can be used to capture how much income or jobs are generated per dollar of sales. These ratios will vary from region to region and across individual economic sectors due to the relative importance of labour inputs in each industry and different wage and salary rates in different regions of the country. Be aware that job estimates are generally not full time equivalents, making them difficult to compare across industries with different proportions of seasonal and part time jobs. Income or value added are generally the preferred measures of the contribution of tourism to a region's economy.

THE TYPICAL APPROACHES FOR AN ECONOMIC ASSESSMENT

At the simple, "quick and dirty" end of the spectrum are

highly aggregate approaches that rely mostly on judgement to determine tourism activity, spending and multipliers. Such estimates can be completed in a couple hours at little cost and rest largely on the expertise and judgement of the analyst. At the other extreme are studies that gather primary data from visitor spending studies and apply the spending estimates to formal regional economic models for the area in question. In between are a wide range of options that employ varying degrees of judgement, secondary data, primary data, and formal models.

Different levels of detail and corresponding expense (time and money) and accuracy are possible for each of the three steps—estimating tourist volume, spending, and multiplier effects. Four typical approaches illustrate the levels of detail that are possible and the associated methods to sales estimates. With sound judgement in choosing the parameters, the MGM model can yield reasonable ballpark estimates of economic impacts at minimal cost. This approach, however, provides little detail on spending categories or which sectors of the economy benefit from either direct or secondary effects. The aggregate nature of the approach also makes it difficult to adjust recommended spending rates or multipliers to different applications. The Bureau of Economic Analysis's (BEA) RIMS II user handbook illustrates how to apply published multipliers to estimate economic impacts. This approach starts with visitor spending (from survey or secondary sources) divided into a number of spending categories and makes use of sector specific multipliers to estimate the direct and total sales, income and employment effects. Multipliers from the BEA's RIMS II models are used to estimate secondary effects. Multipliers are reported for 39 sectors for each state in the second edition of their report.

This method uses margins to properly account for retail purchases of goods and makes use of disaggregate sector-specific multipliers for each state. Multipliers for sub-state regions are not as readily available, but can be acquired from BEA or other sources. Secondary effects cannot be disaggregated to individual sectors using the BEA approach.

The MI-REC/IMPLAN System: Stynes and Propst have developed a fairly complete micro-computer-based system for estimating economic impacts of recreation and tourism. The system combines spreadsheets for estimating spending with the IMPLAN input-output modeling system. IMPLAN uses county level data to estimate 528 sector input-output models for regions down to account level. IMPLAN generates a complete set of economic accounts for the region including multipliers and trade flows. MI-REC spreadsheets estimate visitor spending within up to 33categories based on the number and types of visitors attracted to an area. Spending is then bridged to the IMPLAN model sectors to estimate direct, indirect and induced effects in terms of sales, income and employment. Users may estimate spending via visitor surveys or use the MI-REC database of spending profiles, compiled from previous studies. The system also includes price indices to easily update spending data to a current year.

Two other systems for estimating economic impacts of tourism should be noted. The TEIM or Travel Economic Impact Model developed by the U.S. Travel Data Centre has been widely used to estimate tourism and travel impacts at state and national levels. A more recent development is the satellite accounting approach developed by the World Travel and Tourism Council.

Both of these systems are primarily designed for estimating the overall economic significance of tourism at national or state levels. They are not readily applied to estimate the impacts of particular policies and actions at the local level.

The TEIM relies on national travel surveys to estimate trip volume and spending on a state-by-state basis. Local estimates of impacts are obtained using simple allocation formulas to distribute statewide impacts to counties and cities within the state. These local estimates do not account very well for the distinct types of tourism activity or spending patterns in different sub-regions of a state. The WTTC effort also focuses on national and statewide accounting of tourism's economic significance. Their satellite tourism account identifies the contribution of travel and tourism to gross national product

(GNP) or gross state product (GSP). Using the standard national system of accounts, they identify the portion of sales, taxes and investment attributable directly to travel and tourism. The WTTC system does not use multipliers or attempt to estimate secondary effects. It does, however, capture a great deal of travel-related economic activity, not covered by visitor trip spending, such as durable goods purchases (boats and RV's), construction and investment in tourism, and government expenditures.

An economic impact study involves four basic:

1. Define the problem
2. Estimate the change in final demand (tourism spending).
3. Estimate the regional economic effects of this change
4. Interpret, apply, and communicate the results

The most important part of any study is the first step—clarifying the nature of the problem being addressed and intended uses of the results. Before launching an economic impact study, be sure this is the kind of study that is needed rather than one or more of the other kinds of economic analyses. Stynes and Propst (1996) identify seven factors that should be specified as part of defining a problem for an economic impact assessment:

- Define the action to be evaluated. Begin by clarifying the action or actions involved in the problem. Actions may include construction, government investment, changes in marketing, management, or policies, or changes in the quality or quantity of tourist facilities. If evaluating impacts of existing tourism activity, be sure to define what is to be included as "tourism".
- Identify the change in the amount and kinds of recreation/tourism activity resulting from the action. The action must be defined precisely enough in step one to be able to estimate the changes in the number and types of visitors to the area and/or their spending patterns. As a general rule, the analysis should be with vs. without the action rather than simply before vs. after. Thus, if tourism has been growing by 5%

per year and a new promotional programme increases this to 10% this year, only half of the 10% growth can likely be attributed to the promotional programme. Identifying the net changes in activity that are attributable to an action can be a complex and difficult task. Assessments of economic impact, however, rest firmly on such estimates, so attention to these details is very important. In situations of some uncertainty, we recommend evaluating impacts using a range of estimates in order to establish rough confidence intervals around your estimates. Evaluating a range of alternatives also helps to evaluate the sensitivity of the results to your initial estimates of changes in activity levels.

- Identify the kinds of spending to be included. Tourism may impact the local economy through visitor trip spending, durable goods purchases, government spending, or investment and construction. Which to include in a given analysis depends on how the problem is defined, and again, on attributing given spending changes to the proposed action.
- Identify the study region. Perhaps the most important, yet often neglected part of a recreation and tourism impact assessment is the definition of a study region. The region defines the area for which impacts are desired, as well as the portions of visitor spending that are relevant. An impact assessment evaluates the impacts on households, businesses, and organizations within the given region. Spending that visitors make outside of a study region either at home or en route are not included in assessing impacts of spending on the designated region. For an economic impact analysis, the study region should be large enough to constitute a viable economic region. Since little economic data exists below the county level, the county is generally the smallest region one should consider for a tourism impact assessment.

- Identify key economic sectors and desired sectoral detail. The proposed action and anticipated uses/ users of the results should suggest the key sectors that will be impacted. Recreation and tourism activity typically impact the lodging, restaurant, amusements, retail, transportation and government sectors most directly. In the problem definition stage consideration of impacted sectors helps to identify relevant categories of spending. The desired sectoral detail plays an important role in structuring the presentation of results. In some cases only an aggregate measure of impacts may be desired. In other cases, clients may be interested in which particular sectors are most heavily affected and will want estimates of sales and jobs broken down by sector. If formal input-output models are used, impacts may be estimated in considerable sectoral detail. This is not possible if an aggregate spending estimate or multiplier is used.
- Identify the most important measures of economic activity. Tourism impacts may be reported in terms of visitor spending, business receipts/sales/ production, wage and salary income, proprietors income and profits, value added, and employment. The direct effects are the most important and are captured well by estimates of visitor spending. Simple ratios can be used to convert direct spending or sales to the associated income and jobs. Input-output models and multipliers are needed only if one is interested in secondary effects.
- Identify the tolerable levels of error in the results. Although confidence intervals and estimates of error are rare in economic impact studies, this doesn't mean they are not important. You should have at least a ballpark idea of how much error you can tolerate in the analysis, as this will dictate how much effort and expense you must put into it. The more accuracy you demand, the greater the requirements

to gather up-to-date local data on visitation, spending and economic activity. These data allow you to fine tune the spending estimates and input-output models or multipliers. Such fine tuning will require time, knowledge, and money that must be weighed against the benefits of the improved estimates. Estimates of impacts are based on three components: visits, spending, and multipliers. You should try to balance the errors across these components.

- What are some questions to ask when evaluating or interpreting a tourism economic impact study? Evaluating, interpreting and applying an economic impact study requires a clear understanding of the findings and at least some knowledge of the underlying concepts and methods. Judging the accuracy or quality of a study can be based on the reputation of the author or the quality of presentation, although a careful evaluation of the methods that were used is the best approach. Here's some questions to ask when reading or evaluating a tourism economic impact study.
- *Impact of what?* The report should identify the action being evaluated. An economic impact assessment is most useful when evaluating the effects of a particular action or policy. If so, the action and assumptions about alternatives should be spelled out in presenting a with vs. without scenario. If the study reports impacts of existing tourism activity, identify how tourism is defined (if at all). What kinds of tourism activity and spending are included? Which trip expenses are included? Does the study include all visitor spending or only spending of tourists who live outside the local region? Does the study address impacts of visitor trip spending, durable goods purchases, operational expenses of a programme, or construction and investment?
- *On what region?* The study region should be defined (preferably with a map). It should be viable both

economically and as a distinct tourism destination area. Spending that is included should be restricted to spending in this region and multipliers should represent the given region of interest. A short profile of tourism and economic activity in the region provides useful background for an economic impact study.

- *Sources and quality of the data:* The report should identify the sources of the data for estimating visits, spending, and regional economic multipliers/models. The methods that were used to estimate impacts should be clear. Judgements of the quality of the estimates must be based largely on an understanding of the data and methods that were used. A more disaggregate analysis reporting spending within at least six categories, visitors for two or more distinct segments, and multipliers and results broken down by sector will generally be more accurate and meaningful than a study that only uses aggregate data. Disaggregation is particularly helpful when adjusting secondary data taken from government reports or other studies to a new situation. The fundamental question is whether the visit estimates, spending profiles and multipliers adequately represent the intended population and study area.
- *Quality of methods:* There are a number of issues to watch for in evaluating methods.
- *Visits:* Has the study clearly defined which visits/visitors will be affected by the proposed action, separated local visitors from tourists, and identified which visitors would be lost or gained due to the action (with vs. without the action)? Are secondary sources of visitation reliable? If models are used, how good are they and do the assumptions hold for the intended application? Has the study handled potential double counting problems in estimating visits?
- *Spending:* How accurate are the spending estimates?

Do the spending averages or totals seem reasonable? If spending averages are taken from a secondary source, evaluate the source, as well as how well these averages may apply to the intended application. What year does the spending represent? Has the data been price adjusted to the current (or model) year? If spending data come from a visitor survey, evaluate the survey methods-how was spending measured, what was the sample size, the response rate, soundness of the analysis? Are variances and confidence intervals reported for the spending estimates? Are visitors divided into distinct segments to reduce variances? Also make sure the units for which spending is reported match the units for visits, *i.e.*, the study doesn't multiply a per party spending average times the number of person visits. If adjustments are made in units of analysis, evaluate the assumed or estimated average length of stay or party size assumptions.

- *Multipliers:* If "off-the-shelf" or borrowed multipliers are used, investigate the source. Does the study clearly define what type of multiplier is being used (Type I, Type III, income, sales or employment, ratio or Keynesian) and use the multiplier appropriately? In particular, watch for studies that multiply tourism spending by a multiplier taken from an input-output model. They should adjust for the capture rate either by reducing spending, only using retail margins on goods purchased by tourists, or using a "tourist spending" multiplier that takes the capture rate into account. If an input-output model is used, the report should summarize where it came from, what year it represents, the levels of sectoral aggregation, and the basic assumptions of the model.
- *Communication and reporting of results:* The study should communicate the study results in terms that are understandable to the intended audience. For most audiences, a summary and glossary of economic

terms is helpful. Most readers will not fully understand terms like indirect and induced effects, Type I and Type III multipliers, and input-output models. Formal definitions of the measures of sales, income, and jobs that are reported are also needed to clarify what each of these terms include and the measurement units. For example, is income only wage and salary income or does it also include proprietors income, rents and profits? Study limitations and errors should be indicated.

STUDY COST

The costs of a tourism economic impact study can range from $500 to $50,000 and more. Costs will depend largely on the size and scope of tourism activity to be covered, the size and complexity of the study region, how much primary data are to be gathered and the level of accuracy and detail desired. The greatest and perhaps most significant cost will be the technical expertise of the analysts involved.

Tourism economic impact studies require considerable technical judgement of specialists and a mix of corresponding skills:

- Knowledge of tourism
- Expertise in conducting tourism surveys, particularly spending studies
- Regional economic modeling skills, including knowledge and access to economic data bases, multipliers and input-output modeling systems
- Communication skills

The cost of conducting economic impact studies has dropped substantially in the past ten years due to improvements in microcomputer programmes for estimating spending and regional economic models. The three principal components of an economic impact estimate (visits, spending, and multipliers) each involve different costs and somewhat different skills. The costs and needed skills will vary considerably depending on whether primary or existing data are to be used. If levels and types of tourism activity are known and spending averages and multipliers may be taken from secondary sources, a complete economic impact assessment can be conducted in less than a month and in many cases for under $5,000.

You are paying primarily for the time, judgement and skills of the analyst. A small visitor spending survey may add another $5,000. For a more complete analysis of secondary effects using a

formal input-output model, figure another $2,000-$5,000. Increase the cost estimate if several distinct alternatives are to be evaluated or multiple regions are involved. There will generally be scale economies in these situations with additional impact analyses costing less than half of the initial one. Costs will increase significantly if the number and types of visitors must be estimated using a general visitor survey or a demand model. Large scale spending surveys and custom input-output models based on primary data will also increase costs considerably. In many cases, the tourism activity and visitor spending data needed for an economic impact analysis can be gathered in a general visitor survey or market study. Spending averages for particular tourist segments can be estimated by having a portion of the general survey respondents complete an extra page of spending questions. Armed with good estimates of the number and types of visitors and their spending patterns, one can complete an economic impact study at little additional cost.

The principal motivations for a business or region to serve tourists are generally economic. An individual business is interested primarily in its own revenues and costs, while a community or region is concerned with tourism's overall contribution to the economy, as well as its social, fiscal and environmental impacts. A good understanding of tourism's economic impacts is therefore important for the tourism industry, government officials, and the community as a whole.

Tourism economics is unfortunately a technical area, involving concepts, methods, and models that are unfamiliar to most non-economists. In this bulletin I've attempted to define the key concepts and explain the basic methods for estimating the economic impacts of tourism, hopefully in as "non-technical" a way as the subject allows. Understanding the concepts and methods is critical to interpreting, evaluating, and applying economic impact results. This bulletin should be read along with one or more economic impact reports that can be used as examples and opportunities to test your grasp of the issues.

At the risk of oversimplifying a complex topic, let me conclude with the five pieces of advice, most frequently give to people who ask about tourism economic impacts. First, tell them that the most important information for estimating tourism impacts is a good estimate of the number of tourists. This requires clearly defining what one wishes to include as "tourism" and the region of interest. Secondly, recommend that tourists be divided into distinct subgroups (segments) with distinct spending patterns and likely reacting differently to various policy and marketing actions. In particular, local customers should be distinguished from visitors from outside the region and day users from overnight visitors.

Thirdly, focus most of your effort on estimating the direct effects of tourism, usually as tourist spending in the area. Multiplier effects are not nearly as important in most cases, as their use in tourism would suggest and multipliers tend to introduce complexities that most users of the results do not fully understand. Even if multiplier effects are important to the study purpose, remember that any errors in estimates of the direct effects will also be multiplied by any multiplier. Fourth, if you must use multipliers be sure you understand them.

E-COMMERCE TOURISM

Tourism is growing fastest in the developing countries, where it is a major component of most economies. Tourism is one of the world's largest industries, and it is a natural partner for the Internet, where it is also the world's largest on-line industry. Community-based tourism (CBT) has been shown to foster local development in developing countries, particularly in the poorer rural areas. At the same time, Information and Communication Technologies are being deployed within poor communities in developing countries and are beginning to demonstrate their potential for inducing local development. This paper describes an action research initiative for introducing electronic commerce for community based tourism (e-CBT) in three Asian rural communities in order to reveal its potential for community development.

E-CBT targets an important and growing market segment in the developing world, consisting of individual travellers for whom travel is an essential component of their life-style and who seek new and authentic experiences that are not directed towards a mass market. The proposal describes strategic partnerships between a University in Hong Kong and three other Asian universities who will work with local communities and tourism authorities for the eventual propagation of the development benefits of e-CBT among wider rural populations in their countries.

The WTO forecasts that international arrivals are expected to reach over 1.56 billion by the year 2020. The total expected tourist arrivals by region shows that by 2020 the top three receiving regions will be Europe (717 million tourists), East Asia and the Pacific (397 million) and Americas (282 million). East Asia and the Pacific, South Asia, the Middle East and Africa are forecasted to record growth at rates of over 5% per year, compared to the world average of 4.1 per cent. By 2010, WTO forecasts that the Americas will lose its number two position, behind Europe, to East Asia and the Pacific, which will receive 25% of world arrivals.

Tourism offers huge opportunities for developing countries to increase incomes from the growing number of arrivals that land on their shores. However, it has been recognized that many tourism policies developed from central governments without local involvement fail to cater for the sensibilities and aspirations of the communities that tourists visit. The conference on Community Based Ecotourism in Southeast Asia agreed that local communities should have the right to self-determination and to decide whether to accept or not accept the policies that affect their livelihood. As tourism is essentially a micro-enterprise, tourism lends itself to local entrepreneurial activity, and community-based tourism has emerged as a mechanism for fostering locally based tourism operations, as opposed to those whose financial interests are often located away from the tourist destination.

Moreover, as Information and Communication Technologies (ICTs) are beginning to be deployed in rural communities for the purpose of fostering local development, communities are able to implement electronic commerce in support of their CBT operations, and engage in e-CBT. Furthermore, it will be shown that the Internet is not only a natural partner for tourism, it also a natural partner for the market segment that e-CBT should target. With more than 600 million people on-line by September 2002, and more than 60% of them residing in Europe or North America, even small and remote communities with an Internet connection can address huge global markets.

The purpose of this paper is to introduce the concept of electronic commerce for community based tourism, e-CBT, as a mechanism for local development. E-CBT involves the operation of local tourism activities which are promoted across the internet by a community using a community based telecentre, which provides community access to information and communication technologies. The concept is presented as a method for fostering rural development in developing countries. Tourism is a principal export for developing countries and the least developed countries (LDCs). It is growing rapidly and is the most significant source of foreign exchange after petroleum. There is a general shift of tourism arrivals towards developing countries. Growth rates of international tourism receipts during the 1990s were, on average, 50% higher in the major developing country destinations than in comparison with the major developed country destinations. By far the largest single developing country international tourism destination is China.

The People's Republic accounted for US$10 billion in international tourism receipts in 1996, receiving 22.7 million international visitors, experiencing 19% annual growth rates of receipts since 1980. Together with earnings generated by the Hong Kong Special Administrative Region, China's 1996 receipts surpass US$20 billion. In 2001, China ranked fifth in the world's top tourism destinations, measured both by the number of international arrivals and by international tourism receipts. Yet in terms of Gross National Income per capita, China ranks 108 out of 173 countries in the World Bank's statistical indicators for 2001. China, Thailand and Indonesia together generated 40% of all international tourism receipts accruing to developing countries in 1996.

The World Tourism Organisation says there is a strong economic case for promoting tourism in developing countries, suggesting that affirmative action and pro-poor policies are able to go beyond trickle down and multiplier affects by unlocking opportunities for the poor within tourism (WTO 2002). Success in poverty alleviation through tourism depends, says the WTO, partly on effective community-public-private partnerships that serve to reduce financial leakages and increase economic linkages to the local economy. Financial leakages occur where a disproportionately low percentage of tourism revenues stays in the local market, and they reduce the development impact of tourism. Linkages with the local economy foster revenue retention from tourism activities, and they depend on quality, reliability and competitiveness of local products. WTO suggest various steps that can be taken to increase the benefits to the local economy in tourist destination areas, by;

- Facilitating local community access to the tourism market,
- Minimising the financial leakages from the local economy,
- Maximising the linkages of tourism to the local economy,
- Building on and complimenting existing livelihood strategies through employment and small enterprise development,
- Ensuring that tourism products contribute to local economic development not just to national revenue generation.

- Tourism is a principal export for 83% of developing countries and it is the principal export for one third of them.
- Developing countries had 292.6 million arrivals in 2000, an increase since 1990 of nearly 95%. The 40 least developed countries had 5.1 million international arrivals in 2000; they achieved an increase of 75% in the decade.
- 80% of the world's poor, those living on less than US$1 per day, live in 12countries. In 11 of these countries, tourism is significant and growing
- The developing countries are attracting an increasing share of global international tourist arrivals up from 20% in 1973 to 42% in 2000.

The developing countries and particularly the LDCs secured a larger increase in the income per international arrival between 1990 and 2000 than did the OECD or the European Union countries. The LDCs secured an increase of 45% between1990 and 2000 and the developing countries nearly 20%. This compares with18% for the OECD countries and 7.8% for the EU.

In 2000, tourism ranked third among the major merchandise export sectors for both developing countries and LDCs. If petroleum industry exports are discounted (and they are significant in only three) tourism is the primary source of foreign exchange in the 49 LDCs.

COMMUNITY BASED TOURISM

Community-based tourism provides alternative economic opportunities, which are in essence in rural areas. Community-based tourism is regarded as a tool for natural and cultural resource conservation and community development and it is closely associated with ecotourism, sometimes referred to as community-based ecotourism.

It is a community-based practice that provides contributions and incentives for natural and cultural conservation as well as providing opportunities for improved community livelihood. It has the potential to create jobs and generate entrepreneurial opportunities for people from a variety of backgrounds, skills and experiences, including rural communities and especially women.

Community-based tourism has been implemented in many developing countries, often in support of wildlife management, environmental protection and/or development for indigenous peoples.

Community tourism should;

- Be run with the involvement and consent of local communities. (Local people should participate in planning and managing the tour.)
- Give a fair share of profits back to the local community. (Ideally this will include community projects (health, schools, etc).)
- Involve communities rather than individuals. (Working with individuals can disrupt social structures.)
- Be environmentally sustainable. (Local people must be involved if conservation projects are to succeed.)
- Respect traditional culture and social structures.
- Have mechanisms to help communities cope with the impact of western tourists.
- Keep groups small to minimise cultural/ environmental impact.
- Brief tourists before the trip on appropriate behaviour.
- Not make local people perform inappropriate ceremonies, etc.
- Leave communities alone if they don't want tourism. (People should have the right to say 'no' to tourism.)

Community based tourism occurs when decisions about tourism activity and development are driven by the host community. It usually involves some form of cultural exchange where tourists meet with local communities and witness aspects of their lifestyle. Eco-tourism also emphasises observation and learning by the tourist, alongside economic and cultural conservation, and the delivery of benefits that ensure long-term sustainability of communities and natural resources. In Nepal, the Tourism for Rural Poverty Alleviation Programme began in 2001, jointly funded by the United Nations Development Programme (UNDP), the UK Department for International Development (DFID) with advisory services from SNV (Stichting Nederlandse Vrijwilligers) a Dutch development organisation.

Operating in six remote locations, the programme employed social mobilisation and tourist awareness programmes in villages to empower local communities to manage their own tourism development. In Vietnam, the International Union for Conservation of Nature and Natural Resources (IUCN) or World Conservation Union, is operating a community based tourism pilot in Sa Pa, a highly visited area with colourful ethnic minorities. Funded mainly by the Ford Foundation, the goal of the project is to assist local stakeholders to achieve an environmentally, culturally and socio-economically sustainable form of tourism, establishing mechanisms that support the active participation of the community in tourism decision-making and implementation.

The Nam Ha ecotourism project in Lao PDR uses community-based tourism as a vehicle to integrate environmental and cultural conservation with sustainable socio and economic development. Working closely with local villagers, limits were set on the number of trekking tourists allowed each year so as not to overwhelm the communities and to ensure that tourist incomes supplement rather than replace other economic activities.

Typically, with community-based tourism, the community runs all of the activities that a tourist engages in; lodging, food, guiding and craft sales. Benefits include; economic growth in rural regions; the distribution of tourism revenue, which can foster improved welfare and equity in the industry; improved resource conservation by local people; and diversification of the regional and national tourism product.

Intertwined with community-based tourism in developing countries is the concept of pro-poor tourism. In most counties with high levels of poverty, tourism is a significant and/or growing component of the economy. Governments and aid agencies acknowledge that whilst economic growth is essential for poverty reduction, of itself, it is insufficient to ensure a significant reduction. Growth that is specifically pro-poor is a pre-requisite for significant progress towards agreed targets for poverty reduction.

Tourism has many characteristics that make it potentially pro-poor:

- It is a diverse industry, which increases the scope for wide participation,
- The customer comes to the product, providing important opportunities for linkages(*e.g.*, souvenir sales),
- It is highly dependent on natural capital (wildlife, scenery) and culture, assets that some of the poor have in abundance, even if they have few financial resources,
- Tourism can be more labour intensive than manufacturing,
- A higher proportion of benefits (jobs, trade opportunities) go to women.

Pro-poor tourism is defined as tourism that generates net benefits for the poor. It maximises the potential for eradicating poverty by developing appropriate strategies in co-operation with all major groups, indigenous and local communities. Benefits may be economic, but they may also be social, environmental or cultural. Pro-poor tourism is not a specific product or sector of tourism, but an approach to the tourism industry. The core activity is to increase access of the poor to economic benefits. Pro-poor tourism strategies unlock opportunities for the poor; whether for economic gain, other livelihood benefits, or participation in decision-making.

Early experience shows that pro-poor tourism strategies do appear able to 'tilt' the industry at the margin, to expand opportunities for the poor and have potentially wide application across the industry. Poverty reduction through pro-poor tourism can therefore be significant at a local or district level. Moreover, the poverty impact may be greater in remote areas, though the tourism itself may be on a limited scale. Most examples of community-based in tourism in developing countries qualify as pro-poor tourism as they are designed to foster development at grassroots levels.

EFFECTS OF TOURISM TAXATION

The analysis reveals that, unlike the traditional outcome of a deadweight loss associated with higher taxes, increasing taxes on tourism can be welfare improving. Tourism is being targeted as a growing source of tax revenue by governments across the world. However, tourism taxation can have significant effects on welfare, which should be taken into account when taxes are levied. Little research has been undertaken on the welfare effects of tourism taxation and, given the special characteristics of tourism as an export sector, direct application of the literature on commodity taxation and export taxation to tourism taxation is not appropriate. This paper examines the welfare effects of tourism taxation on residents of a tourist destination country within a partial equilibrium framework, in the context of fixed and variable prices.

It is also found that the higher the proportion of tourism demand in total demand, and the more inelastic tourism demand is relative to domestic demand, the higher will be the welfare gain. Tourism's role as one of the fastest growing economic activities in the world makes it a key target for taxation. As a major source of foreign currency receipts, tourism appears to be the salvation for governments faced with budgetary constraints and pressures to decrease their reliance on income tax and tariffs as sources of revenue. On the other hand, taxes on tourism have proliferated and there are now calls from international bodies and tourism businesses and consumers for reductions in the range and levels of taxes on tourism.

Although the revenue gained from tourism taxation can be used to benefit the public by such means as increasing the provision of public services, it may also reduce welfare and act as a disincentive to tourism demand. Given the increasing importance of tourism taxation in both developed and developing countries, greater understanding of the economic underpinnings of tourism taxation and its effects is necessary, so that modeling of tourism taxation can be undertaken and appropriate policies for tourism taxation can be formulated. Tourism taxes thus have a direct effect on domestic consumption and hence domestic welfare.

Moreover, trade policies such as import tariffs aimed at the tradable sector also affect the tourism sector, with the tourists paying the domestic price instead of the world price. Most importantly, the burden of a tax on the tourism sector falls on both domestic residents and foreigners (tourists). Therefore, the burden of a tourism tax is a combination of the burden of an export tax and a domestic tax. Formal analysis of the welfare effects of tourism taxation is undertaken in section 4, and the fifth section of the paper includes some parameter values in the equations for the welfare effects in order to determine the results of tourism taxation in alternative contexts

TAXING THE TOURISM SECTOR

In practice, the tourism sector can be taxed either by taxing the businesses in the tourism sector or by taxing the tourists directly. Both methods may be implemented either via the general tax system of the economy or through special tourism taxes. The World Tourism Organisation (WTO, 1998) has identified 40 different types of taxes applied to the tourism sector in both developed and developing countries. They are given in the tourism tax typology.

Additional taxes relating to tourists' use of the natural environment and general taxes that also fall on tourists have also been included. Of the 45 taxes, 30 are directly payable by the tourists and 15 are levied on tourism businesses. Five broad sectors involved in tourism taxation can be identified, namely airlines and airports, hotels and other accommodation, road transportation, food and beverages and provider of tourism services. The practicality of taxing each of these sectors is highlighted below.

- *Airlines and airports:* In long haul destinations,

international transport occupies a major part in the total cost of holiday packages and hence taxing this sector should, in principle, be lucrative. However, although this is an option for developed countries, this is beyond the reach of most developing countries because they normally do not own an airline company or if they do own one, it is often unprofitable. Revenue may, instead, be generated from airport-related taxes.

- *Hotels and other accommodation*: This is normally the most important revenue generator of the tourism industry and is also easier to tax. However, the practicality of taxing the accommodation sector also varies between developed and developing countries and tends to be more problematic in the latter. The hotel sector is often highly subsidised or receives investment and tax incentives from the government in developing countries, with the aim of attracting foreign and domestic investment to the sector. The motivation is twofold, first to expand the sector as a part of a policy to expand the tourism industry and second, to protect the sector because it is a relatively unstable one due to its highly seasonal nature. The contradicting implication is that the easiest and major target for tourism taxation is most likely to be freed from taxation.
- *Taxis, food and beverages and tourism services:* These sectors are relatively easy to tax in industrialised countries but form part of fragmented small business sectors and do not normally contribute a major proportion of tourism revenue. They include such sectors as entertainments, handicrafts, jewellery and other souvenirs. In most developing countries, these activities form part of the informal sector or of the hard-to-tax formal sector and it is difficult to raise much revenue from this source. Ecotourism tax is a relatively new form of taxation that destinations such as the Balearics levy in an attempt to counter the

environmental damage caused by mass tourism. Carbon tax and landfill tax are more general environmental taxes on the level of carbon emissions and wastes respectively, but are borne by tourists as well.

Although gambling (in-shop and racing) is not legal in some countries mainly due to religious opposition, casinos are socially accepted in several countries. Tourists are involved in gambling and casinos, and hence bear the tax associated with those activities. The tax can be levied on the suppliers rather than tourists as in the case of the UK where the betting tax that was initially levied on the gamblers is now levied on the gross profit of bookmakers.

TAXING TOURISTS

Since taxing tourism businesses is not always a lucrative way of raising tax revenue, much tax revenue from tourism is generated from consumption taxes and special tourism taxes applied directly to tourists' consumption. Consumption taxes take the form of general sales taxes or value added tax (VAT). Sales tax/VAT is levied in almost all countries, regardless of the tourism taxation policies.

Therefore, in the presence of this type of sales tax, tourists are being taxed without any deliberate tourism tax policy on the part of the government. In the spirit of optimal taxation, some countries discriminate between domestic and tourism consumption, such that the latter is taxed at a higher rate or an additional tourism tax is applied to tourists' consumption. However, this entails administration problems in enforcing and monitoring such taxes. Special tourism taxes are generally levied directly on tourists and they can take several forms.

Common forms include taxes on hotels and restaurants, passenger services, tourist transport, entry/exit taxes and hotel accommodation taxes. The last tax is the most common and, as the name suggests, hotel accommodation tax is simply a tax on the tourists' expenditure on accommodation. The rate levied usually depends on hotel class and the season. It is relatively easy to collect, although discrimination across hotel classes sometimes creates administrative problems. In countries such as Jamaica, it is levied at a flat rate amounting to around $4-12 per night, and in other countries it is an ad valorem tax, which differs across countries: for example, 13% in South Africa, 12.5% in Senegal and 7.5% in Grenada. Entry/exit taxes include those on airport departures, which are fixed amounts that have to be paid when leaving the country, on airport embarkation, which is paid on entering the country, and the visa fee.

These taxes are usually levied at a flat rate and are relatively small in amount: for example, the airport departure tax has been within the range $1-6 in Singapore, Indonesia, Malaysia, Philippines, and Thailand, and was set at $10 in Malawi, Tanzania and Zambia.

CONTROVERSY

The WTO (1998) posits that the nature of the tourism sector makes it a target for tax revenue not only because tourism taxes are easy to collect and easy to administer but also because international tourists are rarely voters in the destination country they visit. Most of the arguments in favour of taxing the tourism sector are based on the fact that tourism products are consumed jointly with unpriced natural amenities and public goods.

Unpriced natural amenities include the sun, sea and wildlife, while public goods can include security and health services. As Gray (1982) argues, "the question of public goods, their supply and their pricing, is relatively more important in tourism than in many other industries, in part, because of the needed role of the government in asset preservation and, in part, because of the greater role of the government in the normal routine when foreigners reside temporarily within its own borders."

The main reasons for tourism taxation can be considered under the following categories. Besides providing law and order, under which contracts can be enforced and property rights protected, so ensuring that the private sector is operating efficiently, one of the main roles of the government is to provide 'public goods'. The technical definition of public goods comprises the following: indivisibility, ie. commodities are not divisible into units that can be sold individually; non-excludability, ie. no one can be excluded from benefiting from the product; the free-rider problem, where it is difficult to charge users an appropriate fee.

Common examples of public goods include national defence and street lighting. The distinctive characteristics of public goods makes it difficult to provide them via the private sector because there is no price mechanism that controls the market. They can be provided only by the government, which uses its right to tax to generate the resources necessary to supply them. Domestic taxpayers usually finance the provision of such goods. The influx of tourists imposes an extra cost on the government relating to the provision of items such as greater security and an improved environment. As non-residents, tourists do not pay to finance these extra costs.

A tourist tax will, therefore, serve to redress the balance and impose the burden on those who are responsible for them. There are often user charges for some attractions, such as parks and safaris, but in other cases, such as street lighting and public security, enforcing payment is difficult. In such circumstances, taxing the may be the only way of 'charging' them for the public goods they consume.

Higher government revenue can increase welfare by such means as financing improvements in public services. Furthermore, it may help to reduce the burden of income taxation on domestic residents, and it may also be an alternative policy for countries that want to reduce their dependency on trade taxes while, at the same time, not imposing an additional burden on domestic residents.

The WTO (1988) estimates that 'tourist countries' obtain around 10-25% of their tax revenue from the tourism sector. In some small specialised tourism countries such as the Bahamas, over 50% of government revenue is generated from the tourism sector. In Mauritius, about 12-15% of tax revenue is collected directly and indirectly from the tourism sector. The tourism sector is an unusual sector for revenue generation. Bird

(1992) believes that developing countries tend to under tax their tourism sector, failing to exploiting fully the economic rent emerging from the sector.

Such rent results from less than perfectly elastic demand for their tourism products, due to the differentiated nature of their natural amenities. The degree of inelasticity of demand depends, in part, on the degree of differentiation of the destination and affects the ability to tax. The greater the degree of differentiation of the destination, the more inelastic demand will be and, hence, the greater the scope for taxation.

Tourism product differentiation generally occurs in terms of types and quality of attractions (endowments), types and quality of goods and services sold in the country, geographical location and distance. Examples of attractions with very inelastic demand are the pyramids of Egypt, the Taj Mahal and the Grand Canyon. Gray (1987) associates the demand for differentiated tourism products with 'wanderlust' tourism, involving seeing or doing something that is unique to the destination, as opposed to 'sunlust' tourism which refers to the sun, sea and sand destinations such as Mauritius and the Caribbean countries. 'Sunlust' destinations tend to have less inelastic demand because the tourism products tend to be less differentiated across countries.

Less than perfectly elastic demand implies that tourism gives rise to 'economic rents' which suppliers of tourism services may try to maximise and governments may attempt to tax. However, tourism is a composite product with multiple components, and each of the components can be taxed at a different rate. For example, Bonham *et al.* considered a room tax on hotel receipts in Hawaii and found that the tax resulted in an insignificant change in hotel revenue. Combs and Elledge found that a small ad-valorem tax room tax imposed on motels and other forms of tourist accommodation in the USA would have very little impact on the industry and would generate substantial revenue for the government.

However, an increase in taxation on one component of tourism can result in lower expenditure on another. In one of the first systematic tourism taxation studies, Mak and

Nishimura investigated the effect of a hotel room tax on the length of stay of tourists in Hawaii. The results were that visitors' length of stay was insensitive to price changes and that an increase in the room tax would not reduce tourist arrivals in Hawaii significantly.

However, Mak and Nishimura also examined the effect of a hotel room tax on non-lodging consumption and find that tourists 'respond to marginal increases in price of lodging partly by reducing some of their non-lodging expenditures and partly by reducing their savings and/or spending at home'.

EXPORTABILITY

Taxation on tourism may be exportable in the sense that tourists bear the major burden of the taxation. The issue of tax incidence is important in this respect, as discussed in the context of the UK by Durbarry and Sinclair. One of the first studies that examined the tax incidence of tourism taxes explicitly was by Fujii *et al.*, who examined the incidence and the exportability of an ad valorem hotel room tax for Hawaii in a partial equilibrium framework.

Tax incidence refers to the distribution of the tax burden between the buyers and the hoteliers whereas tax exporting refers to the extent to which the burden of the tax is distributed between the residents and the non-residents. If the hotel industry is an enclave with a high proportion of foreign investment, then the distinction between tax incidence and tax exporting is minor because the incidence of the tax on the supplier is actually exported. Under a partial equilibrium framework, the incidence of a hotel room tax depends on the relative sizes of the elasticities of demand and of supply. Fujii *et al.* calculated the relative burden of the hotel tax on tourists and the tourism industry as the ratio of the supply and demand elasticities for accommodation.

They estimated the demand function for accommodation and found that the price elasticities of demand were negative and significant, and also found supply to be less than perfectly elastic. Their results suggested that one-third of the hotel room tax was borne by the tourism industry and the rest by the tourists. They also showed that the hotel room tax was more readily exported than similar taxes levied on meals, drinks and entertainment and the general sales tax. Hence the exportability of tourism taxes is liable to vary between different components of the tourism product.

SUSTAINABILITY OF THE ENVIRONMENT

Many developing countries under balance of payments and foreign exchange pressure have targeted tourism as a means of development. In many cases, no proper management strategies have been formulated especially at the initial stage of the tourism development. Natural resources have been degraded to the point where environmental sustainability is threatened. Regulating the inflow of tourists and taxation are the two most popular tools used, or considered, to remedy the problem.

However, regulating the inflow of tourists may not be the ideal solution because it deliberately contracts the tourism sector and this may have negative repercussions on the economy. It should also be remembered that many countries are investing resources to expand the tourism sector, and therefore it would be contradictory to pursue these two policies simultaneously. Moreover, it is believed that unconstrained growth (not limiting tourist arrivals) is usually beneficial in the sense that it increases the level of per capita income, thus providing more funds for maintaining the environment and sustaining growth. On the other hand, regulation through taxation not only provides the government with revenue (if designed properly) but also targets only the activities and individuals involved in the environmental degradation process and is, therefore, an efficient way to tackle the problem.

Furthermore, with higher revenues, more resources will be available to sustain the development of the industry. The tourism sector does not only rely on the natural amenities in the country but also on public goods. A strong regulatory framework, such as maintaining high health and food preparation standards, is also important in the success of the tourism sector. Taxation can generate the necessary resources to provide these requirements. Of course, the tourism industry has no inherent right to have the taxes it pays ploughed back into the industry.

However, appropriate earmarking of tax revenue can help to sustain the tourism industry and also help to reduce and combat the associated degradation of the environment. The taxation issues involved in controlling environment degradation and sustaining tourism are similar. The basic method is to use the Pigouvian tax, whereby the tax rate should correct for the divergence between the market price and the social marginal cost. Such taxes should be applied to all users, including both domestic residents and tourists, and should as far as possible be directed to the goods and services that generate the externalities so as to avoid inefficiencies.

If resources are to be exploited only to the economically desirable limit, then the social marginal cost (hence tax rate) should be set sufficiently high to include not only the opportunity costs to local residents in terms of environmental damage and congestion costs, but also the maximum possible rent extractable. On the other hand the price, hence the tax rate, should not be set so high as to hinder consumption of the product and tourist arrivals in the country. Congestion is an important facet of sustainability. High congestion, often caused by tourists themselves, reduces the quality of tourism services, which can lead to a reduction in arrivals, especially of high class and high spending tourists. The presence of crowds may detract from the enjoyment of tourists seeking solitude and privacy.

Discomfort in crowds, long queues at popular places, traffic congestion and an untidy environment will not only affect the quality of tourism services but also the quality of life of domestic residents. Tourism taxation may be used both to reduce the inflow of tourists and to compensate the local residents. However, many tourism activities are not priced, for example, sun, sea and sand, and if some are priced, the associated transaction costs relating to monitoring and enforcement are generally very high.

Thus, they are supplied at a zero fee to all users and the

problem of free riders is difficult to avoid. In this context, regulatory processes such as parking fees near crowded beaches and taxes on car rental can be applied. An entry/exit tax, which is a fixed amount of money that tourists pay when they enter and leave the destination country, can also be used. An entry/exit tax is an easy way of extracting economic rents from the tourism services the destination country is selling because it is often a tax included in the airfare, unnoticed by many travellers. Sometimes countries discriminate between domestic residents and tourists, so that only tourists pay the tax. However, an entry/exit tax has some disadvantages.

First, by capturing rents from tourists, an entry/exit tax does not provide any incentive for tourism to reduce their demand for the specific good that is causing the externalities, as should optimally be the case. The tax will reduce the number of tourist arrivals. Hence not only the demand of the externality generating commodity will fall but demand for other tourism services will also fall because of the complementary nature of tourism demand. The economic benefits normally attached to expanding the tourism sector may then be constrained.

Second, a uniform entry/exit tax does not offer first degree price discrimination in the sense that both low and high income tourists or short and long stay tourists pay the same amount of tax. This may discourage short stay tourists. Third, since it is levied mainly on foreigners, or at a higher rate on foreigners, it may fail to take full account of the full contribution of residents to environmental degradation.

Despite the advantages of tourism taxation, governments have been cautious about the magnitude of the taxes levied on the tourism sector because there are also negative effects associated with tourism taxation. A range of arguments has been levelled against tourism taxation, and some of the key arguments can be included under the following headings.

COSTS OF COMPLIANCE

Taxes levied directly on the tourism sector are sometimes difficult to justify. The amount of tax collected may be small but the tax can still have a substantial negative impact on the tourism sector, with repercussions on the overall economy. This happens especially with taxes levied directly on tourists, such as visa fees. It is not only the high fees required; there is often unnecessary bureaucracy (indeed discrimination between tourists of different nationalities) that can greatly raise the compliance costs for the tax payer and act as a deterrent to visiting the country.

This may contract tourist arrivals and affect other sectors related to the tourism sector. For countries where tourism comprises a major part of the economy, this can adversely affect the employment level and the balance of payments resulting in an overall contraction of the level of economic activity of the economy. The fiscal effects are likely to differ from country to country and from time to time, for three main reasons.

First, the effects depend on the policy of the government. If the government wants to maximise revenue, the tax rates will tend to be high. On the other hand, if the government wants to promote the sector, tax rates can be very low. In some case the government goes further by providing subsidies, such as subsidies for airport and parking infrastructure, and investment incentives to businesses. Second, the effects also depend on how important tourism is to the economy. Obviously, the higher the contribution of tourism in the economy, the higher will be the effects of tourism taxes on the government budget.

Thirdly, the number and types of linkages with other sectors in the economy and leakages from the economy that the tourism sector brings about are also important. As a general rule, linkages tend to increase government revenue and leakages lead to a reduction in revenue. The amount of revenue that is obtained from tourism taxation depends, in part, upon the value of the price elasticity of demand for tourism. If the price elasticity of demand is high, the effect of an increase in tax may be to decrease revenue.

In the case of tourist accommodation, all obtained demand elasticities for accommodation that were significantly different from zero. Hiemstra and Ismail reported a significant price elasticity of demand for the lodging industry based on a survey of the properties owned and managed by the American Hotel and Motel Association.

RETALIATION

Taxation generates revenue but, as in the case of trade taxes, it invites retaliation by other countries if they feel that the other government is unfairly treating their citizens. For example, Kenya and Tanzania introduced visa charges for UK citizens in retaliation to the application of visa fees by the UK on their citizens. Retaliation is always a threat and in most cases the eventual outcome is lower welfare for both countries. Tisdell (1983) showed how retaliation in the case of tourism taxes can lead to a lower economic surplus for both countries. [illegible]s because the consumer surplus that the tourists from the leader country were enjoying in the retaliating country will disappear after the tax. The country with a more inelastic demand for tourism will lose less but, compared with the case without retaliation, both countries lose. However, if a developing country imposes, say, an entry tax on tourists who are mainly from developed countries, then retaliation will tend to affect the developing country to a lesser extent. This is because the number of tourists from the developing country visiting the developed is fewer than the number of tourists from the developed countries who visit developing country.

WELFARE IMPLICATIONS OF TOURISM TAXATION

It is widely accepted in the literature that taxation should comply with three main principles: efficiency, equity and having a low disincentive to work effect. Tourism taxation may meet all three criteria or only some of them. The efficiency principle can be achieved because, unlike other taxes, tourism taxes can lead to an increase in welfare, thereby rendering tourism taxation more efficient than taxing other sectors. The main reason why this occurs is that the presence of tourists increases the tax base for commodity taxation and hence higher tax revenue is generated. However, the welfare loss corresponding to a tax increase is not reflected in domestic welfare since utility of tourists is not included in the social welfare function. This is explained in more detail below.

The equity principle can also be achieved as some tourism products are classified as luxuries. Following the redistributive effect of taxation literature, taxing such products entails positive equity effects because they are consumed mainly by individuals from the higher income brackets. The disincentive to work effect of taxation is also considered to be an important criterion for good taxation principles. It is believed that taxation leads to a disincentive to work because the more a person works, the more tax the person pays, so that to avoid paying high taxes, people work less and take more leisure. This effect is more notable with direct income taxation, but Corlette and Hague demonstrate how commodity taxation can be used to circumvent the problem. They argue that goods that complement leisure more can be taxed at a higher rate. The intuition is that by taxing goods that are complementary to leisure, the price of leisure will increase.

Hence, people will be less willing to undertake leisure activities, thereby reducing the disincentive to work effect of taxation. Taxing tourism products reinforces the above proposition because taxing tourism is equivalent to taxing commodities that are complementary to leisure, thereby not only reducing the disincentive effects inflicted by the commodity tax but also reducing those introduced by income taxation, hence making the overall taxation system more efficient. The latter two principles will not be considered further here but the focus of the analysis will be on the first principle and will concern the welfare implications of tourism taxation, based on the normative analysis of the taxation literature using demand and supply analysis.

A practical and common method of taxing the tourism sector is through consumption taxes. Consumption taxes can either take the form of special taxes designed specifically to tax the tourism sector, such as a hotel room tax, or can be levied through the general sales tax system. Tourism may be the only export sector that can be taxed using the domestic sales tax.

This is because of the special nature of the tourism product as an exported commodity. In contrast to conventional commodity exports, foreign tourists who want to consume tourism travel to the exporting country; ie. rather than sending goods across boundaries, consumers move across boundaries to consume the product. Consumption of goods and services will thus have a non-tourism consumption and a tourism consumption component.

Therefore, in an economy where a sales tax already exists, the tourism sector is taxed even without any deliberate actions from the government. This is, of course, true unless there is price discrimination between local consumers and tourists in the sense that tourists are exempted from sales tax. However, this happens rarely, especially in developing countries, and if price discrimination is present, it is generally in favour of the domestic residents rather than the tourists. It is widely accepted in economics that there is a deadweight loss (a reduction in social welfare) attached to almost all taxes.

Sales tax may not always be welfare diminishing in the presence of tourists. Taxing tourists using the existing sales tax can be welfare improving. The presence of tourists means higher demand and, thus, a higher tax base that will generate more tax revenue. On the other hand, part of the burden of this additional tax revenue is borne by the tourists and is not accounted for in domestic welfare. Therefore with higher tax revenue and a relatively lower reduction in domestic consumer surplus, the increase in the tax rate in the presence of tourists will have a lower deadweight loss, and in some cases a windfall gain may emerge. In this section, we examine this issue within a one commodity partial equilibrium framework. Although, the latter does not take account of general equilibrium effects, it provides a range of interesting insights about the possible sources and directions of welfare gains or losses. We consider two cases, the fixed producer price and the variable producer price case.

Bibliography

Airey, D.: *Tourism Management,* London: The National Liaison Group for Higher Education in Tourism, 2002.

Comic, D. K.: *Tourism as a Subject of Philosophical Reflection,* London: Picador, 2007.

Conlin, M. V.: *Tourism: Building Credibility for a Credible Industry,* Princeton: Princeton University Press, 2008.

Conroy, B.: *Quality in Education and Training for Tourism,* New Delhi: Har-Anand Publications, 2001.

Cooper, C.: *Tourism Education and Training for Tourism,* New Delhi: Penguin Books, 1997.

Cristureanu, C.: *Tourism in Central and Eastern Europe: Educating for Quality,* Tilberg: Tilberg University Press, 1998.

Cross, J.: *Tourism Education: The International Dimension Tourism,* New Delhi: Oxford University Press, 2005.

Daniele, R.: *Information and Communication Technologies,* London: Ernest Benn, 2007.

Daurer, C.: *Tourism and Hospitality Management,* Delhi: Orient Longman, 2004.

Echtner, C.: *Annals of Tourism Research,* New Delhi: Oxford University Press, 2000.

Enghagen, L.K.: *Hospitality Research Journal,* New York: Routledge, 2000.

Fennell, D.: *Tourism Recreation Research,* New Delhi: Sage Publications, 1996.

Formica, S.: *Journal of Hospitality and Tourism Education*, New Delhi: Oxford University Press, 2006.

Getz, D.: *International Journal of Hospitality Management*, Bombay: Government of Maharashtra, 2001.

Guerrier, Y.: *Tourism and Hospitality Education*, Cambridge: Cambridge University Press, 2006.

Hall, C. M.: *Trends and Issues in Tertiary Tourism*, New England: University of New England, 2005.

Korzay, M.: *International Journal of Hospitality Management*, London: BBC Books, 2006.

Ladkin, A.: *The ATTT Tourism Education Handbook*, London: Tourism Society, 2005.

Lam, T.: *International Journal of Contemporary Hospitality Management*, New Delhi: Oxford University Press, 1999.

Lawson, M.: *Teaching Tourism: Education and Training*, London: Tourism International Press, 2002.

Medlik, S.: *Tourism, Past, Present and Future*, London: Heinemann, 2001.

Middleton, V.: *Tourism Education Course*, UK: A Review, 2008.

Moutinho, L.: *Tourism Marketing and Management Handbook*, London: Prentice Hall, 2001.

Shepherd, R.: *Tourism and Hospitality Education*, Guildford: University of Surrey, 2000.

Westlake, J.: *Educating the Educators: A Manual of Tourism and Hospitality Education*, London: Yale University Press, 2003.

Yale, L.J.: *Hospitality and Tourism Educator*, New Delhi: Oxford University Press, 1998.

Index

I

N

O

P

R

S

T

U

V

W